# Quick
# Country Quilting

## Over 80 Projects Featuring Easy, Timesaving Techniques

**Debbie Mumm**

Rodale Press
Emmaus, Pennsylvania

*To my husband, Steve, for his never ending support and encouragement. Thank you for ignoring your "friend" who once asked you, "When is your wife going to get a real job?"*

Senior Managing Editor: Margaret Lydic Balitas
Crafts Editor: Suzanne Nelson
Associate Crafts Editor: Mary V. Green
Copy Editor: Ellen Pahl
Administrative Assistant: Stacy A. Brobst

Book Designer: Sandy Freeman
Cover Designer: Darlene Schneck

Illustrations:  Wayne Michaud pp. 6, 33, 34, 35, 36
          Pat O'Brien pp. 9, 10, 11, 16, 20, 27, 29, 30
             (Diagram 9), 31
          All other illustrations are by Debbie Mumm.

Interior and Front Cover Photography by Mitch Mandel
Photo Stylist: Dee Schlagel
Back Cover Photography by Robert Barros

Cover Quilts: The quilts shown on the front cover include (clockwise from the bottom) Crazy for Cats! (page 49), Autumn Leaves (page 135), and An Apple a Day (page 85). The stuffed cat on the windowsill is found in the Alley Cats project (page 183).

If you have any questions or comments concerning this book, please write:

  Rodale Press
  Book Reader Service
  33 East Minor Street
  Emmaus, PA 18098

**Library of Congress Cataloging-in-Publication Data**

Mumm, Debbie.
   Quick country quilting : over 80 projects featuring easy, timesaving techniques / Debbie Mumm.
       p.    cm.
   Includes bibliographical references.
   ISBN 0-87857-984-2   hardcover
   1. Quilting—Patterns.   I. Title.
TT835.M84   1991
746.46—dc20                                      91-27283
                                                 CIP

**Distributed in the book trade by St. Martin's Press**

   4  6  8  10  9  7  5  3        hardcover

**NOTICE**
The author and editors who compiled this book have tried to make all the contents as accurate and as correct as possible. Illustrations, photographs, and text have all been carefully checked and cross-checked. However, due to the variability of materials, personal skill, and so on, neither the author nor Rodale Press assumes any responsibility for any damages or other losses incurred that result from the material presented herein. All instructions and diagrams should be carefully studied and clearly understood before beginning any project.

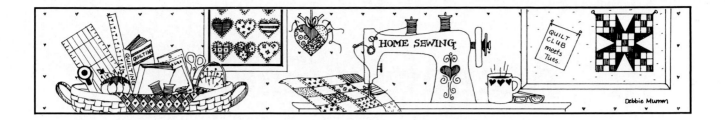

# Contents

# Acknowledgments

First, I want to thank my husband, Steve Mumm, who has always given me generous support in everything I've done. No one has encouraged me or believed in me more than he when it came to developing my talents. He has supported me in every risk I've taken and given me the pushes I've needed when necessary. I thank him for helping me become who I am, which is better than I would have been without him.

Thank you to my parents, Ardis Kvare and Richard Kvare, for teaching me all the skills I need to achieve the goals I set. And for encouraging me to work hard (but not too hard!) to give me balance and enjoyment in my work. Thank you, too, for providing the opportunities to develop my artistic talent. But most of all, thank you for loving me no matter what I do.

My friend Ann Weisbeck is not only one of my great supporters but she actually picks up a needle and thread and works on my quilts with me. I appreciate and admire her skills and am grateful that she works with me and shares this interest. It's been such a pleasure. What would I do without her?

Thank you, Jackie Wolff, for helping me to get to my first Quilt Market. Teaching at your shop has kept me in touch with quilters (and has also kept me supplied with fabric!).

A heartfelt thank you to all the ladies who work for me both in and out of the office: Kathy Grabowski, Kristy Paulson, Ann Weisbeck, Darlene Linahan, Carol Von Stubbe, Janet Buege, Gayle Gregory, Julie Linahan, Retta Warehime, and Gail Abeloe (who taught me how to use a computer!). I appreciate all you do for me and your dedication.

Mairi Fischer has the gifted hands that quilted many of the quilts shown in this book. If only you could see her work up close! Not only is she good but she always meets my demanding deadlines. Thank you's are also due to Vi McDonald and Chris Mewhinney for their quilting contributions.

Thanks to my friends from Fiddlesticks (Kathy Meyers, Michele Sink, Carol Von Stubbe, Carol Barany, Janni Stelzer, and all the others) for introducing me to the world of quilts. Janni Stelzer was the one who taught me how to quilt and made it fun. I also learned that work can be a lot of fun!

And a special thank you to all my other family and friends who have given me encouragement along the way.

Last, but certainly not least, thank you to my editor, Suzanne Nelson. It was a joy to work with her, not only because she is so good at what she does, but because she made me feel so good about what I do. Thank you for giving me this marvelous opportunity!

## A Note from the Editor

It takes a very special family to allow a photography crew to invade their lovely home for eight very long days. Keith, Bev, and Carrie Haselhorst were the picture of patience as the furniture in their rooms was rearranged, armfuls of props were brought in and out, and quilts were hung on the walls. Their hospitality, understanding, and unflagging cheerfulness (not to mention the delicious aroma of Carrie's brownies) were truly appreciated.

# Introduction

I've been teaching quilting classes for many years, and I will admit that it is a different experience to talk to quilters through the pages of a book rather than in person! But I'll start out just as I do in my quilt classes, by explaining a little bit about myself and my quilt projects and then give you some helpful guidelines on how to use this book.

## How I Got Started

Quilting entered my life nine years ago in a totally unexpected way. That was the year my husband and I relocated from Seattle to Yakima, Washington, for his first on-air television job. I was not looking forward to the move but would have felt much better about it if I could have peeked into the future and foreseen that this new home was where I would launch a wonderful new career as a quilt designer.

I started working at a shop called Fiddlesticks, which was half quilt/cross-stitch shop and half gift shop. I was hired for my graphic art skills to create signs and displays and to help customers with their projects. It was the first time I had ever really enjoyed my job! Better yet, I took my first quilt class there and was amazed that I could do it. Making quilts was more fun and not nearly as hard as I had thought it would be. My first quilt was a Double Irish Chain using Mary Ellen Hopkins's techniques. I gave the quilt to my sister for her wedding gift. I was hooked!

This first hands-on experience and lots of reading about quilting techniques made me begin to think about the general methods of quilt construction. I wondered whether streamlined, timesaving methods could be applied to other sorts of quilt designs. I answered the question by designing the next quilt I made—it's called Heart's Content and you can see it on page 79. Not long after, I taught a quilting class using Heart's Content as the project and was encouraged by the way everyone liked the quick-cutting and quick-sewing methods it featured. From this very humble beginning, my career as a quilt designer began to take off.

### The Birth of a Business

As I continued to learn about quilt techniques, I incorporated the best of what I had learned into quilt designs and other types of appliqué projects. I also taught classes, which was a wonderful way to find out immediately whether people liked my designs and whether my directions were clear! Students and quilting peers kept suggesting I turn my designs into patterns. I decided it was time to take the plunge. I developed a test pattern using Heart's Content and marketed it in the local area. I learned a lot from that experience, and a few years later I did my first official nationwide release of seven patterns.

When you're in the quilting business, you soon realize that the place to go with any new products is the annual Quilt Market held in Houston, Texas. Quilt-shop owners from across the country come to see the latest quilt patterns, fabrics, and supplies that are available to stock in their shops. I took my seven patterns to Quilt Market in 1986 and kept my fingers crossed that shop owners would like my designs. As the orders poured in, I realized I could uncross my fingers! And I also realized that what had been a hobby up to that point had turned into a full-fledged business.

Since that first trip to Houston, my mail-order business, Mumm's the Word, has continued to grow. I'm pleased that quilters like my designs, and I'm also gratified that they find my directions and diagrams easy to follow. It's not unusual for me to get letters or phone calls from quilters who just have to tell me how much fun they have making my projects. One of the reasons why I decided to do this book is that I thought it would be nice to collect all of my patterns in one handy place for quilters to use.

## What Inspires My Designs?

I'm often asked where I get inspiration for my quilt designs. I love antiques and the country style, so that look is a big part of what I do. I also turn to artwork and magazines for inspiration. When I was pregnant with my son Murphy (now two years old), I found myself naturally gravitating toward nursery theme projects. I always keep my eyes open for popular trends so that my designs will be appealing to others as well. Once I have an idea for a quilt project, I actually do my work with graph paper, colored pencils, and calculator.

Like many of you, my life is quite a juggling act. Running my business, designing patterns, illustrating for my stationery products, and trying to have a happy personal and family life keep me busy. And as quilters, we all want and *need* to make time for our creativity. I design my patterns with that in mind. I want you to be able to enjoy the creative quiltmaking process, but I also know it has to be worked into your already jam-packed life. So I try to make my designs as simple as possible. Then I use timesaving cutting and sewing techniques. I also make my projects small in scale. This not only allows you to finish your project in a reasonable amount of time but leaves you encouraged and eager to start your next project.

## The Time-Savers Built Into My Projects

My timesaving approach to quilting uses no patterns for piecing templates. That's why you won't find pattern pieces on the pages of my book! With the traditional template method, you need to first make a template for every pattern piece in the quilt, then trace around those templates for each piece of fabric you cut. This cutting process can take a long time. Plus, some people find it hard to be precise when cutting with scissors, and pattern pieces that aren't cut accurately don't fit together well.

For template-free cutting, you forget about the scissors and templates. Instead, you use a see-through type of ruler with a rotary cutter. Each project gives you a list of pieces to cut. With your ruler and rotary cutter you can cut through four layers of fabric at once with great accuracy, allowing you to cut out your project pieces quickly and precisely. All of my pieced quilts are based on a very simple "building block" formula. You cut out squares, rectangles, and strips, and then assemble them to form the design.

There are other quick and easy techniques that I incorporate into my projects. The Speedy Triangle technique allows you to make several triangle sets at one time. Assembly Line Piecing and the Continuous Seam technique speed up assembling the blocks. With Strip Sets you can put together complex-looking checkerboard and scrap borders in no time flat. On the appliqué projects, I recommend a number of quick techniques that give you great results. I've even developed a timesaving technique of my own, called Penstitch appliqué. All of these techniques are described in detail in the chapters that follow.

My hope is that no matter how busy your life, my projects will enable you to find the time to enjoy making a quilt.

## How to Use This Book

I would recommend that you start by reading through the two chapters in Techniques for Quick Country Quilting. In these chapters, I describe the general

materials and supplies you will need to make any of the projects in this book. I also give you a detailed account of the basic techniques that are used for the projects.

The projects in this book cover the range of crib quilts and wallhangings to holiday decorations, table accessories, appliquéd sweatshirts, and baby gifts. They have been grouped according to the type of construction that is used—piecing or appliqué. In Pieced Country Quilting Projects, you'll find quilts that are made of strips and triangles sewn together to create the quilt top. Appliqué Country Quilting Projects are quilts made by arranging and attaching smaller pieces of fabric to a background piece to create a design.

## Features in the Projects

As I wrote the directions for each project, my motivation was to make sure that you would have *all* the information you need in a very clear, easy-to-use format. You'll notice that every project begins with a materials list that includes all the fabric yardage you will need, plus batting and any other special items such as appliqué film or embroidery floss. Be sure to read through the list to make sure you have everything on hand. Check Tools and Accessories You Will Need on page 6 to make sure you're all set.

For the Pieced Country Quilting Projects, very precise cutting directions for the strips and pieces are given in a handy chart format. There are two columns in each chart. The first column gives you the dimensions for the first strip to be cut; if that strip is to be cut into smaller pieces, those dimensions are given in the second column. (Sometimes this second cut won't be necessary, so the second column will be empty.)

It has been my experience that detailed step-by-step directions are a help to *any* quilter, no matter how much or how little experience you have. I've broken down the assembly for each quilt into a very simple-to-follow sequence of steps. (At times, these steps will refer you back to details provided in Techniques for Quick Country Quilting. If you're not sure about the details of a certain technique, it really does help to flip back and refresh your memory.) Numbered diagrams help make the step-by-step directions even clearer. You should never feel lost when making one of these quilts! Always read the instructions for a project from start to finish before you begin. This perspective can help you avoid unnecessary mistakes.

There are lots of extra features that you should find helpful. Whenever I can share a hint that makes a certain step quicker or easier, I've turned it into a Sew Smart tip. Look for the little spool of thread that starts each of these tips.

For certain quilts, I have supplied quilting templates. These appear full size so you can trace them directly from the pages of the book and use them to mark your quilt. All of the appliqué designs appear full size as well, so you will never have to waste time enlarging any of the patterns.

To help with the assembly directions, I've provided a Fabric Key that shows a different kind of shading for each of the fabrics used in the quilt. This Fabric Key is included in the step-by-step directions, so it's there, handy for you to refer to as you're sewing.

And now the fun part begins . . . page through the book and pick out the project you want to make first. Happy quilting!

# Enlarging a Wall Quilt to Fit a Bed

Nearly all of the quilts in this book are intended to be hung on a wall. However, you may fall in love with one of the designs and decide that you would like to expand it to fit a full-size bed. Here's the way I suggest you adapt a smaller quilt to fit a bed.

**STEP 1.** Note that every project will give you the size of the finished quilt, plus the individual block size. Look up these dimensions for the quilt you want to enlarge.

**STEP 2.** First, measure the top of your bed. Knowing the finished block size, determine how many blocks it will take to cover the mattress top. Don't forget to include the measurement for the lattice. For some quilts, you could choose to increase the width of the lattice so you wouldn't need to make so many extra blocks. (When you figure the yardage for the lattice strips, make sure you measure so they're ½ inch wider than the finished size you desire.) Once you have determined how many blocks you will need, refigure the yardage required to make the blocks. For example, if there are twice as many blocks, double the yardage requirements for the block fabrics.

**STEP 3.** Measure from the top of the mattress down the side of the bed (toward the floor). Add two or three borders to the sides of the quilt to acquire that needed length.

**STEP 4.** Draw your bed quilt top with borders on graph paper. Use a scale of one square per inch. This important step will help you determine the fabric requirements for your lattice, borders, backing, and batting. (You'll need your calculator, too!) It will also help you visualize your project and confirm that the plan that is now in your head will actually work. When it comes time to translate your drawing into yards of fabric, keep in mind that most cotton fabrics run 44 inches wide. The width of the fabric is crucial in determining how much you need for the lattice, borders, and backing. If you do your figuring at home based on a 44-inch width and find out when you get to the fabric store that the fabric you want happens to be narrower or perhaps even wider, you will need to do some refiguring.

# Techniques for
# Quick Country Quilting

In this section you'll find all of the details for certain techniques that are used over and over for quilting projects throughout the book. Speedy Quilting Methods highlights the timesaving cutting and sewing techniques I incorporate into all my projects. Quiltmaking Essentials gives you the basic techniques you'll need to assemble and add the finishing touches to your projects. Here's a handy checklist with pointers on how to use this section of the book.

☐ Before you make your first project, read both chapters, Speedy Quilting Methods and Quiltmaking Essentials. They don't take long to read and are an easy way to familiarize yourself with all the techniques that appear in the projects.

☐ Watch for the Sew Simple tips marked with a spool of thread. These are handy hints you can use as you make your projects.

☐ Pay special attention to Tools and Accessories You Will Need on page 6. Take this book to the quilting store with you in case you have any questions about some of the items you may need to buy.

☐ Once your project is underway, be sure to flip back to these chapters when you need to refresh your memory about the specific details of a certain technique.

# Speedy Quilting Methods

"Speedy," "quick," and "timesaving" are not usually the first words that come to mind when the word quilt is mentioned. Most people have the impression that a quilt takes months, maybe even *years* to complete. Thankfully, for those of us who have hectic lives, there are lots of ways to make quiltmaking a quicker, less time-consuming process—and still end up with projects we're proud of. In the quilts that follow later in the book, I've combined a variety of quick-cutting and quick-sewing methods that really do make it possible for you to enjoy the whole process of making a quilt in *one week or less.*

This chapter is where I really explain all of the details and special tricks that make these timesaving techniques work. Before you start any of the projects in the book, it would be a good idea to read through the methods I describe in this chapter. Once you start an individual project, there will be certain places in the directions that refer you back to these pages for a refresher on details of the techniques.

## Tools and Accessories You Will Need

The "latest" in sewing and quilting tool technology is always changing. New products are continually being developed to make what we do easier, faster, and more precise. Befriend the staff in your local fabric or quilting shop to keep yourself informed of the latest and the best that is available. Also, make sure you're on the mailing lists for the mail-order sources of quilting supplies provided on page 251.

### Sewing Machine

Keep your sewing machine in good working order. Don't overlook the fact that sewing machines are complex pieces of machinery and need occasional maintenance just like cars. If you're having problems with your machine, you'll have problems with your projects. Use the best machine you can afford, and maintain it in good condition to prevent frustration. Remember—quiltmaking is supposed to be *fun!*

### Rotary Cutter

This simple gadget, which looks like nothing more than a pizza cutter, has revolutionized quiltmaking. Thanks to the rotary cutter, cutting the pieces for a quilt has become much quicker and much more accurate than in the Dark Ages when we all had to use scissors. All of the strips for the pieced projects and portions of the appliquéd projects are intended to be cut with a rotary cutter. Using scissors would defeat the whole timesaving aspect of these quilts!

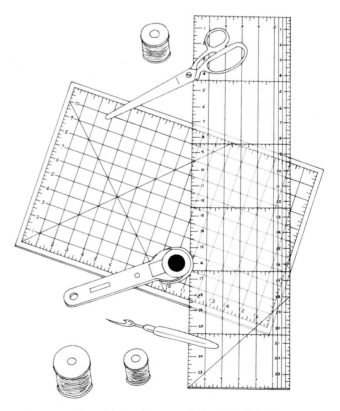

**Diagram 1.** *Essential quilting tools include (clockwise from top) sewing and quilting thread; good, sharp scissors; a see-through ruler; a self-healing cutting mat; a seam ripper; and a rotary cutter.*

If you don't already own a rotary cutter, don't worry—they are easy to find and affordable (usually around $10 through mail-order catalogs or in fabric stores). Be sure to select a rotary cutter with the large-size blade. It will give you much more control, and it will last longer. It doesn't matter whether you're left- or right-handed—a rotary cutter works comfortably either way. (Be sure to note the next item, the Cutting Mat. You should never use a rotary cutter without one.)

When your cutter starts skipping, it's time for a new blade. Don't put replacing off too long; you'll run the risk of mistakes and less-than-accurate cutting. Replacement blades are easy to find wherever you bought the cutter, and they are very simple to install.

For the sake of your fingers and those of your loved ones, get in the habit of retracting the blade every time you set your cutter down. It's a good idea to always be sure to keep the cutter out of reach of inquisitive little hands—the blade is sharp!

## Cutting Mat

A rotary cutter and cutting mat go together like a needle and thread—you can't use one without the other! The cutting mat is the surface on which you lay your fabric before slicing with the cutter. The mat protects the tabletop or floor on which you are cutting, and it also provides handy grid marks and measurements to use as you are preparing the fabric for cutting. Most mats are "self-healing," meaning you won't see the cutting lines in the surface. Under normal use, most mats will last for years.

Get the largest-size mat you have room for. The 24 × 36-inch mat is an all-around good size. If your mat is small, you will end up moving your fabric all the time while cutting. Even though most mat instructions recommend using the rough side up, I like to use the grid side up to help with aligning the fabric.

## See-Through Ruler

To complete the trio of quick-cutting tools, you will need a special rigid plastic see-through ruler to use with your rotary cutter and cutting mat. Although it is possible to use a metal straightedge as a guide against which to push the cutter, the projects in this book require a see-through ruler with measurements.

A 6 × 24-inch ruler is a convenient size. Your ruler needs to have ⅛-inch increments to draw the Speedy Triangle grids. I use the Salem brand, but there are other brands that have the necessary features. If you feel like splurging on an extra accessory, the 6 × 12-inch ruler is also a very handy size to have in addition to your larger ruler.

## Pen

There's nothing high-tech about this, but a pen will come in handy when you are drawing the Speedy Triangle grids. Use a fine- or medium-point ballpoint pen or a fine- or extra-fine felt-tip pen.

## Sewing Thread

We've probably all been tempted by the bargain bins at the fabric store offering many spools of thread for a very low price. Just keep in mind that what you gain in pennies saved may be lost in terms of quality. You should expect your quilts to become family heirlooms. You want them to outlive you and not come apart at the seams! Use good quality thread. If you're not sure about the quality of a certain thread, ask the shop clerk. Quality materials are essential.

## Thread and Needles for Handquilting

For handquilting you must always use special quilting thread, which is easy to find in sewing or quilting shops. Once again, the quality of the thread is critical. If you happen to have some very old spools of quilting thread sitting around, you'll be better off tossing them out. Old thread can become brittle, and if it doesn't snap while you're quilting, it is likely to break after you've stitched it into the quilt.

Quilting thread comes in a variety of colors. When you are quilting in the background of a project, use a coordinating color of thread if you want to create the special texture of quilting but want the design to blend with the background. Use a contrasting color of thread if you want the background stitching design to really stand out.

Quilting needles are also called "betweens." Look for them under either name. Many quilters find the number 10 size to be their favorite size needle for quilting. If you are not sure which size you prefer, buy a package with assorted sizes. The larger the number, the smaller the needle.

## Needles for Basting and Handsewing

A "sharp" is a type of needle that is longer and has a larger eye than the needles you use for quilting. This is a handy needle to do the handbasting. Some people also like to use it for hand appliqué.

Another convenient needle for basting quilt layers together is a darning needle. This longer and larger needle can be easier to grasp as you're basting across large areas, and it can make the work go faster.

For handstitching various parts of the quilt, you should have on hand whatever size sewing needle you find most convenient to use.

## Iron and Ironing Board

Use your iron on the cotton setting and keep the ironing surface clean. Set your ironing board right next to your sewing machine, and position it at the same height as your sewing machine table. This saves on steps (literally) between your machine and ironing board. You can also use the ironing board as a work surface to keep your fabric pieces organized.

## Seam Ripper

There are times (hopefully not too many) when nothing but a sharp seam ripper will do. The tiny, sharp point can rip out stitches much more effectively and carefully than the tips of scissor blades. Aside from the occasional mistake, there are also times when the seam ripper is needed to help construct the quilt. For example, when you make checkerboard and scrap borders, the directions have you make extra and trim the excess to fit the sides of the quilt exactly. A seam ripper is the perfect tool to remove those extra border pieces.

## Walking Foot

This sewing machine attachment is not essential for making the quilts in this book, but it certainly can come in handy. It is sometimes called an even feed foot. Whenever you are sewing two layers of fabric together, the sewing machine pushes the top piece of fabric through at a faster rate than the bottom piece. This can make perfect or nearly perfect piecing very difficult. A walking foot helps correct this tendency. I use one throughout my entire project. This attachment also comes in handy if you plan to do any machine quilting.

## Scissors

Most fabric cutting for the projects is done with the rotary cutter. But for cutting threads and trimming the extra backing, you still need a good, sharp pair of fabric scissors handy.

Use your "second-string" scissors for cutting appliqué designs out of the appliqué film and cutting and trimming batting. These scissors need to be sharp, but you don't want to use your top quality scissors for these steps.

## Appliqué Film

Nearly all of the appliqué projects in this book are perfectly suited for appliqué film. This paper-backed, fusible webbing is sold in precut packets or on bolts at your local fabric or quilting store. Appliqué film replaces laborious handstitching with a simple stroke

of the iron to hold pieces of fabric in place on a background. You simply trace your appliqué designs onto the paper side of the film, fuse with an iron to the wrong side of the appliqué fabrics, cut out the shapes, peel off the paper, then fuse onto the background fabric.

Wonder-Under, Heat 'N Bond and Aleene's are all brands of appliqué film that I use. I'm sure there are other good quality appliqué films available. Inquire at your local fabric shop. Wonder-Under and Aleene's are great for machine appliqué. Appliqué designs attached with Heat 'N Bond and Aleene's can be laundered without finishing the edges with sewing. This makes them perfect for my Penstitch method. Always check the manufacturer's instructions and restrictions before using any appliqué film.

## Tear-Away Paper

Use tear-away paper (sold with interfacings under names like Stitch-n-Tear) as a stabilizer behind the background fabric when doing machine appliqué. This keeps your fabrics from puckering. You may also use paper, but it can dull your needle.

## Extra-Fine Point, Permanent Felt-Tip Pen

For Penstitch appliqué, use this type of felt-tip pen to draw your stitches. You can also use the pen to add details like eyes, noses, mouths, and buttons to various appliqué designs. If you have trouble finding these pens at your quilt or fabric store, check at the local art supply store. Bring a fabric swatch along to test the pens.

## Embroidery Floss

For certain projects, the directions will tell you to add details like noses, eyes, and mouths with embroidery floss. Choose a floss color that works well for the details you are adding.

Embroidery floss is also used for the buttonhole embroidery hand appliqué technique. Coordinate embroidery floss color with your appliqué fabrics.

# Timesaving Techniques for Piecing

The techniques described in detail below are sure to make your cutting and piecing quick and trouble-free!

## Cutting in No Time Flat

Your basic tools for cutting include a rotary cutter, see-through ruler, and a cutting mat. If you haven't used these tools before, you'll be thrilled at how they can work for you. You can cut quickly and accurately

## THE QUILTER'S SEWING BASKET

### Tools and Supplies for Piecing

Fabric requirements as listed for each pattern

Sewing machine

Rotary cutter

Cutting mat

See-through ruler

Ballpoint pen

Straight pins

Sewing thread

Quilting thread and needles

Needles for basting and handstitching

Iron and ironing board

Seam ripper

Scissors

Walking foot attachment for sewing machine (optional)

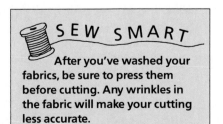

through four or more layers of fabric at a time. If cutting out the pieces of a quilt is your least favorite part of the process, rotary cutting will let you zip through that part and get on with the fun.

If you will be using a rotary cutter and see-through ruler for the first time on these projects, read through these general directions first. Then take some time to practice on scrap fabrics. It's a sensible idea to master this technique on miscellaneous bits of fabric before you get into your project fabric.

Precise cutting is the first step in precision sewing. All of the pieced quilts in this book require accurate cutting and sewing for the best results. Take your time to measure and cut your strips and pieces accurately.

**SEW SMART**

After you've washed your fabrics, be sure to press them before cutting. Any wrinkles in the fabric will make your cutting less accurate.

If possible, a work surface that is kitchen-counter height will be easiest on your back and bring you closer to your work. Lay your cutting mat on your work surface. Use the lines of the grid on the mat to help you straighten and line up the fabric. However, I do not recommend using these thick lines for precision cutting. Both their thickness and the fact that they can "erode" over time greatly reduce their accuracy. But they work great as general guidelines.

**SEW SMART**

If your cutting mat is not normally stored on your work surface, be sure to store it flat, out of sunlight, and away from other heat sources to prevent warpage.

When you are cutting strips, often the dimension for the first strip cut is 44 inches long. This is based on the 44-inch width of the fabric. But don't worry if your fabric is only 42 or 43 inches wide. Cut the strip whatever width your fabric is. This variance has been considered in the yardage and cutting dimensions.

### Making the Cut

**STEP 1.** The average 44-inch-wide fabric comes off the bolt folded in half selvage to selvage (finished edge) to measure approximately 22 inches wide. (If you have washed your fabric, refold selvage to selvage.) Make sure the fabric is straight and then fold again, bringing the fold up to the selvages. It will now be approximately 11 inches wide and four layers thick. Refer to **Diagram 2.** Position the folded fabric so that the edge with the selvages is facing away from you and the double folded edge is facing toward you. Again, be very careful that the fabric is straight. From this folded length of fabric, you can now start to cut your strips.

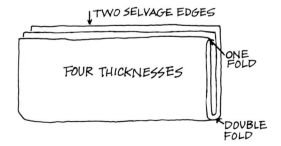

**Diagram 2.** *Fold the fabric in half, selvage to selvage. Make sure it is straight, and fold it in half again.*

**STEP 2.** Use your see-through ruler as a cutting guide. Align one of the horizontal lines of the ruler with the double folded edge of the fabric so the ruler is square with the fabric. See **Diagram 3.** Using some pressure, hold the ruler in position and trim off the uneven edges on the right end of the fabric with the rotary cutter. Make sure you've cut through all four layers. You should now have a perfectly straight edge of fabric.

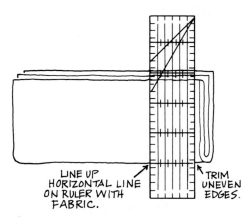

LINE UP HORIZONTAL LINE ON RULER WITH FABRIC.

TRIM UNEVEN EDGES.

**Diagram 3.** *Using a see-through ruler and rotary cutter, trim the uneven edge on the right end of the folded fabric.*

**STEP 3.** You now need to rotate your fabric so that the end you have trimmed is on your left. All of the cutting of strips and pieces for your quilt will be made measuring from this trimmed end of fabric. To move your fabric into the correct position, simply rotate your cutting mat. If you pick up the fabric, you'll risk messing up the four layers of straight edges.

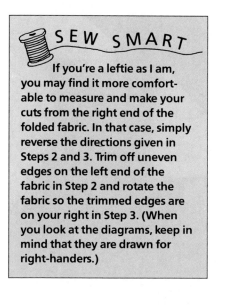

**SEW SMART**

If you're a leftie as I am, you may find it more comfortable to measure and make your cuts from the right end of the folded fabric. In that case, simply reverse the directions given in Steps 2 and 3. Trim off uneven edges on the left end of the fabric in Step 2 and rotate the fabric so the trimmed edges are on your right in Step 3. (When you look at the diagrams, keep in mind that they are drawn for right-handers.)

**STEP 4.** On your ruler there should be several horizontal lines that run across the width. Each of these lines should be marked in increments (on the Salem ruler I use, these are ⅛-inch increments). Use these horizontal lines as your point of reference as you make the next cuts. From the edge of the ruler, going across one of these lines, find the width of the first strip you want to cut. For example, if the strip is 2½ inches wide by 44 inches long, find 2½ inches from the edge of your ruler. Align the 2½-inch line on the ruler with the straight edge of the fabric. See **Diagram 4.** To make sure your ruler is lined up perfectly straight, look for the 2½-inch mark on two or three of the lines that cross the ruler. These marks should also lie directly over the straight edge of the fabric. When the ruler is lined up perfectly with the fabric edge, hold it in position and cut.

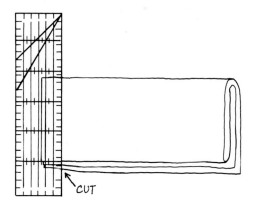

CUT

**Diagram 4.** *Rotate the mat so that the trimmed end of the fabric is on the left. Align the ruler with the straight edge of the fabric, hold it in position, and cut the strips.*

**STEP 5.** After cutting strips, many of the projects then require you to cut pieces from those strips. The width of the strip is usually the same as the width or length of the pieces you will be cutting. If you're cutting several pieces that are the same size, you can leave your strip folded in quarters or in half, so you can cut more than one piece at a time. Lay the ruler on top of the strip. Line up one of the horizontal lines on your ruler with the long edge of your strip. Trim off one end of the strip to square and straighten the edge of the fabric. (For fabric folded in quarters, trim the end with one fold and the selvages; for fabric folded in half, trim the end with the selvages. See **Diagrams 5 and 6.**) Rotate the fabric so this cut end is on the left, as described above in Step 3. Following the cutting procedure explained in Step 4, cut the pieces as specified in the pattern. See **Diagram 7.** In some cases you may be cutting several different size pieces from one strip. Cut the largest pieces first, and then trim down strips or pieces to make the smaller pieces.

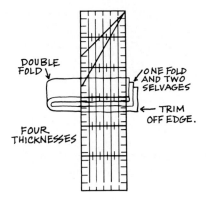

**Diagram 5.** *To cut smaller pieces off a strip, leave the strip folded in fourths so you can cut more than one piece at a time. Align one of the horizontal lines on the ruler with the long edge of the strip, and trim off the edge.*

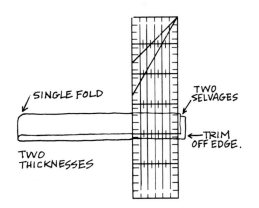
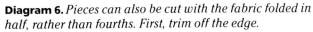

**Diagram 6.** *Pieces can also be cut with the fabric folded in half, rather than fourths. First, trim off the edge.*

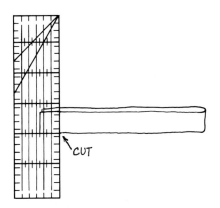

**Diagram 7.** *Once the edge has been trimmed, rotate the mat so that the cut end of the fabric is on the left, and cut the pieces specified in the pattern.*

## How to Get the Best Results with a Rotary Cutter

✄ When cutting with a rotary cutter, you should always stand. You will have more control and a straight perspective on your work.

✄ To keep the ruler from slipping while you cut, put a few small pieces of masking tape on the back side. (If you'll be taking that ruler to any quilting classes, use one of those pieces of tape to write your name on!)

✄ When the ruler is in position, hold it in place with your fingers flexed. If your palm is flat on the ruler, it can easily slide out of position.

✄ Make sure the blade in your rotary cutter is sharp. There are telltale signs that the blade is getting dull: it will start skipping, leaving small sections of fabric uncut. When you find yourself going back over your cutting lines, it is definitely time for a blade change.

✄ Always cut *away* from you. This is not only a safety precaution, but you will also have more control when cutting in that direction.

### Speedy Triangles

One of the basic building blocks of many quilt designs is a square or rectangle made of two triangles sewn together along the long edge. The traditional method for preparing these units is to cut two individual triangles, then stitch them together. You can imagine how long that sort of piecing would take, especially if you were stitching by hand!

In my quilts, I feature a quick-sew method for making these units that will save you lots of time and aggravation. I call them triangle sets, even though when you are done sewing and pressing you end up with a square shape. Refer to each specific pattern for fabric color, size of fabric pieces, and size of the grid you will mark. Read through the step-by-step directions below for details on this quick and easy technique.

## Marking, Sewing, and Cutting Speedy Triangles

**STEP 1.** Line up and position your selected fabrics with right sides together.

**STEP 2.** To mark the grid, you need a ballpoint pen, see-through ruler, and good light. A bright lamp directly over your work area is a good idea. The specific project will list the size and number of squares in the grid. For an example, let's say our pattern requires a 2⅞-inch grid of eight squares. As you get ready to mark the grid, keep in mind that you want to draw on the wrong side of the lightest fabric.

**STEP 3.** The size of fabric pieces used for the Speedy Triangles allows a ½- to 1-inch margin of fabric all the way around the grid. Line up your ruler approximately ½ to 1 inch from the edge of your fabric lengthwise and draw a line.

**STEP 4.** Rotate your fabric and line up your ruler to draw a second line exactly 2⅞ inches from the first line. Align your ruler with the second line to draw a third line exactly 2⅞ inches from the second line.

**STEP 5.** Rotate your fabric a quarter turn to get ready to draw perpendicular lines to make the squares. Line up one of the horizontal lines on your ruler with one of the lines drawn on your fabric to square your ruler. Draw your first perpendicular line about ½ to 1 inch from the edge of the fabric.

**STEP 6.** Rotate your fabric and line your ruler up to draw a second line exactly 2⅞ inches from the first perpendicular line. Align your ruler with the second line to draw a third line 2⅞ inches away. Repeat two more times to draw a fourth and fifth line. Your grid is now complete.

**STEP 7.** The next step is to draw diagonal lines that will exactly intersect the corners of the squares. Drop the point of your pen exactly on the corners you will intersect and then butt the ruler up to the pen. You will need to move the pen from point to point until you get your ruler lined up so that the line you draw will precisely intersect the corners. Refer to **Diagram 8**.

**STEP 8.** Now you're ready to sew. Using a ¼-inch seam allowance, stitch along *both* sides of the diagonal lines. Use the edge of your presser foot as a ¼-inch guide, or draw a line ¼ inch away from both sides of the pen lines if your presser foot doesn't equal exactly ¼ inch. When you're done sewing, you should have a piece of fabric that looks like **Diagram 9**.

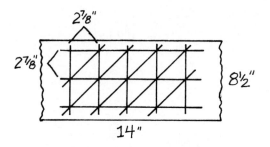

**Diagram 8.** *To make Speedy Triangles, first mark a grid on your fabric. Then, draw diagonal lines that intersect the squares on the grid.*

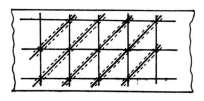

**Diagram 9.** *Stitch along both sides of the diagonal lines, using a ¼-inch seam allowance.*

**STEP 9.** Use your rotary cutter and ruler to cut along all the pen lines. On many of the points of the triangles, there will remain a couple of stitches as shown in the triangle set at the left in **Diagram 10**. Just open up the triangle set with a gentle tug and the stitches will pull out. Do not tug with force or you can stretch your triangle set out of shape. Based on our example, you will have made a total of sixteen 2½-inch triangle sets. Each square from the grid you drew makes two triangle sets.

**STEP 10.** Gently press open the triangle sets. See the individual projects for which direction to press the seam allowances. Triangle sets should be right side up while pressing. Your finished sets should look like the one in **Diagram 11**.

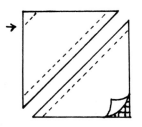 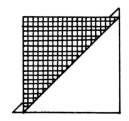

**Diagram 10.** *Cut along the diagonal pen lines. A gentle tug will remove any stitches remaining in the corners.*

**Diagram 11.** *Press open the triangle sets.*

Accuracy is critical in every step of making triangle sets (marking, cutting, sewing, and pressing). If you don't pay close attention, you can alter the size of your triangle set, making piecing the blocks together more difficult.

## Troubleshooting Triangles

| DILEMMA | POSSIBLE CAUSES |
| --- | --- |
| The finished triangle set isn't perfectly square. | Did you mark your grid accurately? |
| | Were the diagonal lines connected exactly across the corners? |
| | Did you tug them out of whack while pressing? Try gently finger-pressing the triangle sets open before using the iron. |
| The size of the triangle sets varies slightly from set to set. | Did you mark your grid accurately? |
| | Did you sew with an accurate ¼-inch seam? |
| | Did you cut exactly along the pen lines? |
| | Did you fail to open the seams fully when pressing the set open? |
| Little "tails" of fabric (the seam allowance) stick out on the sides. | If you find these distracting, trim off the seam allowance carefully so it is even with the sides of the square. |

## Speedy Sewing Techniques

There are several ways you can speed up the sewing portion of your quiltmaking (not including making your machine go faster!). Three of these techniques are discussed in detail here. As you read through specific projects later in the book, the instructions will tell you when it is appropriate to use one or more of these methods.

## Assembly Line Piecing

Your inclination might be to sew *all* the pieces for one block together before moving on to complete the second block, third block, and so on. Although your quilt would certainly get done, that is not necessarily the quickest way to go about assembling the blocks.

I've found that if you work on the same principle as an assembly line, repeating the same step over and over, your piecing can go much more quickly. Basically, you will assemble the blocks one step at a time, and you will repeat the same step for each block at the same time. Instead of finishing the blocks one by one, you will finish the blocks all at the same time. For example, let's say you are working on a quilt that has twelve blocks. The first step calls for you to sew together four triangle sets. You repeat this step *twelve* times (once for each block). If the next step calls for you to sew a rectangle to the triangle set units, you repeat *that* step twelve times. As you proceed through the rest of the assembly steps, repeating each step twelve times, all of your blocks will take shape at the same time and will be completed all together.

Take an extra minute to double-check that you are sewing the right pieces together and that all the pieces are positioned correctly. If you make a mistake, you don't want to keep repeating it for all the blocks!

Besides speeding up your piecing, this assembly line technique will help keep you organized. You think once, repeat the step for the number of blocks in the quilt, and then move on to the next step.

You may want to start out by putting one entire block together to use as a guide for piecing the rest. It's fun to see a block put together right away, and it will help you to see how the Assembly Line works!

To keep track of which strips and pieces to use in each assembly step, make a pile for each different size piece as you're cutting the fabric for your blocks. You may even want to use a small scrap of paper or a piece of masking tape to mark each pile with the size of the piece. For example, one pile might read, Fabric A—2½ × 2½ inches.

When working with a scrap design, you may be using different fabrics for each of the blocks. For example, there may be four different Fabric A's. In this case, I suggest you stack your fabrics in the same order for each pile. The same Fabric A will be on top of the pile and in the same sequence throughout each of the piles.

### Continuous Seam

Assembly Line Piecing and the Continuous Seam technique go hand in hand. Any time you are using the assembly line method to piece your blocks, you can use the Continuous Seam method of sewing them together.

Line up all the same pieces for the first step for each block next to your sewing machine. With right sides together, stitch the first two pieces together. Instead of removing those pieces from under the presser foot and clipping the threads, keep them where they are. Butt the next set of pieces directly behind the set you have just sewn and continue sewing. Add each set without breaking your seam until you have joined all the sets together. (The hardest part about learning this technique is to overcome the natural tendency to want to clip the threads.)

You will end up with a long chain of pieces joined together by thread (see **Diagram 12**). Take this chain to your ironing board and press, following the directions for pressing given in the project text. Once you've pressed the seams, you can clip the threads that join all the pieces.

**Diagram 12.** *Sew the first set of pieces together. Without lifting the presser foot or clipping threads, butt the second set directly behind the first and continue sewing. Add each set in a continuous seam until you have joined all the sets together.*

### Speedy Strips

With this very basic and easy technique, you will be able to assemble very complex looking quilt blocks and create two or three color checkerboards or multicolored scrap borders in no time flat. For an example of a project that makes good use of this technique, look at Trio of Trees on page 151. Both the

tree blocks and the checkerboard accent were created using Speedy Strips.

The unit assembled using the Speedy Strip technique is called a strip set. The directions for each project will tell you the number of strips to cut and which fabrics to use to create the required strip sets.

To make a checkerboard or scrap border, you sew the strips together along the long edges, alternating the fabrics as directed. As you add each strip, always pause to press the seam. The general rule for pressing is to press seams toward the darkest fabric or all in the same direction.

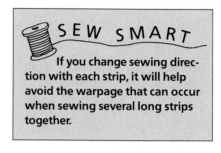

**SEW SMART**

If you change sewing direction with each strip, it will help avoid the warpage that can occur when sewing several long strips together.

Once you have joined together all the strips, you have created a large strip set like the one shown in **Diagram 13**. The directions will then tell you to cut this strip set in half or in thirds. Resew the sections end to end. From this final strip set, you will cut the narrow strips that form the scrap border or checkerboard. (See The Borders on page 26 for more details on making scrap and checkerboard borders.)

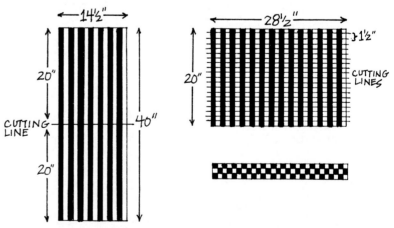

**Diagram 13.** *To make a checkerboard or scrap border, sew strips together to make a large strip set. Cut the strip set in half, and resew the halves together as shown. From this new strip set, cut narrow strips and either rematch them to form a checkerboard, or sew them end to end for a scrap border.*

The same basic principle applies to strip sets you will sew to make quilt blocks. In some of the projects, you will notice that there is a special cutting chart just for cutting these strips. Be sure to read all the directions and cut the strips as described. The step-by-step directions will then tell you how to sew together strips of various widths and different fabrics to create a number of strip sets (see **Diagram 14**).

Once the strip sets are assembled, you will need to slice them into segments with your rotary cutter and group them into piles (see **Diagram 15**). Each pile of segments will make one block. The directions will very clearly explain in what order you are to assemble these segments. (See **Diagram 16** for an example of how the strips are sewn together to become a block.)

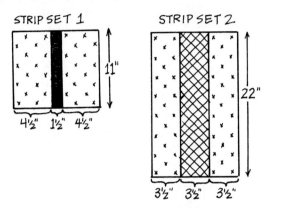

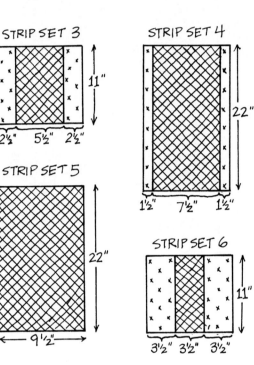

**Diagram 14.** *Strip sets are created by sewing together strips of various widths and fabrics.*

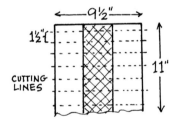

**Diagram 15.** *The strip sets are then cut into segments.*

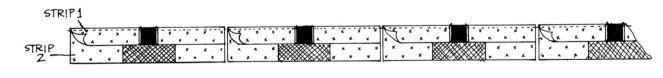

**Diagram 16.** *The segments are sewn together into blocks using the Continuous Seam technique.*

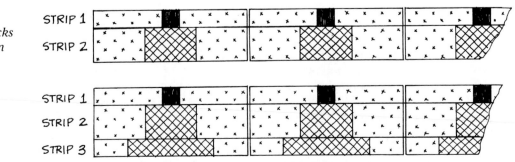

## Stitches for Special Touches

Some of the projects call for adding features like eyes, noses, and mouths with embroidery floss. **Diagram 17** illustrates three embroidery stitches you can use to add these extra details.

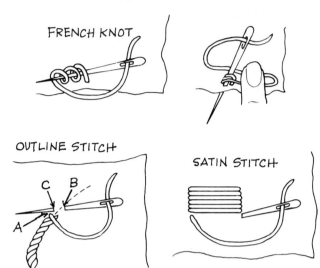

**Diagram 17.** *These simple embroidery stitches are great for adding details.*

### French Knot

These knots make wonderful eyes! Thread the needle with four to six strands of floss. Knot one end. Bring the needle up through the fabric at the point where you want the knot. Wrap the thread around the needle three times and hold the thread taut with your finger. Insert the needle back into the fabric close to where it came up. Pull the needle through to the back. The knot will remain on top.

### Outline or Stem Stitch

This is the stitch to use to create smiling faces. Thread the needle with three strands of floss and tie a knot in one end. (You may choose to use fewer strands for tiny details or more for a heavier look.) Pull the needle up at A, insert at B, then pull the needle up at C, a point approximately halfway between A and B.

### Satin Stitch

This stitch is good for filling in solid areas like animal noses. Thread the needle with three strands of floss and tie a knot in one end. (You may choose to use fewer strands for tiny details or more for a heavier look.) Start at the widest part of the area you want to fill in. Bring the needle up through the fabric on one edge and insert it on the opposite side. Make the second stitch as close as possible to the first stitch. Continue until the area has been filled in.

## Timesaving Techniques for Appliqué

The basic theory behind appliqué has not really changed over the years: You cut out shapes, then apply them to a background fabric. But the techniques and tools we use have changed over time. In the past, a quilter's only options were to use a needle to turn under raw edges of the appliquéd pieces and finish by stitching or embroidering by hand. Quilts made this way were certainly very traditional and beautiful, but they were also very time-consuming.

---

### THE QUILTER'S SEWING BASKET

**Tools and Supplies for Appliqué**

Fabric requirements as listed for
   each pattern

Sewing machine

Rotary cutter

Cutting mat

See-through ruler

Sewing thread

Straight pins

Quilting thread and needles

Needles for handstitching and hand
   appliqué

Seam ripper

Scissors (fabric and paper)

Iron and ironing board

Appliqué film

Tear-away paper (for machine
   appliqué only)

Extra-fine point, permanent felt-tip
   pen (for Penstitch
   appliqué only)

Embroidery floss
   (for buttonhole
   embroidery and
   adding details)

---

Now we have fancy sewing machines to finish the edges with machine stitches, appliqué film to hold our fabric pieces in position while we sew them, tear-away paper to stabilize our fabrics to keep them from puckering, and threads made especially for machine embroidery. Plus, there's a great new technique I've developed called Penstitch appliqué—you don't even need to finish the edges with sewing. All of these advances in appliqué technique mean you can create a lovely appliqué project in a mere fraction of the time it takes using traditional methods.

In the appliqué projects that follow later in the book, you are reminded to select an appliqué technique to use to complete the project. You are asked to choose from machine, buttonhole embroidery, Penstitch, or hand appliqué. All of these techniques are discussed in detail below. In some cases, if I believe one technique gives a better result, I will recommend that particular method. But for the most part, the choice of technique is up to you.

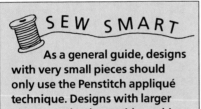

**S E W  S M A R T**

As a general guide, designs with very small pieces should only use the Penstitch appliqué technique. Designs with larger pieces may be done with machine, buttonhole embroidery, or hand appliqué.

## General Directions for Using Appliqué Film

For Penstitch, machine, and buttonhole embroidery appliqué you will need to fuse your appliqué pieces onto a background. The quickest and easiest way to do this is to use appliqué film (see Appliqué Film on page 8 for more on how to select appliqué film).

**STEP 1.** Trace each of the parts of the selected appliqué design individually onto the paper side of the appliqué film. Since you can see through the film, you can lay it directly over the design in the book and trace. Remember your design will be the mirror image of what you see on the book page. If you want to avoid this, first trace the design from the book onto a white piece of paper using a dark felt-tip pen. Turn the paper over so the lines you've traced are facing down. Retrace the design to the side of the paper that is facing up using the felt-tip pen. From this second tracing, transfer the design onto the appliqué film. Keep in mind that letters *must* be traced in reverse.

**STEP 2.** Using paper scissors, cut loosely around the traced designs on the appliqué film as shown in **Diagram 18.** Do not cut along the lines at this point.

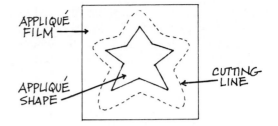

**Diagram 18.** *Trace the appliqué shape onto the appliqué film and cut it out, loosely following the outline of the design.*

**STEP 3.** Before you fuse, check the manufacturer's instructions for the proper iron setting to use with that brand of appliqué film. Fuse each piece of appliqué film to the wrong side of your selected fabrics. Place the appliqué film with paper side up and webbing side against your fabric.

**STEP 4.** When all the pieces are fused, cut out the appliqué shapes following the tracing lines (see **Diagram 19**). Remove the paper backing of the appliqué film. A thin fusing film will remain on the wrong side of the fabric.

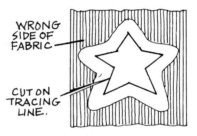

**Diagram 19.** *Fuse the appliqué film to the wrong side of the fabric. Following the tracing lines, cut out the appliqué shape.*

**S E W  S M A R T**

After you've fused the appliqué film to the fabric and have cut out the shapes, let the pieces cool for a while before removing the paper backing.

**STEP 5.** Arrange and center all the pieces of the appliqué design on the background fabric. Remember to allow ¼ inch for seam allowances on the edges of background fabric. Refer to the appliqué patterns as you position the pieces; the dotted lines will indicate where certain pieces should be placed underneath others. When everything is arranged, fuse the pieces in position with your iron. After the fabric is fused to the background, choose which appliqué technique you prefer, Penstitch, buttonhole embroidery, or machine appliqué.

**SEW SMART**
You may find that your fingers are clumsy when it comes to laying out all the tiny pieces in an appliqué design. Use a straight pin instead to move all the pieces into place. I also suggest laying them out on your ironing board because you won't want to move them once you've got them arranged.

## Penstitch Appliqué

I developed this technique for small projects where you want the look of appliqué without having to spend a lot of time. Penstitch is a pseudo-stitch done with an extra-fine point, permanent felt-tip pen. After you fuse the appliqué pieces to the background fabric, you use the pen to draw in stitches along the edges of the appliqué. Since there is no real stitching done, the fusing is what holds the appliqué pieces in place. This technique allows you to use very small pieces of fabric and gives much greater detail to the appliqué design. It is simple to do, lots of fun, and very effective. It's great if you want quick results. After all, the pen is much quicker than the needle!

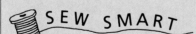

**SEW SMART**
With very dark fabrics, skip the Penstitch for those pieces of the design. Penstitch won't show up on dark colors.

This technique is best used in smaller projects that have a lot of detail and that won't have a lot of stress put on them. I wouldn't recommend Penstitch for items like pillows and baby bibs that will be handled a lot or that will need to be laundered frequently. But for other projects like wallhangings or ornaments, Penstitch is perfect. In the appliqué project text I will often mention whether I feel the project is suited to Penstitch or not.

Once the edges of the appliquéd pieces are held in position with the appliqué film, you can then finish them with your choice of Penstitch (Style 1 or Style 2, described below). Some appliqué films, like Heat 'N Bond, can be laundered without finishing the edges with sewing, making them a good choice for Penstitch appliqué. Be sure to check the manufacturer's instructions for projects that you may wish to launder.

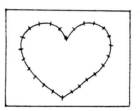

**SEW SMART**
If the edges of your appliquéd pieces ever lift up, don't worry! Just repress them back in position with your iron.

### Penstitch Style 1

The stitches should look like they overlap from the edge of the appliqué onto the background. With your pen, use just one continuous stroke per stitch. Your Penstitch should be only about ¹⁄₁₆ inch long and spaced fairly evenly. See **Diagram 20** for an example of this style.

**Diagram 20.** *Using your felt-tip pen, make tiny stitches from the edge of the appliqué piece onto the background.*

### Penstitch Style 2

The stitches should appear along the outer edges of the appliqué shapes. The idea is to have them resemble a running stitch. Working about ¹⁄₁₆ inch from the outer edge of the appliqué pieces, draw lines about ¹⁄₁₆ inch long on the appliqué fabric. See **Diagram 21** for reference.

**Diagram 21.** *In this style of Penstitch, the stitches resemble a running stitch outlining the appliqué piece.*

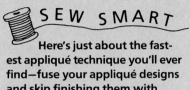

**SEW SMART**

Here's just about the fastest appliqué technique you'll ever find—fuse your appliqué designs and skip finishing them with Penstitch. The best use for this method is on ornaments.

## Machine Appliqué

After fusing your appliqué pieces in place you can outline the edges with a machine embroidery stitch. This technique may be your best choice for larger projects with larger pieces, like Alley Cats on page 175. This technique takes some practice and a sewing machine in good working order. Be sure to spend some time with practice fabrics before starting your project.

**STEP 1.** Fuse all the appliqué pieces in place on the background fabric, following the steps given in General Directions for Using Appliqué Film on page 17.

**STEP 2.** Use tear-away paper as a stabilizer underneath the machine stitches. Cut a piece of paper large enough to cover the area you'll be stitching. Hold or pin the tear-away paper to the *wrong* side of the background fabric in the stitching areas. This keeps your fabrics from puckering when you do your appliqué stitching. (You may also use paper, but it can dull the sewing machine needle.)

**STEP 3.** Use a neutral colored bobbin thread for all of the appliqué. Coordinate several thread colors to match the various appliqué fabric colors. These you will use for the top threads, changing them as needed as you work on the appliqué. For best results, use machine embroidery thread.

**STEP 4.** To get a good appliqué stitch, make sure your sewing machine is working properly. Set it on satin stitch at about 80 stitches per inch (about the same as you'd use for a machine buttonhole stitch). Be sure to practice on test fabric so you can adjust your machine settings to just where you want them.

**STEP 5.** Stitch along all the edges of all the appliqué pieces. Begin by appliquéing along the edges of the pieces that go underneath another appliqué piece. Change top thread color as necessary. When you're all finished, pull away the paper from the back side of the fabric.

## Buttonhole Embroidery Appliqué

Although this technique does call for handstitching, it is fairly simple and it gives a very traditional, old-fashioned look to your quilt. The real advantage is that you can take your project along with you in the car, to the doctor's office, or on a plane and continue your stitching. Buttonhole embroidery is best suited to appliqué projects with relatively large, simple pieces. If the appliqué pieces are too small or there are too many small pieces, Penstitch appliqué may be a better choice.

After you have fused the appliqué design to the background fabric, you outline the edges of the appliqué pieces with the buttonhole stitch done in embroidery floss. You can pick out an assortment of different floss colors to coordinate with the different appliqué fabric colors, or you can use one standard color throughout (black can be quite effective).

Use two to three strands of embroidery floss and refer to **Diagram 22** for guidance on how to do the stitch. For very small pieces, use just one strand of floss.

**Diagram 22.** *Use embroidery floss and the buttonhole stitch to outline appliqué pieces that have been fused in position.*

## Hand Appliqué

In many of the appliqué projects in this book, you will be asked to select the technique you want to use. One of your options is hand appliqué. Take your choice from the two hand appliqué methods described below.

### Quick and Easy Hand Appliqué

For larger, relatively simple shapes like hearts, this technique is a quicker alternative to the laborious, needle-turning hand appliqué method our grandmothers used.

**STEP 1.** For this example, let's assume we're making an appliquéd heart. First, make a heart template. Then, put two pieces of your selected fabric right sides together. With a pen, trace around the heart template onto the wrong side of the fabric.

**STEP 2.** Holding the two pieces of fabric together, cut ¼ inch outside the traced line. Stitch all the way around the heart shape on the pen line. Clip the curves and trim the seam allowance down to ⅛ inch as shown in **Diagram 23.**

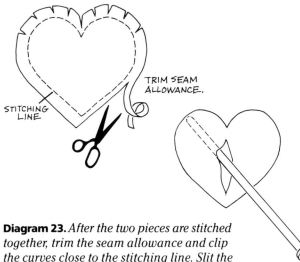

STITCHING LINE

TRIM SEAM ALLOWANCE.

**Diagram 23.** *After the two pieces are stitched together, trim the seam allowance and clip the curves close to the stitching line. Slit the back, turn the heart right side out, and smooth the seams with a knitting needle or other object.*

**STEP 3.** Slit the back of the heart and turn right side out. Use a blunt but pointy object (like a knitting needle) to smooth out seams and create smooth curves. Press flat.

**STEP 4.** Pin the heart in position and handstitch in place.

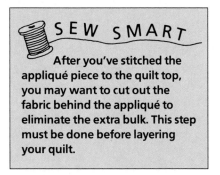

**SEW SMART**

After you've stitched the appliqué piece to the quilt top, you may want to cut out the fabric behind the appliqué to eliminate the extra bulk. This step must be done before layering your quilt.

### Freezer Paper Appliqué

Like the technique described above, freezer paper appliqué works best with larger, simpler shapes. It is a great way to create nice smooth curves on appliqué pieces.

**STEP 1.** Trace the appliqué design from the book onto freezer paper, and cut out the shape for each piece.

**STEP 2.** Using the freezer paper shape as your pattern, cut out the fabric piece, adding ¼ inch all the way around. (See **Diagram 24.**)

RIGHT SIDE OF FABRIC

FREEZER PAPER SHAPE

**Diagram 24.** *Cut the appliqué shape out of freezer paper. Using the shape as a pattern, cut out the fabric piece, allowing ¼-inch seam allowance. Place the freezer paper (waxy side up) on the wrong side of the fabric, fold over the seam allowance, and press it in place with the tip of your iron.*

**STEP 3.** Lay the freezer paper on top of the wrong side of the fabric piece. The waxy side of the freezer paper should be facing up.

**STEP 4.** Fold the ¼-inch seam allowance of fabric up and over the edge of the freezer paper shape, referring to **Diagram 24.** Curves and corners will need to be clipped. Use the tip of your iron to press the seam allowances to the waxy side of the freezer paper. The heat will fuse the edges of the fabric in position, creating a perfect appliqué shape.

**STEP 5.** Leaving the freezer paper in for now, pin the appliqué in position and handstitch in place.

**STEP 6.** Cut out the fabric behind the appliqué piece (leaving a ¼-inch seam allowance), and remove the freezer paper. See **Diagram 25.** Press.

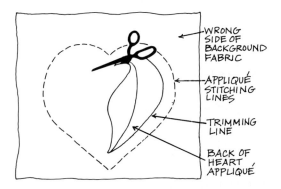

WRONG SIDE OF BACKGROUND FABRIC

APPLIQUÉ STITCHING LINES

TRIMMING LINE

BACK OF HEART APPLIQUÉ

**Diagram 25.** *After the piece is appliquéd in place, cut away the fabric from the back side and remove the freezer paper.*

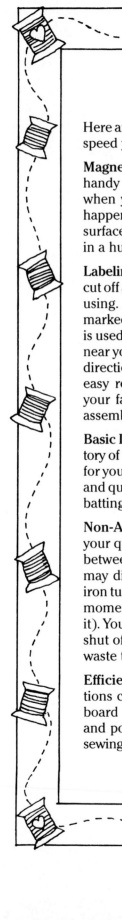

# Ten Tried-and-True Timesavers

Here are some tricks and tools that can help speed your quiltmaking along.

**Magnetic Pin Holder:** This keeps your pins handy in one place so they're always ready when you need them. Plus, if you should happen to knock the holder off your work surface, the magnet picks up scattered pins in a hurry.

**Labeling System:** At the start of your project, cut off a small snip of each fabric you will be using. Attach it to a piece of masking tape marked with the letter ID of the fabric as it is used in the project. Tape these fabric bits near your work table, sewing machine, and directions. They will serve as a quick and easy reminder to help you keep track of your fabrics while cutting the pieces and assembling the blocks.

**Basic Inventory:** Keep a well-stocked inventory of the basics such as replacement blades for your rotary cutter, basic colors of sewing and quilting thread, needles, appliqué film, batting, or anything else you use a lot.

**Non-Automatic Iron:** As you're working on your quilting projects, there will be pauses between sewing and pressing seams. You may discover that your automatic-shut-off iron turns itself off at the most inconvenient moments (like right before you want to use it). You may want to use an iron that doesn't shut off automatically so you don't have to waste time waiting for the iron to reheat!

**Efficient Floor Plan:** Keep your work stations close to each other. Set your ironing board right next to your sewing machine, and position it at the same height as your sewing machine table. This saves many steps back and forth between your sewing machine and iron.

**Thread Reserves:** Use neutral colors of thread like gray and natural for your sewing. Keep large spools of these on hand and wind several bobbins of these colors before starting your project. Nothing is more annoying than having to stop, unthread your machine, and wind another bobbin to replace one that has run out.

**Pins on the Top:** When pinning the binding in place to handstitch, put the pins on the top side of your quilt. This way your thread won't constantly wrap around the pins while you're stitching.

**Thread Needles Ahead:** For handbasting and quilting, thread several needles at once (try four to six needles) and keep them in reserve. As you're working, you won't constantly have to stop and rethread.

**Masking Tape Guides:** Use quilter's ¼-inch masking tape for the quickest, most reliable way to mark outline quilting. This saves you the time of drawing the lines on your quilt plus the time to erase them once you're done. A word of warning however: Don't leave any tape on your project for an extended period of time or leave it in sunlight; otherwise, tape residue may remain on your quilt.

**Portable Projects:** Have a small handquilting project ready to go in a tote bag with thread, needle, scissors, and a thimble. It's amazing how much quilting you can get done while waiting in traffic, at the doctor's office, or any other place when you have 15 to 20 idle minutes.

# Quiltmaking Essentials

In this chapter, we'll get back to basics by discussing all the basic procedures you follow to make a quilt, from the very first step of choosing fabric, through joining the blocks together, all the way to the finishing touches of binding and quilting.

## Fun with Fabric

For many people, the hardest part of making a quilt is selecting the fabrics. What colors work well together? What sort of prints will go together nicely without clashing? Because there are so many options of colors and prints, it's easy to become overwhelmed. To aid you in this important first step, I've put together some practical pointers. No one should have to suffer from fabric-phobia!

### Is 100 Percent Cotton Really the Best?

In my opinion, you should buy only 100 percent cotton fabric. This fabric is much easier to work with when piecing and appliquéing. Cotton fabrics have more "give," which can assist in piecing. Cotton fabrics also handle much more easily when you are creating curves and points on appliqué pieces. The polyester fibers in cotton/poly blends can cause puckering and don't give when they need to during piecing. If you've ever tried to hand appliqué with a cotton/poly blend, you know what it's like to have to wrestle with the fabric to get nice smooth curves and crisp points. Beside all these drawbacks to polyester fibers, 100 percent cotton fabric is the traditional choice of quilters and gives the old-fashioned, country look that is perfectly suited to my quilt designs.

### Coordinating Colors

Does "color theory" mystify you? It does most people who aren't trained as artists. But understanding how colors relate to each other can give you the confidence to mix and match colors that you might not have considered before. Enrolling in a Color Theory for Quilting class can give you some great tools and knowledge on which to base your fabric choices.

Check for a class like this at your local quilting shop. Color classes are usually offered in conjunction with quilt shows, so check for any shows in your area and request a schedule of classes. In the meantime, you can continue reading for some practical ideas to help you out.

SEW SMART

When choosing your quilt backing fabric, think about whether you want the quilting stitch to stand out or not. If the fabric is a contrast to your thread color, the stitches will be more prominent. If you use an active print, your stitches will be hidden.

As a starting point, ask yourself a few questions. What is the purpose of this project? Are you making it for yourself? Will it be a gift for a friend who has specific color preferences? Is the quilt a homecoming gift for a new baby? Can you use any colors that you want? Or does your quilt need to coordinate with colors in a certain room or theme? Would any specific colors lend themselves particularly well to this project (seasonal red and green for a holiday quilt, for example)? What colors do you enjoy looking at?

Once you've thought about answers to those questions, start to study the colors you see around you every day. Continually observe the use of color and make mental notes about what combinations work, which ones don't work, and what you like. The following are some great resources for color observation.

### Quilts

Quilts made by others are a natural place to start. Look at the photos in quilting magazines or quilting books. Visit a quilting shop where quilts are on display. Attend a quilt show. See what color combinations work. Also look at what doesn't seem to be working and see if you can figure out why. When you see a color combination you love, make notes and borrow the same colors for your quilt.

## Multi-Color Print Fabrics

Print fabrics that include a variety of colors in one piece can be a good starting point for inspiration. Fabrics are a very handy resource you can find easily in your favorite fabric shop. Find a particular multi-color fabric that you like, and then use that set of colors as the basis for matching and coordinating several fabrics for your quilt.

## Other Textiles

Also observe other textiles such as clothing, linens, and draperies. Keep your eyes open when you go shopping or page through mail-order catalogs. You never know where you'll see something that really inspires you.

## Artwork

Artwork is another related medium in which the use of color is very important. Look at photographs, paintings, and pottery for ideas on how to combine colors for a certain effect.

## Mother Nature

Don't forget the greatest artist of all! Mother Nature has created beautiful blendings of colors in sunsets, autumn foliage, winter skies, and spring flowers. Keep your eyes open and learn from her!

Benefit from others who know how to use color and put colors together. Observe and use those ideas, and soon your color intuition will develop. After experience and experimentation with color, you will begin to assimilate what you have learned and develop your own color sense and style.

### SEW SMART

If you have a bulging collection of scrap fabrics that you would like to use for a project instead of purchasing something new, here's how to adapt the yardage requirements. Refer to the cutting chart for the project you want to make. Determine the number and sizes of the pieces that need to be cut. Compare those numbers to the amount of scrap fabric you have available to use.

## My Favorite Country Color Combinations

It is no surprise that our tastes and favorite colors usually change over time. The colors I loved when I was newly married are not the same colors I've used to decorate my home some fourteen years later. Plus, our minds are often involuntarily governed by trends, and the availability of colors is often governed by fabric manufacturers.

As you glance through the photographs of the projects in this book, you'll see that I've tried to present a wide range of color combinations to provide you with as much inspiration as possible. However, you may also notice that certain color combinations do occur a little more frequently than others. I will admit that I do have favorite color pairings (subject, as always, to change!). If I were to write this book twenty years from now, these favorites would probably be different. But for now, here are my favorite color combinations that create what I feel is a country look.

✂ Pastels with a grayed undertone (These soft pastels have probably been the colors most closely associated with the country look.)

✂ Steel blue with deep dusty rose

✂ Soft mint green with dusty pink

✂ Dark forest green with berry red

✂ Black with burgundy or deep red

✂ Warm tans instead of whites for background fabrics (to create more of an antique country look)

## Texture for the Eyes

When you hear the word texture, you probably think about how something feels to your fingers. When you're selecting fabrics for your quilts, you need to expand that definition of texture and start thinking about how your eyes respond to the fabric. Visual texture means all the elements of the fabric, in combination with color, that give it its particular look. These elements include any shapes that create a print, their size, and how they appear against the background.

The key to a successful quilt is to use a variety of textures and vary the scale (size) of the prints. To help you understand and recognize different visual textures, here are some basic categories:

Geometric—angular, repetitive shapes like squares, triangles, diamonds, plaids, stripes, and checks
Circular—print filled with dots or circles
Abstract—nonrepetitive, nonsymmetrical, uneven
Floral Prints
Leafy Prints
Paisley Prints—swirly, overall patterns
Combination—two or more textures in one print

Any of those textures in the list can have a busy look when the print pattern is very dense and very little background shows through. When the print is very open and the background shows up more, the background color becomes more prominent.

All of these textures can vary even more depending on the scale of the print. Tiny, medium, and large-sized floral prints will all look different from each other because the scale varies, even though the patterns are similar.

Your goal in varying print textures and scale is to make a project that is interesting to look at. Contrast creates quilts that are visually exciting. If you use several prints that have the same look (scale and texture), your project can easily become busy or boring. Don't forget to incorporate solid fabrics into your projects. They can have a calming effect on the look of your quilt.

When you find several fabrics that you are considering for a project, look at each one and define which texture category it falls into. See if you have a pleasing variety. Really study the quilt pattern you are working with, and see which fabrics will be next to each other. Then lay your chosen fabrics next to each other to see how they will look.

## Should You Use Directional Prints?

Many of the quilt projects in the book will tell you that obvious directional prints are not recommended. In other projects, you can use directional prints as long as you pay attention to how you cut and sew them. Here I'll tell you a little bit about directional prints, and then you can make your choice.

A directional print has a pattern that runs in one direction only. This means if you turn the fabric any way but up, the print will be upside down or sideways. (There are some prints that are two way directional instead of just one way as shown in

Diagram 1.) When using one of these prints in a quilt, problems can arise when the pieces you cut appear in the quilt with the print running in all different directions—creating a chaotic and haphazard look.

**Diagram 1.** *Fabric prints can be one-way directional (left), two-way directional (center), or nondirectional (right).*

There are many directional prints available, and many are so appealing they are very tempting to use in your quilt projects. You shouldn't necessarily rule them out. If a print is very small, the fact that it is directional may not be so apparent, especially if you step back from it a bit. A fabric like this would not be an obvious directional print. If this fabric is your best choice, I would not eliminate it because it was technically a directional print. You should be able to use it effectively in your quilt.

When the directional print is large, the one-way pattern is much more obvious. If the print was turned on its side anywhere in the quilt, it might look funny. You could save yourself a lot of headaches by choosing another fabric without an obvious directional pattern.

S E W   S M A R T

To help you cut and sew directional prints for specific projects, look for the Sew Smart tips with diagrams. These will appear near the cutting information.

However, if you find an obvious directional print that you love and want to use it anyway, you can sometimes work with it. Look at the last diagram in Assembling the Blocks for your project. Observe how the pieces are laid out. As you cut your fabric, cut the pieces so the direction of the print will be correct when the block is pieced together.

For example, look at the neck section of the goose in the quilt shown in **Diagram 2.** Cut the rectangular and square pieces that combine to make the neck so the hearts are running up and down and not sideways. This will require more planning and usually a little extra fabric.

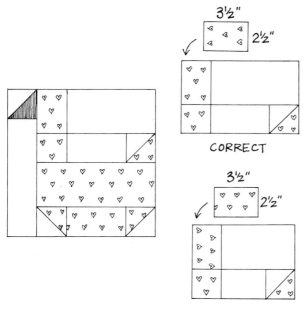

**Diagram 2.** *When using a directional print, cut the pieces carefully so that the print runs the right way when the pieces are sewn together.*

If you are adapting a pattern to work with an obvious directional print, keep in mind that when using the Speedy Triangle technique, your triangle sets will be going in different directions. You have two choices here. The first is to accept that some triangles will be going the wrong direction. Or, you can recut a triangle going the right direction to replace it.

Unless you want to purchase a lot of extra fabric, don't select a directional print for the background, lattice, or borders. However, if having the print run in different directions doesn't bother you, you may choose to use one of these prints.

## Stripes and Plaids

Stripes and plaids can add a lot of interest to your designs. But be aware that they are not usually printed or woven straight. This means you can drive yourself crazy if you try to cut and sew them so they appear straight!

If the plaid or stripe is just slightly off grain, you can cut your pieces following the lines of the pattern. But most of the time when working with plaid and stripe patterns, my philosophy is "throw caution to the wind," and let them fall where they may.

Besides reducing your frustration level, this can give a spontaneous country look! To see what I mean,

## How to Tea-Dye Fabric

To get that warm country look, I sometimes tea-dye some of my fabrics. (It can also add instant "antique" status to a quilt!) This dye won't work on dark-colored fabrics. But you can use it to create a nice effect on light to medium solids and prints. Tea dying comes in handy when you have white fabric that you'd like to transform into a warm natural or tan coloring.

**STEP 1.** Find the largest pot you have. I use a 6-quart pot and find that it comfortably holds about ½ yard of fabric.

**STEP 2.** Fill the pot three-quarters full of water. Add tea bags and bring to a boil. I use about two bags per quart of water. I suggest experimenting to see what works best for you. The more tea bags you use, the darker the resulting dye (up to a point, however, since fabric will only darken so much). Also, different brands of tea vary slightly in color.

**STEP 3.** Once the water starts boiling, remove the tea bags and add the fabric. Don't over-load the pot with fabric. The fabric should be completely immersed and easily stirred. It's better to tea-dye in several batches than to cram too much fabric in at once.

**STEP 4.** Reduce heat and simmer about 20 minutes. Use a wooden spoon to stir frequently.

**STEP 5.** Using tongs, lift the fabric from the pot into a large bowl or clean bucket (be careful—it will be hot). Once the fabric has cooled, rinse out the excess tea in cool water, wring out the fabric, and heat set in the dryer.

look at the Checkerboard Crossing quilt photograph on page 104.

If you are using stripes or plaids for a lattice or border, it is important that your strips look straight and be cut on the grain. Otherwise these parts of the quilt will look "wavy" and give the impression that the fabric strip was not cut straight. So be more selective about choosing stripes or plaids for the lattice or border.

## Contrast

Contrast is the difference between two fabrics when placed next to each other. The contrast between fabrics is what defines the shapes of your quilt design. If there was no contrast between your background fabric and your main block design, you wouldn't be able to distinguish what was quilt block and what was background. Contrast is created by such things as the difference in darkness and lightness of the colors, the texture, the scale of the print, and print versus solid.

When you are selecting fabrics for a project, make sure there is a contrast between fabrics that are positioned next to each other. For example, look at the Flock of Sheep quilt on page 56. All three fabrics need to have a strong contrast with one another because they are all positioned next to each other in different parts of the block.

## Putting It All Together

Once you've selected and cut your fabrics, and your blocks are pieced or appliquéd, you are ready to join them together to make the quilt top. Lattice strips and the borders are the "glue" that holds the individual quilt blocks together, defining and enhancing the overall quilt design. The directions for each of the projects will tell you anything special you need to know about attaching the lattice and borders. In this chapter, I'll give you some general pointers that can make fitting and attaching these parts of the quilt foolproof.

### The Lattice

The lattice includes the strips of fabric that go between and around each of the blocks. (See **Diagram 3.**) In most cases, the lattice fabric I choose is the same as the background of the blocks. If you use a contrasting fabric instead, the lattice will act more like a frame around each block.

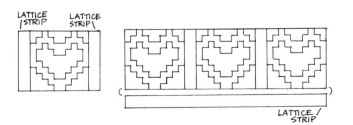

**Diagram 3.** *Lattice strips run between blocks and along rows.*

Each project has specific cutting and sewing directions for attaching the lattice to the blocks. Here I'll share some hints to make sewing and fitting your blocks together go smoothly.

### Trimming the Blocks

Before sewing on the lattice strips, compare the size of your blocks. They should all be about the same size (within about ⅛ to ¼ of an inch). If they are not, you may need to do a *little* trimming with your rotary cutter to make them more similar. Do not trim your blocks unless it is really necessary.

### Match the Lattice to the Blocks

Before cutting your strips for the lattice, measure the height of the finished blocks. This measurement should be the same as the length you cut your lattice strips for between the blocks. If you cut the lattice strips before the blocks were done and find they are too long, trim the excess lattice. If the lattice strips are less than ¼ inch too short, center the lattice strip along the side of the block. If lattice strips are *more* than ¼ inch short, cut new strips and match the block dimensions.

### Overcoming Uneven Edges

When sewing lattice strips to your blocks, lay the strips on top of the blocks with right sides together. The edge of your block may not have a perfectly straight edge (not uncommon with pieced blocks) but your lattice strip will (since you were able to cut perfectly straight with a rotary cutter). Use the lattice strip as your sewing guide for your ¼-inch seam allowance and average over the inconsistent edges of your quilt block.

### Press As You Go

For a smooth and flat quilt top, always press as you sew, and press all the seam allowances toward the lattice.

### The Borders

The borders are the strips that go around the joined blocks and lattice. Think of a piece of matted and framed artwork; without the mat in place between the art and the frame, the total effect would be much less dramatic. The same thing is true for quilts; think of the borders as the mats and the binding as the frame.

In many of the projects, the first border I've used outlines the blocks with a thin strip (frequently about ½ inch wide) using an accent color from the quilt blocks. This border sets off the quilt top.

The second border is usually a wider border that picks up one of the main colors or fabrics of the quilt. A print fabric that incorporates many of the quilt colors often works well. In many of the projects, I combine several of the quilt colors into a scrap border or two or three of the colors into a checkerboard border. In these kinds of multi-fabric borders, I always include the background fabric as one of the fabrics to tie it all together.

Each of the projects will list specific cutting and sewing directions for adding the borders. In this section, I will include some general hints for sewing plain borders, scrap borders, checkerboard borders, and borders with corner squares.

### Plain Border

A plain border, made of strips of just one fabric, is obviously the simplest to do. Basically you sew strips to the quilt top and bottom and then to the sides (in some projects I will specify when you need to add border strips to the sides first). Be sure to press as you sew and press all seam allowances toward the border.

### Scrap Border

I've named this type of border "scrap" because of the finished effect it creates, not because you literally make it out of leftover fabric scraps. As you can see in the photograph of the three Elsie and Co. quilts on page 68, a scrap border is made up of several or all the fabrics used in the quilt top itself. In each project featuring a scrap border, you will find the fabric yardage listed, as well as specific cutting and sewing requirements. Here I'll provide some helpful hints.

**STEP 1.** Scrap borders always start with a strip set made using the Speedy Strip technique described earlier on page 14. Arrange all the strips you've cut in a pleasing order and sew them together side by side along the long edges. As you sew, press the seam allowances in the same direction. The project directions may have you cut this strip set in half (or sometimes in thirds), then resew the halves together before cutting the border strips. In the example shown in **Diagram 4**, this particular strip set is cut and resewn twice before the border strips are finally cut.

**STEP 2.** Fit and sew the border to the quilt top and bottom (or sides first if indicated in the project directions), raw edge to raw edge. Use your seam ripper to remove excess strips from the border to make sure there's a perfect fit.

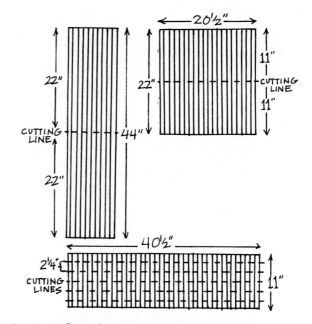

**Diagram 4.** *Scrap borders are made from strip sets made up of several or all of the fabrics used in the quilt top. The sets are cut apart and resewn together to make long multi-colored border strips.*

**STEP 3.** Compare and fit the remaining two scrap borders to the sides of the quilt. Pay attention so you do not end up with borders that are too short. Measure up to but do not include the top and bottom borders you just added. *Then add ¼ inch to each end of the side border strip.* (See **Diagram 5**.) If you do not add this extra ½ inch, the border will be too short. Add corner squares (see page 29) to these border strips, then sew to the quilt sides.

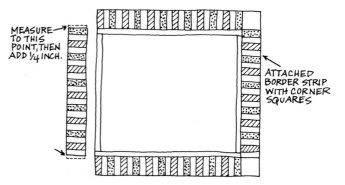

**Diagram 5.** *When measuring border strips that will have corner squares attached, be sure to add ¼-inch seam allowance on each end or the border will be too short.*

## Hints on Fitting a Scrap Border

✂ Count the scrap strips in the border. There should be the same amount in each border strip used for the top and bottom. The same should be true for the side border strips; each of those two borders should contain an equal number of strips. (But the side borders don't have to match the top and bottom borders.)

✂ The border will have a fair amount of give and can be stretched to fit, ¼ to ⅜ inch if necessary. Be careful not to overstretch, however.

✂ If stretching still doesn't make your border fit, make adjustments by taking in or letting out a few of the seam allowances (keeping in mind that it is always easier to take in than it is to let out). As one example, let's say the border strip is ¾ inch too long. You can remove one strip and stretch the remaining border ¼ inch to perfectly match the side of the quilt. For another example, let's use a border strip that is ½ inch too long. You can reasonably expect to take in a seam by 1/16 inch without disrupting the overall look of the scrap border. To "swallow" the excess ½ inch, that means you would need to take in eight seam allowances by 1/16 inch each. If a border strip is inadvertently trimmed too short, sew one scrap strip back on and take in seams as needed to adjust to the correct size.

✂ Because the scrap border will stretch, always pin it in position before sewing it to the quilt top. And press all the seam allowances away from the scrap border.

## Checkerboard Border

Checkerboards look so hard and so time-consuming—but looks can be deceiving! Using the Speedy Strip technique and your rotary cutter, you can put these together in no time at all. And as you can see from projects like A Bunch of Bunnies on page 41, a checkerboard can really add a delightful finishing touch to the design. Each project with a checkerboard will give you specific dimensions and quantities of strips to cut. Here are some general rules.

**STEP 1.** Checkerboards always start with a strip set made using the Speedy Strip technique described earlier on page 14. Arrange all the strips in the order given in the directions and sew them together side by side along the long edges. As you sew, press the seam allowances in the same direction.

**STEP 2.** The project directions will have you cut this strip set in half or thirds, then resew the sections together before cutting the strips for the checkerboard. In the example shown in **Diagram 6**, the strip set is first cut into thirds, resewn, then cut in half, resewn, and finally cut into strips to use in the checkerboard.

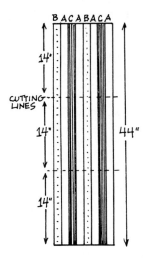

**Diagram 6.** *Checkerboard borders are easy if you use the Speedy Strip technique. Simply follow project directions for making and cutting the strip set. Rematch the final strips to form the checkerboard pattern.*

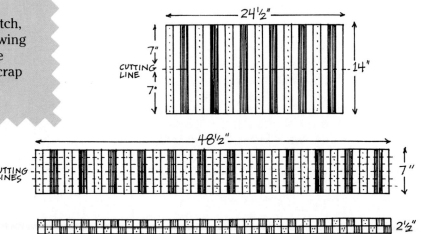

**STEP 3.** Take two or three of these strips, as directed, and rematch to form the checkerboard pattern.

**STEP 4.** Fit the border strips to the top and bottom of the quilt (or sides first if indicated in the project directions). Use your seam ripper as needed to fit the borders perfectly to the quilt.

**STEP 5.** In some projects the checkerboard border will not have corner squares (check Flock of Sheep on page 56). In this case, you will need to match the checkerboard where the top/bottom and side borders meet in the corners. Be sure to align the checkerboard on the two adjacent borders so that the pattern of alternating colors continues unbroken (see **Diagram 7**). Fit these remaining two borders, pin in place, and sew to the sides. (Then, if someone asks you how you have the time and patience to sew together all those tiny squares to make a checkerboard, it's up to you whether you want to tell them the truth!)

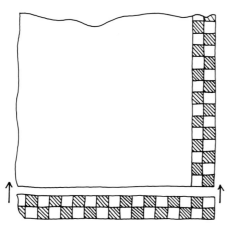

**Diagram 7.** *When the border does not have corner squares, check to make sure the pattern matches correctly at the corners.*

### Borders with Corner Squares

Corner squares at the ends of the borders can add some "action" to plain borders and have a calming effect on busier borders. But most importantly, they can add that spark of accent color that helps bring the borders of your quilt alive.

Each of the projects will list specific cutting and sewing requirements for adding the corner squares. Some basic pointers are given here to help you make sure your corner squares come out perfectly.

**STEP 1.** Fit and sew a plain, scrap, or checkerboard border to the top and bottom of the quilt top (or sides first if specified by the directions).

## Hints on Fitting a Checkerboard Border

✂ Count the squares. There should be the same number in the top and bottom borders. Then count the squares in the side borders; the number should be equal for each of those borders. (The side and top and bottom borders don't have to be equal, though.)

✂ The checkerboard will have a fair amount of give and can be stretched to fit, ¼ to ⅜ inch if necessary.

✂ If stretching isn't enough to make the border fit, make adjustments by taking in or letting out a few of the seam allowances. If you do make adjustments, do them in the same place in both strips of the border so they will still match up. (See **Diagram 8.**) As with scrap borders, it is best to let out or take in seams by only ¹⁄₁₆ inch. For example, if your checkerboard is ½ inch too long, take in eight seam allowances by ¹⁄₁₆ inch to absorb the excess.

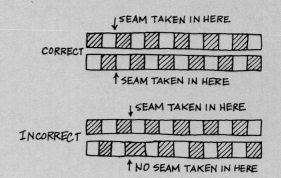

**Diagram 8.** *Make adjustments in the length of the border by taking in (or letting out) seams in both strips of the border so they will still match up.*

**STEP 2.** Compare and fit the border to the sides of the quilt. Pay attention so you do not end up with borders that are too short. Measure up to but do not include the top and bottom borders you just added. *Then add ¼ inch to each end of the side border strip.* If you do not add this extra ½ inch, the border will be too short. See **Diagram 9.**

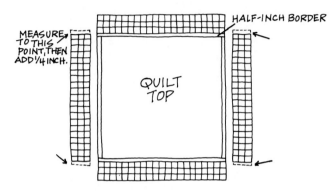

**Diagram 9.** *Before adding corner squares, compare the border strips to the sides of the quilt; then add ¼-inch seam allowance to each end of the strip.*

**STEP 3.** Sew a corner square to each end of both side borders (see **Diagram 10**). Press these seams toward the borders. (The corner squares are always the same size as the width of the border.)

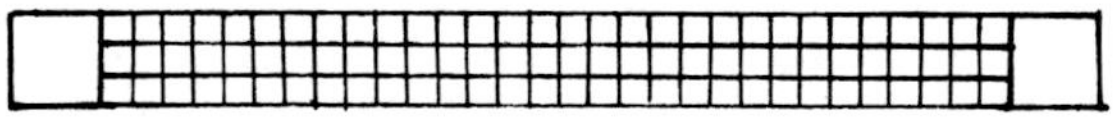

**Diagram 10.** *A checkerboard border strip with corner squares added.*

**STEP 4.** Pin the side borders with corner squares in position and sew to the quilt. Press the seams toward the border.

## How to Choose the Best Batting

Once the quilt top is complete with all the borders sewn on, you are ready to prepare the other two layers, the batting and backing. There are a variety of quilt battings available to you, made from different materials and coming in different sizes and thicknesses. How can you tell what is the best choice for your project?

I generally use the same type of batting for all my projects in this book. Since most of the quilts are used for wallhangings, I prefer a thin, lightweight, polyester batting. This thin batting enhances the country look of the quilts (something a thicker, puffier batting wouldn't do).

For economic reasons, I like to buy my batting in large-size packages. Because my quilts tend to be small, I can get several projects out of one package. (This also provides me with batting on hand so I don't have to run to the store each time I need some.) Batting is also available by the yard. Batting sold this way is usually less expensive (on a per yard basis). However, the width is usually limited to around 45 inches, the loft you desire may not be available, and the batting does not have package protection from dirt and dust.

In addition to my preferences, here are some batting facts to help you determine your best choice.

### Loft

Loft is the term used to describe the thickness of the batting. A thin and lightweight batting with a low loft will give you a flatter quilt. It is also the easiest to slide a quilting needle through. This type of batting would be the best choice for the smaller wallhanging projects and items like the table runners in this book. A thick loft can make a cozy baby or comforter-like quilt. Machine quilting or tying instead of hand-quilting would be easier with a very thick loft.

No matter which thickness you choose, a good quality batting will have an even loft. There shouldn't be thick or thin spots. And it should not pull apart too easily. Always look for good quality products.

### Content

Batting can be made of cotton or polyester or a blend of both. With cotton batting, each row of quilting must be no further than an inch apart, or the cotton fibers will separate and bunch up. That's a lot of quilting! And some people find that cotton is harder to handquilt than polyester. However, in its favor, cotton batting does give a very flat, traditional look to your quilt. With polyester batting, there is no minimum amount of quilting necessary, and the needle slides through the batting easily. One drawback to polyester batting is that the fibers can oftentimes work through the fabric, creating a "batting stubble" on the surface of your quilt. The cotton/polyester blend battings promise to give you the best of both worlds—the easy quilting of polyester plus the more traditional appearance (without migrating fibers) of cotton.

### Color

Batting doesn't just come in white—you can now find it in black. Black batting is perfect when the background or large areas of your quilt are done in very dark colors. This way when the fibers of the batting poke through the grain of the fabric, you won't have fuzzy white "hairs" showing against the dark fabrics.

## Marking the Quilt Top

In every project, I recommend ways to quilt the design to add some nice finishing details. For most projects, the easiest time to mark the quilting design onto the quilt top is before you layer it with the batting and backing fabric.

### Choose Your Marker

First, select a marking tool. New, improved products are always being developed, so get in the habit of checking the displays at your quilt shop or the pages in the quilting supply catalogs. I like to use a sharpened, hard lead pencil for marking. If you have an electric pencil sharpener, you can keep a white chalk pencil sharp enough to mark neat lines on darker fabrics. Whichever marker you end up using, always test it on a scrap of fabric first to make sure that you can clean away any lines that remain after quilting.

### Making a Template

Some of the projects come with a pattern for a full-size quilting template. To use these patterns for making your own template, first buy a sheet of template plastic (available from your favorite quilt supply shop or through mail-order catalogs). Look for a medium-weight, see-through plastic. If the plastic is too heavy, it will be difficult to cut; if it is too thin, it will buckle and slip, making it hard to trace the outline onto the fabric. Lay the sheet of plastic over the template pattern that appears on the book page. With a permanent felt-tip pen, trace the design onto the plastic. Cut it out with a craft knife or paper scissors. Your template is now ready for tracing.

### Marking a Grid Pattern

Many of the projects in this book suggest quilting a grid on the background fabric. Your see-through ruler can make this marking quite easy. There should be a 45-degree angle marked on your ruler. Using that as your reference, mark your first line at a 45-degree angle to the horizontal seam lines of the quilt. (See **Diagram 11.**) Then continue to mark lines across your quilt in regular increments as recommended by the project directions. Next, align the 45-degree angle on your ruler with one of the vertical seam lines

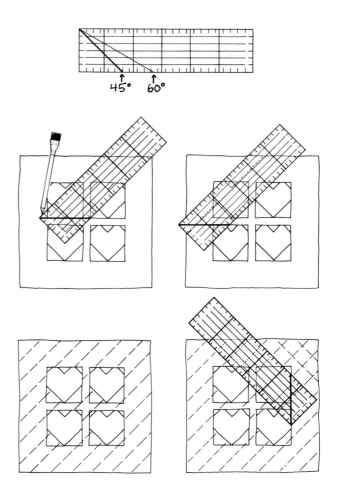

**Diagram 11.** *To mark a diagonal grid for quilting, align the 45-degree line on your ruler with a horizontal seam line on the quilt and mark your first line. Align your ruler with this first line, and mark a second line 1 inch away (or as specified in the project directions). Mark additional lines in regular increments across the quilt. Then, align the 45-degree line on the ruler with a vertical seam line and mark lines in the opposite direction.*

of the quilt and mark your grid lines in the other direction. These intersecting lines will form a grid that you can use to quilt in nice, straight lines.

### Outline Quilting

For outlining the shapes in your quilt designs, there are two options. You can quilt "in the ditch," which means you add a line of stitches directly next to a seam line, or along the outline of an appliqué shape. This sort of quilting requires no marking. It works best when you quilt along the seam line on the side that does not have the seam allowance. If you try to quilt through the seam allowance, you'll be creating extra work for yourself as you push the quilting needle through two extra thicknesses of fabric.

Another option is to outline your design ¼ inch from the seam line. If you do this, I recommend using quilter's ¼-inch masking tape. This will save you from having to mark all the quilting lines on your design. Just position strips of tape around the parts of the design you want to outline and use the edge of the tape as your quilting guide. Lift up the tape and reuse until the stickiness is gone. If you use this tape, wait until right before you are ready to quilt to put it in position. In fact, you shouldn't keep the masking tape on your fabric for long periods of time, or you run the risk of having some sticky residue remain on the fabric.

## Layering the Quilt

Now it's time to turn your quilt top into a quilt. By this point you should have selected your batting, your quilting lines should be marked on the quilt top, and the backing fabric should be on hand. Your next task is to layer these and baste them all together. (For all these steps, refer to **Diagram 12**.)

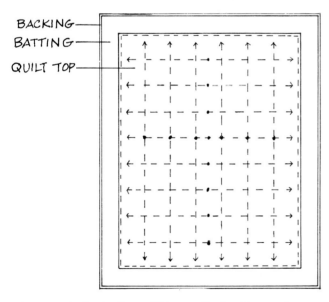

**Diagram 12.** *Center the quilt top on the backing and batting, making sure all three layers are smooth and flat. Pin the layers together to hold them in place while you baste. Begin basting in the center and work out, forming a 3- to 4-inch grid.*

**STEP 1.** Cut the batting and backing pieces 4 to 6 inches larger than the quilt top.

**STEP 2.** Press the quilt top and backing. (Remember, this is your last chance to give both these pieces of fabric a good, thorough pressing.) Find a large work area like the dining room table or the floor. Lay the backing piece down first with the right side facing down. Lay the batting on top of the backing and smooth it out. Then place the quilt top (face up) on top. Make sure everything is centered and that the backing, batting, and top are flat.

**STEP 3.** The backing and batting should extend 2 to 3 inches beyond the quilt top on all the sides. Since some shifting will take place during basting, this extra margin of backing and batting will come in handy.

**STEP 4.** To keep the layers in place as you baste, you may want to pin them together. Place a pin every 6 inches in vertical and horizontal rows. Begin basting in the center and work out to the outer edges of the quilt. Baste vertically and horizontally forming a 3- to 4-inch grid. If you're tempted to skimp on this basting–don't! An adequate amount of basting is critical to keep the layers flat while you are quilting. Last, baste or pin completely around the outer edge of the quilt top.

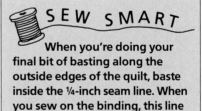

**SEW SMART**

When you're doing your final bit of basting along the outside edges of the quilt, baste inside the ¼-inch seam line. When you sew on the binding, this line of basting won't be visible, saving you from having to rip out the basting threads.

## Basting Hints

✁ Use longer needles than you normally use for handstitching, such as sharps or darning needles. They are easier to handle for this type of stitching and can make the basting go more quickly.

✁ Thread several needles with extra-long lengths of thread before you begin and have them handy.

✁ Take long stitches, about ½ to 1 inch long.

✁ Divide your quilt into quarters for basting. Work in one quarter at a time, basting from the center to the outer edges. This will save wear and tear on your knees and back since you won't have to shift from one part of the quilt to another all the time.

✁ Keep one hand underneath while you're basting, to make sure your backing remains smooth and flat. Before tying off the thread after doing a row of basting, smooth the top and backing with your hand to make sure you haven't slightly gathered the fabric during your stitching.

## Binding the Quilt

For the projects in this book that you will be hand-quilting, I recommend binding the quilt before doing the actual quilting. This step is an important one, since the binding finishes the raw edges left all around your quilt. (If you will be machine quilting, I suggest you quilt *before* binding.)

**STEP 1.** Cut the binding strips as indicated for each project. Press the strips in half with wrong sides together.

**STEP 2.** Trim the batting and backing to within ¼ or ¾ inch of the top, as directed in the individual projects.

**STEP 3.** Align the raw edges of the binding with the front edge of the quilt top and bottom. Pin the binding strips in place. Sew ¼ inch from the quilt

edge, being sure to catch all the layers of the quilt. Trim the excess binding and press the seams toward the binding. (Some quilt projects may specify that you sew the bindings to the sides first, then the top and bottom.)

> **SEW SMART**
> Be sure the weight of the quilt is supported by your sewing table when adding the binding.

**STEP 4.** Align the raw edges of the binding with the edges of the quilt sides. Repeat the sewing and pressing directions given in Step 3. Your quilt should now look like the one shown in **Diagram 13.**

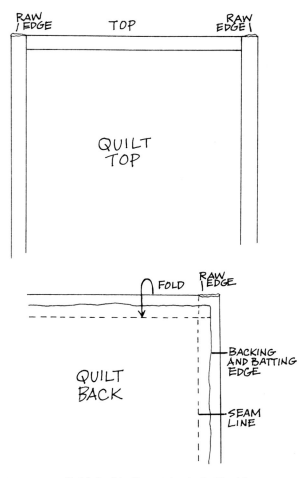

**Diagram 13.** *Fold the binding strips in half with wrong sides together. Align the raw edges of the binding with the edges of the quilt top; pin in position and sew. Your quilt should look like the one shown here.*

**STEP 5.** Bring the top and bottom bindings around to the back. Fold in half so that the outer folded edge of the binding meets the seam line as shown in **Diagram 14.** Press and pin in position.

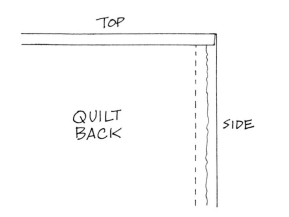

**Diagram 14.** *Fold the top and bottom bindings in half so that the folded edges meet the seam line on the quilt back. Pin, but do not stitch yet.*

**STEP 6.** Fold the side bindings around to the back so that the outer folded edges meet the seam line. Press. Pin in position and handstitch all the way around the binding. Stitch closed the little opening at all four corners as shown on the right in **Diagram 15.**

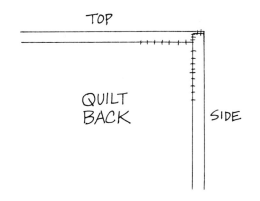

**Diagram 15.** *Fold the side bindings in half to the seam line in back. Pin in position and handstitch all the way around the binding.*

## Helpful Hints for Attaching Binding

Be careful not to stretch the binding when sewing it onto the quilt. When sewing through several layers, the top layer is pushed forward and that can stretch and warp your binding. To prevent this from happening:

✂ Increase the stitch length on your sewing machine (it should look about average or a little longer than average in length).

✂ Don't skimp on pins when you're attaching the binding to the quilt. Use enough to be sure it is held securely in place while you're stitching.

✂ Sew at a slow pace. If you sew too quickly, it is easy to lose the extra control you need to make sure the binding goes on smoothly.

✂ Use a walking foot or even feed attachment if you have one for your machine. It will feed all the layers through at the same rate.

## How to Quilt

Part of the reason the quilts in this book are so quick and easy is that they do not call for a lot of quilting. The quilting I recommend for each project serves the dual function of holding the batting in place between the quilt top and backing, plus adding decorative stitching. Since my projects are not heavily quilted, handstitching is much less time-consuming than you might expect. If you're in a real hurry however, you can always let your sewing machine do the quilting. Here I'll give you the basics for both techniques, handquilting and machine quilting, and you can take your pick.

### Quilting by Hand

Handquilting is similar to playing the piano—the more you do it the better your fingers get. With enough practice you'll find that your fingers fly along and you really don't have to think about what you're doing! Good quilting stitches are small and even.

---

# THE QUILTER'S SEWING BASKET

## Tools for Handquilting

**Quilting Needles:** These are also called "betweens." If you are a beginning quilter, I suggest starting with a package of needles that carries an assortment of sizes. This way you can experiment until you find the size that suits you best. For your first couple of quilts, you may want to use a larger needle and then progress to smaller ones after you gain some experience. Size 10 is a commonly used size and is the needle I prefer. The larger the number, the smaller the needle.

**Thimble:** This is another tool that requires some trial and error before you settle on one you like. Since I didn't grow up using a thimble, a metal one was difficult for me. I really prefer the leather thimbles. Look for one with elastic (it stays on your finger better), a slit for your fingernail to poke through, and extra reinforcement at the fingertip. These leather thimbles can be very comfortable to wear and are not too cumbersome.

**Quilting Thread:** Always be sure to use extra-strong thread made especially for quilting. The color selection is continually growing, which makes coordinating thread with your project all the more fun. On many of the projects in this book, quilting is done on the background fabric. If you want the background to recede, choose a quilting thread color that coordinates with the background fabric color. If you want the background to attract more attention or to make it more active, use a contrasting color of thread. For a special design feature that you want to stand out (like a heart), contrasting thread will show up more.

**Quilting Hoop or Frame:** Hoops or frames hold the three layers taut and smooth while you are quilting. Some people find it easier to make small, evenly spaced stitches when quilting in a hoop. There's also less likelihood that the fabric will pucker or wrinkle under the stitching. Since the projects in this book are relatively small, you don't need a hoop much larger than lap-size. There are plenty of these hoops available in quilting stores or through quilting catalogs. There are also handy, lightweight, lap-size quilt frames that snap together in a jiffy.

I personally don't use a hoop or frame. I like to use one hand to manipulate my needle and the other to manipulate the fabric (instead of holding the frame). This technique works for smaller projects only (not bed-size quilts).

---

Until you become accustomed to working the needle through the three layers, you should concentrate on even stitches; as you gain experience, your stitches will naturally become smaller.

**STEP 1.** Cut a length of quilting thread (approximately 18 inches), thread the needle, and knot one end.

**STEP 2.** About 1 inch from the point where you want to begin stitching, insert the needle through the top layer of fabric (see **Diagram 16**). Bring it up right where you want to take the first stitch, and pull on the thread until the knot rests against the surface of the fabric. With a gentle tug, pull on the thread to pop the knot through the fabric. The knot will stay securely

anchored in the batting beneath the quilt top, hidden out of sight. Whenever you need to start a new piece of thread, repeat this procedure for burying the knot.

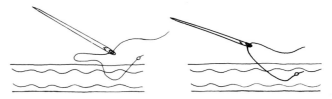

**Diagram 16.** *To hide the knot in the batting, insert the needle through the quilt top and pull the thread until the knot rests on the surface of the fabric. With a gentle tug, pull on the thread to pop the knot through the fabric.*

**STEP 3.** The quilting stitch is a series of running stitches made along the lines of the quilting design you have marked. Many beginners find it easiest to take one stitch at a time, pulling the needle in and out of the fabric. However, I would encourage you to practice "stacking" your stitches on the needle right from the start. This technique, once you get the hang of it, allows you to make many small, nicely aligned stitches at a time and makes the quilting go more quickly.

To stack your stitches, push just the tip of the needle down through the three layers using the finger with the thimble on your top hand as shown in **Diagram 17**. As soon as your hand on the underside feels the needle come through, rock it up again toward the surface. (Simultaneously press down on the head of the needle with the thimble finger and push up against the needle tip with a finger on the underside.) When the needle tip pokes through the top surface, push it down again, then rock it back through the top. Experiment to see how many stitches you feel comfortable stacking at a time. You may start by stacking two stitches, then find as you get more practice you can stack four or five comfortably. Once you've stacked your stitches on the needle, pull it through the fabric using the thumb and forefinger of your top hand. Pull the thread taut, but don't pull it too tight, or the fabric will pucker. See **Diagram 18**.

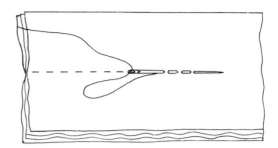

**Diagram 18.** *Stacking several stitches on the needle before pulling it through allows you to make small, even stitches.*

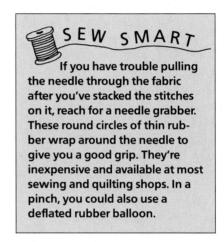

**SEW SMART**

If you have trouble pulling the needle through the fabric after you've stacked the stitches on it, reach for a needle grabber. These round circles of thin rubber wrap around the needle to give you a good grip. They're inexpensive and available at most sewing and quilting shops. In a pinch, you could also use a deflated rubber balloon.

**STEP 4.** To end a line of stitching, bring the needle up where you want to stop. Wrap the thread around the end of the needle two or three times. Pull the needle through these circles of thread to form a knot. Push the needle back down through the top of the quilt only and pull it up about ½ inch away. Tug on the thread to pop the knot through the top of the fabric and bury it in the batting layer as shown in **Diagram 19**. Pull on the thread slightly and clip it close to the surface of the quilt. The end should disappear back beneath the quilt top.

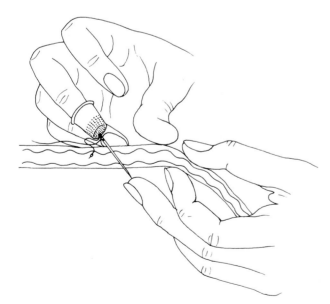

**Diagram 17.** *Push the tip of the needle down through the three layers. As soon as you feel it come through, rock it up again to the top. When it pokes through the top, push it back down through. When you have several stitches stacked on the needle, pull the needle through the fabric.*

**Diagram 19.** *To hide the knot at the end of a line of stitching, push the needle through the quilt top and bring it back up ½ inch away. Gently tug on the thread to pop the knot through the top and into the batting layer.*

## Quilting by Machine

Letting your sewing machine do the quilting can be a quick solution (especially if you're in a last-minute rush to get some holiday gifts done), but it is not necessarily easier than handquilting. Just like hand-stitching, machine quilting takes some practice. It can be difficult to control the layers and keep them from bunching up as you feed them through the machine.

Machine quilting works best on smaller projects like the appliqué wallhangings, where you quilt in the ditch along the borders. These straight quilting lines are a good match for machine stitching. Throughout the projects, I've recommended places where I thought machine quilting would be appropriate. If you are trying machine quilting for the first time, keep in mind that the smaller the project, the easier it will be.

The layering process is the same as for hand-quilting—you sandwich the backing, batting, and quilt top together. However, instead of handbasting the quilt, you could use safety pins to hold the layers together while you stitch. Position the safety pins so they won't get in the way of where you plan to quilt. Do all the quilting *before* you add the binding.

**STEP 1.** Coordinate the thread color with the quilt top or use invisible thread (which is clear). Coordinate the bobbin thread with the backing fabric.

**STEP 2.** Set your machine for normal straight stitching. You may want to increase the stitch length for stitching through the three layers. Starting in the center of the quilt and working out toward the edges, machine stitch in the ditch (right next to the seam lines) to outline the block designs and borders.

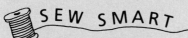

### SEW SMART

A walking foot or even feed attachment is great for machine quilting. It can help avoid the problem of having the three layers bunch up. Check your sewing machine manual to see whether this attachment is available for your model.

## Making Custom-Fit Pillow Forms

Several of the projects in this book provide you with extra blocks that you can turn into pillows. One of the secrets to an attractive finished pillow is a pillow form

that fits perfectly inside the pillow top you've stitched together. This isn't always easy to achieve when you rely on the standard-size pillow forms sold in fabric stores. For very little time and money, you can put together a pillow form that will assure a perfect fit.

The materials list is very short: All you need is some polyester batting or needlepunch and a 1-pound bag of stuffing (the smooth kind, like FiberFil, not shredded foam). In the projects that include pillows, the amount of batting or needlepunch you will need is listed.

**STEP 1.** To determine the size to cut the batting or needlepunch, take the finished size of your pillow and add ½ inch to those measurements. Cut two pieces of batting or needlepunch to those dimensions. For example, if the finished pillow size is listed as 8 inches by 8 inches, you will cut two pieces of batting 8½ inches by 8½ inches.

**STEP 2.** Using a ¼-inch seam allowance, sew the two pieces of batting together, leaving a 3- to 4-inch opening for turning. Turn so the seam allowances are on the inside.

**STEP 3.** Fill the pillow form with stuffing until it reaches the desired firmness. Handstitch the opening.

**STEP 4.** Slip the custom-made pillow form into the opening of your pillow and handstitch the opening. The pillow form should be a perfect fit!

## Hanging Your Wall Quilts

I have found that the best way to hang wall quilts is with fabric tabs and a wooden dowel. Use scraps to make three or four fabric tabs. Cut 1½ × 2½-inch pieces of fabric. Fold in half, right sides together, and stitch a ¼-inch seam along the long edge. Turn right side out. Space the tabs evenly across the top of the quilt back, right under the binding. Handstitch them in place, turning under ¼ inch on each end and stitching across the top and bottom of the tabs. Buy a ½-inch-diameter wooden dowel at your local craft shop or home improvement store, and cut it slightly shorter than the width of the quilt. Slip the dowel through the tabs, and suspend it from the wall with a nail at each end.

# Pieced Country Quilting Projects

Before you begin any of the projects in this section, take a
minute to read through this checklist. These are all important
pointers you should keep in mind to make sure every one of your
country quilts is a success!

☐ Read Tools and Accessories You Will Need on page 6 and the specific materials list for your project to be sure you're all set.

☐ Prewash and press all of your fabrics.

☐ Read the step-by-step directions from start to finish, and look at all the diagrams before you cut and sew any fabric.

☐ Throughout the directions, there will be references to information found in Speedy Quilting Techniques and Quiltmaking Essentials. Take the time to flip back and review the material to make sure you understand everything you need to know about a certain technique.

☐ Always use a ¼-inch seam allowance unless there is a special note that tells you a different seam allowance is required.

☐ Be as accurate and careful as you can when cutting the strips and sewing the seams. Accuracy is your guarantee that all the pieces will fit together smoothly.

☐ When you are cutting strips, often the dimension for the first strip cut may be 44 inches long. This is based on a 44-inch fabric width. Don't worry if your fabric is only 42 or 43 inches wide. Cut the strip to the width of your fabric. This variance has been considered in the yardage and cutting dimensions.

☐ Pay attention to the pressing directions given in the step-by-step text and to the pressing arrows shown in the diagrams.

# A Bunch of Bunnies

46"

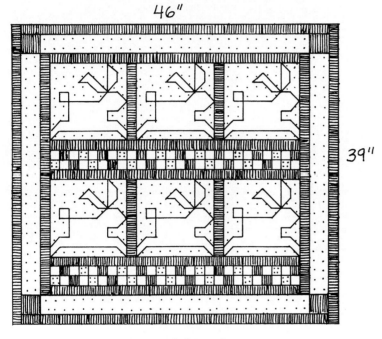

39"

QUILT LAYOUT

Oh boy, bunnies! A half dozen frisky fellows cavort across the front of this delightful quilt. This design makes an irresistible baby gift. Or, done up in an array of cheery pastels, it becomes a perfect decoration to welcome spring. Better yet, make one for the gardeners you know. They'll appreciate having mild-mannered rabbits around who don't raid the garden!

Finished Quilt: 46 × 39 inches
Finished Block: 12 × 12 inches

## Materials

Obvious directional prints are not recommended.

**FABRIC A** *(bunnies, checkerboard)*

| Blocks | ¾ yard |
|---|---|
| Checkerboard | ¼ yard |
| TOTAL | 1 yard |

**FABRIC B** *(background, checkerboard, border)*

| Blocks | 1 yard |
|---|---|
| Checkerboard | ⅛ yard |
| Two-Inch Border | ½ yard |
| TOTAL | 1⅝ yards |

**FABRIC C** *(lattice, checkerboard, binding)*

| Lattice/Corner Squares | ½ yard |
|---|---|
| Checkerboard | ⅛ yard |
| Binding | ⅞ yard |
| TOTAL | 1½ yards |

**BACKING**     1½ yards

**BATTING**     1½ yards or crib-size package (45 × 60 inches)·

## Cutting Directions

Prewash and press all of your fabrics. Using a rotary cutter, see-through ruler, and cutting mat, prepare the strips as described in the first column of the chart below.

Then from those strips, cut the pieces listed in the second column. Some portions of the quilt need to be cut only once, so no additional cutting information will appear in the second column.

| | FIRST CUT | | SECOND CUT | |
|---|---|---|---|---|
| | NO. OF STRIPS | DIMENSIONS | NO. OF PIECES | DIMENSIONS |
| **FABRIC A** | **BUNNIES** | | | |
| | 4 | 2 × 44-inch strips | 12 | 2 × 2-inch pieces |
| | | | 6 | 2 × 3½-inch pieces |
| | | | 6 | 2 × 9½-inch pieces |
| | 1 | 3½ × 44-inch strip | 6 | 3½ × 6½-inch pieces |
| | 1 | 9 × 44-inch strip | 2 | 9 × 20-inch pieces |
| | **CHECKERBOARD ROWS** | | | |
| | 4 | 1½ × 44-inch strips | | |
| **FABRIC B** | **BACKGROUND** | | | |
| | 7 | 2 × 44-inch strips | 18 | 2 × 2-inch pieces |
| | | | 6 | 2 × 3½-inch pieces |
| | | | 6 | 2 × 9½-inch pieces |
| | | | 18 | 2 × 5-inch pieces |
| | 1 | 3½ × 44-inch strip | 6 | 3½ × 3½-inch pieces |
| | 1 | 5 × 44-inch strip | 6 | 5 × 5-inch pieces |
| | 1 | 9 × 44-inch strip | 2 | 9 × 20-inch pieces |
| | **CHECKERBOARD ROWS** | | | |
| | 2 | 1½ × 44-inch strips | | |
| | **TWO-INCH BORDER** | | | |
| | 4 | 2½ × 44-inch strips | | |

| FIRST CUT | | SECOND CUT | |
|---|---|---|---|
| **NO. OF STRIPS** | **DIMENSIONS** | **NO. OF PIECES** | **DIMENSIONS** |
| **FABRIC C** | **CORNER SQUARES** | | |
| 1 | 2½ × 44-inch strip | 4 | 2½ × 2½-inch pieces |
| | **CHECKERBOARD ROWS** | | |
| 2 | 1½ × 44-inch strips | | |
| | **LATTICE** | | |
| | **Before You Cut:** From two of the 44-inch strips, cut the pieces as directed in the second column. The remaining seven 44-inch strips require no further cutting. | | |
| 9 | 1½ × 44-inch strips | 4 | 1½ × 12½-inch pieces |
| | **BINDING** | | |
| 5 | 5½ × 44-inch strips | | |

## Speedy Triangles

**STEP 1.** Refer to Speedy Triangle directions on page 11 for how to mark, sew, and cut.

**STEP 2.** Position the two 9 × 20-inch pieces of Fabrics A and B with right sides together. You will have two sets. On each set, draw a 2⅜-inch grid of twenty-one squares. See **Diagram 1.**

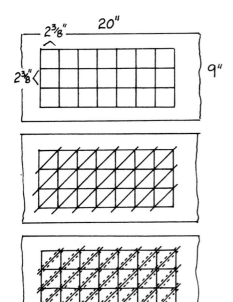

DIAGRAM 1

**STEP 3.** After sewing and cutting are complete, press seam allowances of thirty triangle sets toward Fabric A. Press seam allowances on the remaining forty-eight sets toward Fabric B. You will have made a total of eighty-four triangle sets (there will be a few extra left over after you complete your quilt).

## Assembling the Blocks

Throughout this section, refer to the Fabric Key to identify the fabric placement in the diagrams. Also, it's a good idea to review Assembly Line Piecing on page 13 before you get started. It is more efficient to do the same step for each block at the same time than to piece one entire block together at a time. Be sure to press as you go, and follow the arrows for pressing direction.

FABRIC KEY    FABRIC A □

FABRIC B ⬚

FABRIC C ▥

## SECTION ONE (Ears)

**STEP 1.** Sew six triangle sets (pressed toward Fabric B) to six triangle sets (pressed toward Fabric A). Position them right sides together and line them up next to your sewing machine. Make sure the triangle sets are positioned as shown in **Diagram 2.** Stitch the first set together, then butt the next set directly behind it and continue sewing each set without breaking your seam. Follow the arrow for pressing direction, and cut the joining threads.

DIAGRAM 2

In each of the remaining steps, use the same Continuous Seam method. You will be making a total of six bunny blocks.

**STEP 2.** Sew six triangle sets
(pressed toward Fabric A) to six
2 × 2-inch squares of Fabric B.
Press toward Fabric B. See **Diagram 3.**

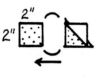

DIAGRAM 3

**STEP 3.** Sew six triangle sets
(pressed toward Fabric B) to six
2 × 2-inch squares of Fabric B.
Press toward Fabric B. See **Diagram 4.**

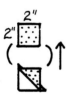

DIAGRAM 4

**STEP 4.** Sew the units from Step 1
to the units from Step 2. Press
toward the Step 2 units, as indicated by the arrow in **Diagram 5.**

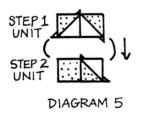

DIAGRAM 5

**STEP 5.** Sew the units from Step 3
to the units from Step 4. Press
toward the Step 3 units, as indicated by the arrow in **Diagram 6.**

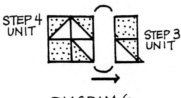

DIAGRAM 6

**STEP 6.** Sew six 5 × 2-inch pieces
of Fabric B to the units from Step
5. Press toward Fabric B. See
**Diagram 7.**

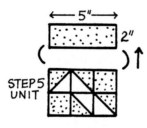

DIAGRAM 7

**STEP 7.** Sew units from Step 6 to
six 5 × 5-inch pieces of Fabric B.
Press toward Fabric B. See **Diagram 8.**

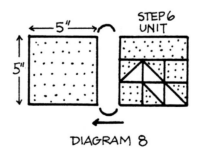

DIAGRAM 8

**STEP 8.** Sew six triangle sets
(pressed toward Fabric B) to six
2 × 2-inch pieces of Fabric A. Press
toward Fabric A. See **Diagram 9.**

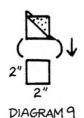

DIAGRAM 9

**STEP 9.** Sew six triangle sets
(pressed toward Fabric B) to the
units from Step 8. Press toward
triangle sets. See **Diagram 10.**

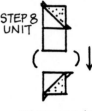

DIAGRAM 10

**STEP 10.** Sew six 2 × 5-inch pieces
of Fabric B to the units from Step
9. Press toward Fabric B. See
**Diagram 11.**

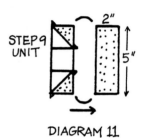

DIAGRAM 11

**STEP 11.** Sew the units from Step
10 to the units from Step 7. Press
toward Step 10 units. See **Diagram 12.**

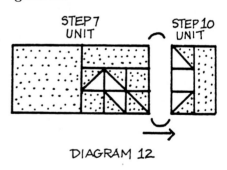

DIAGRAM 12

### SECTION TWO (Body, Head)

**STEP 1.** Sew six 2 × 2-inch pieces of Fabric A to six 2 × 2-inch pieces of Fabric B. Press toward Fabric B. See **Diagram 13**.

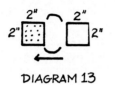

DIAGRAM 13

**STEP 2.** Sew six triangle sets (pressed toward Fabric B) to six 5 × 2-inch pieces of Fabric B. Press toward Fabric B. See **Diagram 14**.

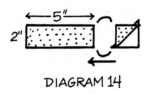

DIAGRAM 14

**STEP 3.** Sew the units from Step 2 to the units from Step 1. Press toward the Step 2 units. See **Diagram 15**.

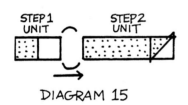

DIAGRAM 15

**STEP 4.** Sew six 6½ × 3½-inch pieces of Fabric A to six 3½ × 3½-inch pieces of Fabric B. Press toward Fabric B. See **Diagram 16**.

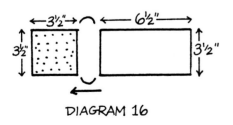

DIAGRAM 16

**STEP 5.** Sew the units from Step 3 to the units from Step 4. Press toward the Step 4 units. See **Diagram 17**.

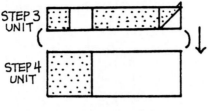

DIAGRAM 17

**STEP 6.** Sew six triangle sets (pressed toward Fabric B) to six triangle sets (pressed toward Fabric A). Follow arrow for pressing direction. See **Diagram 18**.

DIAGRAM 18

**STEP 7.** Sew the units from Step 6 to six 2 × 3½-inch pieces of Fabric A. Press toward Fabric A. See **Diagram 19**.

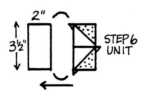

DIAGRAM 19

**STEP 8.** Sew the units from Step 7 to six 3½ × 2-inch pieces of Fabric B. Press toward Fabric B. See **Diagram 20**.

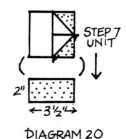

DIAGRAM 20

**STEP 9.** Sew the units from Step 8 to the units from Step 5. Press toward the Step 5 units. See **Diagram 21**.

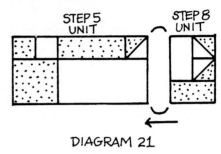

DIAGRAM 21

### SECTION THREE (Legs)

**STEP 1.** Sew six 9½ × 2-inch pieces of Fabric A to six triangle sets (pressed toward Fabric B). Press toward Fabric A. See **Diagram 22**.

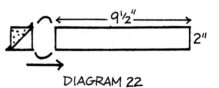

DIAGRAM 22

**STEP 2.** Sew six triangle sets (pressed toward Fabric B) to the units from Step 1. Press toward Step 1 units. See **Diagram 23**.

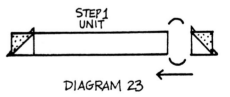

DIAGRAM 23

**STEP 3.** Sew six 9½ × 2-inch pieces of Fabric B to six triangle sets (pressed toward Fabric A). Press toward the triangle sets. See **Diagram 24**.

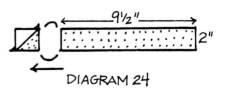

DIAGRAM 24

**STEP 4.** Sew six triangle sets (pressed toward Fabric A) to the units from Step 3. Press toward triangle sets. See **Diagram 25.**

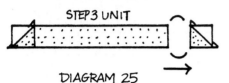

DIAGRAM 25

**STEP 5.** Sew the units from Step 2 to the units from Step 4. Press toward the Step 2 units. See **Diagram 26.**

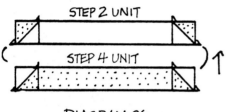

DIAGRAM 26

## SECTION ASSEMBLY

**STEP 1.** Sew the units from Section One to the units from Section Two. Press toward the Section Two units. See **Diagram 27.**

**STEP 2.** Sew the units constructed in Step 1 to the units from Section Three. Press toward the unit in the middle, as shown by arrows in **Diagram 27.**

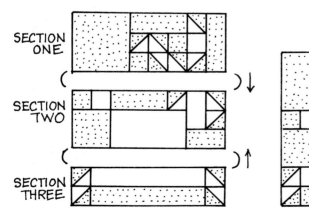

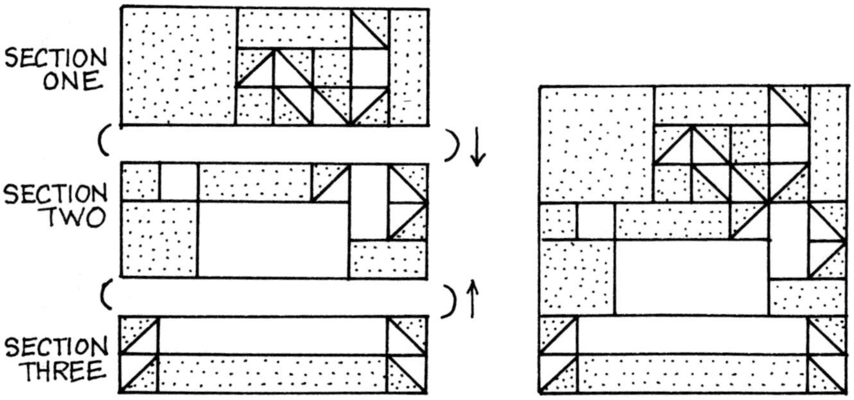

DIAGRAM 27

## Checkerboard Rows

**STEP 1.** Sew together eight 1½ × 44-inch strips of Fabrics A, B, and C, alternating fabrics as shown in **Diagram 28.** Press all seams toward Fabric A as you go.

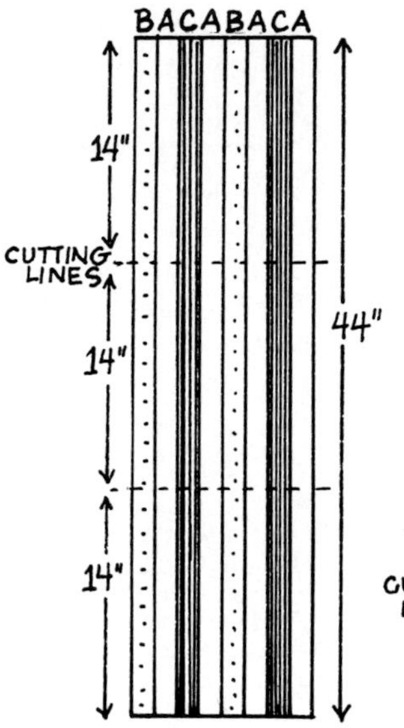

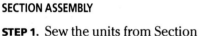

DIAGRAM 28

**STEP 2.** Cut the strip set into thirds (the sections will be approximately 14 inches long). Refer to the cutting lines shown in **Diagram 28.** Resew the thirds together so the strip set is now 24½ × approximately 14 inches. See **Diagram 29.**

**STEP 3.** Cut the strip set in half to end up with two pieces approximately 7 × 24½ inches. The cutting line is indicated in **Diagram 29.** Resew the halves together end to end so the strip set is now 48½ × approximately 7 inches. See **Diagram 30.**

DIAGRAM 29

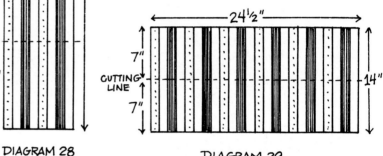

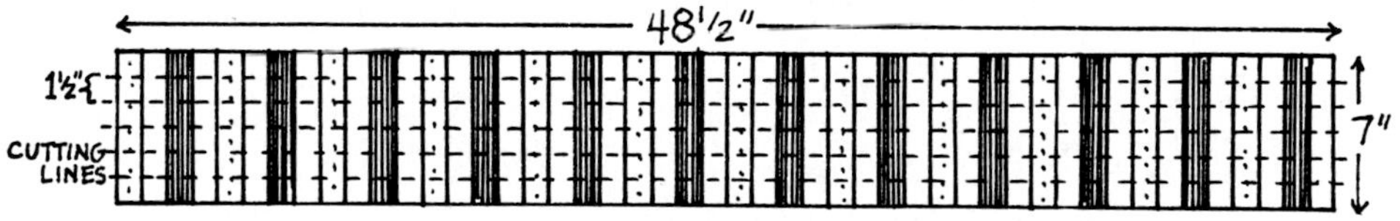

DIAGRAM 30

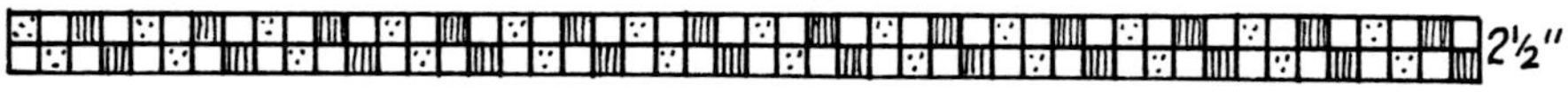

DIAGRAM 31

**STEP 4.** From this 48½-inch strip set, cut four 1½ × 48½-inch strips. Rematch two strips so they form a checkerboard, and stitch them together. Make two 2½ × 48½-inch checkerboard sets like the one in **Diagram 31.**

## The Lattice

**STEP 1.** Sew the 1½ × 12½-inch strips to each side of two bunny blocks. Press all seams toward the lattice. See **Diagram 32.**

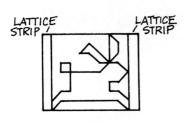

DIAGRAM 32

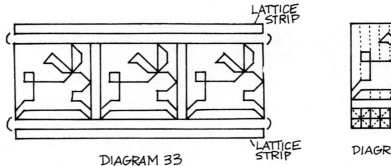

DIAGRAM 33

DIAGRAM 34

**STEP 2.** Using one of the blocks from Step 1, sew a bunny block (without lattice) to each side of those lattice strips to make a row of three bunnies. The bunny block with two lattice strips will be in the middle, as shown in **Diagram 33.** Press. Repeat for the second row.

**STEP 3.** Sew 1½ × 44-inch strips to the top and bottom of both rows of bunnies. Trim the excess and press. Set aside the remaining lattice strips.

## Putting It All Together

Use the **Quilt Layout** on page 41 as a visual guide for putting your quilt top together.

**STEP 1.** See Hints on Fitting a Checkerboard Border on page 29. Fit the checkerboard to the bottom of each row of bunnies. Pin in position and sew. Press all seams toward the lattice.

**STEP 2.** Stitch together the two rows of bunnies. Press.

**STEP 3.** Add a 1½ × 44-inch strip of lattice to the bottom of the quilt (below the checkerboard). Trim the excess and press.

**STEP 4.** Sew lattice strips to the sides of the quilt. Trim the excess and press.

## The Two-Inch Border

**STEP 1.** Sew 2½ × 44-inch strips of Fabric B to the quilt top and bottom. Trim the excess and press all seams toward the border.

**STEP 2.** Compare 44-inch strips to the quilt sides and fit to the correct length. Measure up to but do not include the borders you just added to the top and bottom. Then add ¼ inch to each end of the strips before trimming so they will fit correctly after the corner squares are added.

**STEP 3.** Sew 2½-inch corner squares of Fabric C to each end of the side border strips. Press seams to the borders.

**STEP 4.** Pin in position and sew borders with corner squares to the quilt sides.

## Layering the Quilt

Arrange and baste the backing, batting, and top together following directions for Layering the Quilt on page 32. Trim the batting and backing to ¾ inch from the raw edge of the quilt top.

## Binding the Quilt

**STEP 1.** The 5½ × 44-inch-long binding strips cut from Fabric C will not be long enough to cover the top and bottom edges of the quilt. Cut the fifth strip in half, and sew one half to each of the top and bottom strips.

**STEP 2.** Follow directions on page 33 for Binding the Quilt. Bind the sides first, then the top and bottom.

## The Finishing Stitches

Outline your bunnies by quilting either in the ditch or ¼ inch from the seam line. Diamonds quilted in the checkerboard also look nice (see **Diagram 34**). In the background I stitched straight lines spaced 1 inch apart. I also quilted in the two-inch border using the **Bunny and Heart Quilting Templates** below.

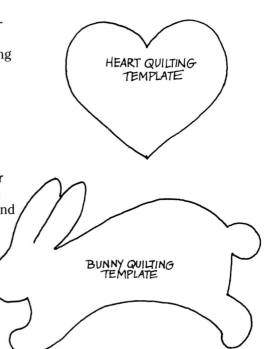

HEART QUILTING TEMPLATE

BUNNY QUILTING TEMPLATE

# Crazy for Cats!

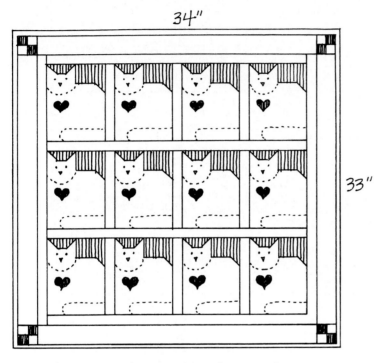

34"

33"

FOUR-PATCH CATS QUILT LAYOUT

## Four-Patch Cats

Finished Quilt: 34 × 33 inches
Finished Block: 6 × 8 inches

**Materials**

Obvious directional prints are not recommended.

**FABRIC A** *(cats, border)*

| | |
|---|---|
| Blocks | ⅔ |
| Two-Inch Border | ⅓ |
| TOTAL | 1 yard |

**FABRIC B** *(background, four-patch corners)*

| | |
|---|---|
| Blocks and Four-Patch | ⅓ yard |

**FABRIC C** *(lattice, binding)*

| | |
|---|---|
| Lattice | ⅓ yard |
| Binding | ½ yard |
| TOTAL | ⅞ yard |

**FABRIC D** *(hearts, four-patch corners)*

| | |
|---|---|
| Hearts and Four-Patch | ⅛ yard |

| | |
|---|---|
| **BACKING** | 1⅛ yards |

| | |
|---|---|
| **BATTING** | 1⅛ yards or crib-size package (45 × 60 inches) |

**Tear-away paper** *(for machine appliqué only)*

Quilters who are crazy for cats will love making this simple-to-sew wall-size quilt. Choose between two interpretations of the same design. The Four-Patch Cats features a dozen cozy cats curled up inside a border marked with four-patch blocks in the corners. Scrap Cats gives you a chance to use leftover bits of fabric in an attractive border highlighted with hearts in the corners. Add face and body details to the contented cats with embroidery and quilting stitches, or simply appliqué a heart on each winsome feline.

## Cutting Directions

Prewash and press all of your fabrics. Using a rotary cutter, see-through ruler, and cutting mat, prepare the strips as described in the first column in the chart below.

Then from those strips, cut the pieces listed in the second column. Some portions of the quilt need to be cut only once, so no additional cutting information will appear in the second column.

| | FIRST CUT | | SECOND CUT | |
| --- | --- | --- | --- | --- |
| | NO. OF STRIPS | DIMENSIONS | NO. OF PIECES | DIMENSIONS |
| **FABRIC A** | **CAT BLOCKS** | | | |
| | 3 | 1½ × 44-inch strips | 12 | 1½ × 3½-inch pieces |
| | | | 12 | 1½ × 5½-inch pieces |
| | 2 | 5½ × 44-inch strips | 12 | 5½ × 6½-inch pieces |
| | 1 | 6 × 20-inch strip | | |
| | **BORDER** | | | |
| | 4 | 2½ × 44-inch strips | | |
| **FABRIC B** | **CAT BLOCKS** | | | |
| | 1 | 1½ × 44-inch strip | 12 | 1½ × 1½-inch pieces |
| | 1 | 2½ × 44-inch strip | 12 | 2½ × 3½-inch pieces |
| | 1 | 6 × 20-inch strip | | |
| | **FOUR-PATCH CORNER SQUARES** | | | |
| | 1 | 1½ × 15-inch strip | | |
| **FABRIC C** | **LATTICE** | | | |
| | **Before You Cut:** From two of the 44-inch strips, cut the pieces as directed in the second column. The remaining six 44-inch strips require no further cutting. | | | |
| | 8 | 1½ × 44-inch strips | 9 | 1½ × 8½-inch pieces |
| | **BINDING** | | | |
| | 4 | 2¾ × 44-inch strips | | |
| **FABRIC D** | **FOUR-PATCH CORNER SQUARES** | | | |
| | 1 | 1½ × 15-inch strip | | |

## Speedy Triangles

**STEP 1.** Refer to Speedy Triangle directions on page 11 for how to mark, sew, and cut.

**STEP 2.** Position the 6 × 20-inch pieces of Fabrics A and B with right sides together. Draw a 1⅞-inch grid of eighteen squares. See **Diagram 1.**

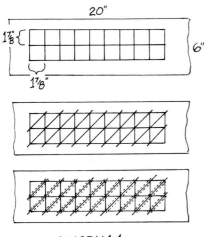

DIAGRAM 1

**STEP 3.** After sewing and cutting are complete, press seam allowances toward Fabric A. You will have made a total of thirty-six triangle sets.

## Assembling the Blocks

Throughout this section, refer to the Fabric Key to identify the fabric placements in the diagrams. Also, it's a good idea to review Assembly Line Piecing on page 13 before you get started. It's more efficient to do the same step for each block at the same time than to piece one entire block together at a time. Be sure to press as you go and follow the arrows for pressing direction.

FABRIC KEY    FABRIC A □
(CATS)
FABRIC B ▥
(BACKGROUND)

### SECTION ONE (Head)

**STEP 1.** Sew twelve triangle sets to twelve 1½ × 1½-inch squares of Fabric B. Position them with right sides of Fabric B together, as shown in **Diagram 2.** Use the Continuous Seam technique described on page 14 to join all twelve sets together. Press seams toward Fabric B and cut joining threads. Pay close attention that the triangle sets are positioned in the same way as shown in **Diagram 2.** You will be making a total of twelve blocks.

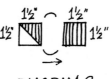

DIAGRAM 2

**STEP 2.** Sew one triangle set to the right side of each of the twelve units from Step 1. Make sure the triangle set being added is positioned as shown in **Diagram 3.** Press away from the new triangle set.

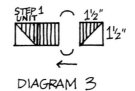

DIAGRAM 3

**STEP 3.** Sew units from Step 2 to twelve 1½ × 3½-inch pieces of Fabric A. See **Diagram 4.** Press toward Fabric A.

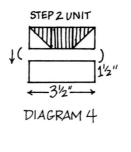

DIAGRAM 4

**STEP 4.** Sew twelve 2½ × 3½-inch pieces of Fabric B to units from Step 3. See **Diagram 5.** Press toward Fabric B.

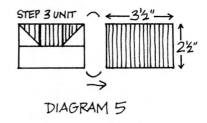

DIAGRAM 5

> ### SEW SMART
> If you've been positioning your triangle sets and rectangles correctly, you should start to see the top of the cat's head take shape.

### SECTION TWO (Upper Back)

Sew twelve triangle sets to twelve 1½ × 5½-inch pieces of Fabric A. Position triangle sets as shown in **Diagram 6.** Press toward Fabric A.

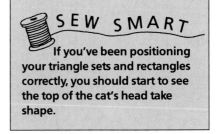

DIAGRAM 6

### SECTION THREE (Body)

The third section is the 5½ × 6½-inch piece of Fabric A as shown in **Diagram 7.** Section Three is complete as is!

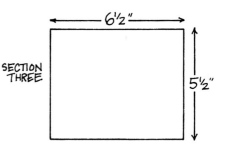

DIAGRAM 7

## SECTION ASSEMBLY

**STEP 1.** Sew units from Section One to units from Section Two as shown in **Diagram 8**. Press toward Section One.

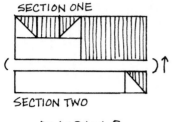

SECTION ONE

SECTION TWO

DIAGRAM 8

**STEP 2.** Sew units from Step 1 to Section Three units as shown in **Diagram 9**. Press toward Section Three units.

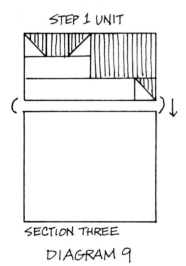

STEP 1 UNIT

SECTION THREE

DIAGRAM 9

## The Hearts

Machine or hand appliqué hearts to the chest of each cat using the **Heart Appliqué Pattern** on page 55. (Refer to Machine or Hand Appliqué on page 19.) If you like, embroider a nose with the satin stitch and use French knots for eyes. It is much easier if you add these details before attaching the lattice. See the photograph and **Quilt Layout** for placement.

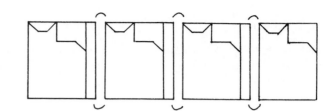

LATTICE STRIP

DIAGRAM 10

DIAGRAM 11

## The Lattice

**STEP 1.** Lay out the cat blocks in a pleasing arrangement, with three rows of four blocks each. Keep track of your layout while sewing on the lattice.

**STEP 2.** Sew the $1\frac{1}{2} \times 8\frac{1}{2}$-inch strips of Fabric C to the right side of nine cat blocks. See **Diagram 10**. Press all seams toward the lattice. Sew three of these blocks, plus one block without lattice together to make a row of four cats. See **Diagram 11**. Press toward lattice. Repeat for two more rows.

**STEP 3.** Sew a $1\frac{1}{2} \times 44$-inch-long lattice strip between each row of cats to join the rows together. Add a strip to the top and bottom of the quilt. Trim the excess and press toward the lattice. Last, add lattice to the quilt sides. Trim and press toward the lattice.

## The Border

**STEP 1.** Prepare the four-patch blocks for each corner. With right sides facing, sew together the two $1\frac{1}{2} \times 15$-inch strips of Fabrics B and D. Press toward the darkest fabric. Following **Diagram 12**, cut eight $1\frac{1}{2} \times 2\frac{1}{2}$-inch strips. Rematch the strips to create a checkerboard effect and sew together to make four $2\frac{1}{2}$-inch corner squares. Press seam open.

**STEP 2.** Attach $2\frac{1}{2} \times 44$-inch border strips of Fabric A to the top and bottom of the quilt. Trim the excess and press toward the border.

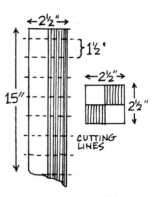

DIAGRAM 12

Measure the sides of the quilt up to but not including the top and bottom borders. Trim side border strips to equal the measurements of the quilt sides plus ¼ inch on each end for seam allowances. Sew a four-patch to the ends of both strips. Press toward the border. Pin in position and sew to the sides of the quilt. See **Quilt Layout** for reference.

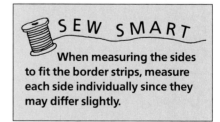

**SEW SMART**

When measuring the sides to fit the border strips, measure each side individually since they may differ slightly.

## Layering the Quilt

Arrange and baste the backing, batting, and top together following directions for Layering The Quilt on page 32. Trim batting and backing to ¼ inch from the raw edge of the quilt top.

## Binding the Quilt

Using the strips cut from Fabric C, follow directions on page 33 for Binding the Quilt.

## The Finishing Stitches

Outline your cats and hearts by quilting in the ditch or ¼ inch away from the seam lines. You may want to outline their tails and faces, too. Use the **Quilt Layout** as your guide. Another nice touch is to fill the border with quilting, using the **Heart and Cat Quilting Templates** provided below. These shapes are alternated in the border of the quilt shown in the photograph.

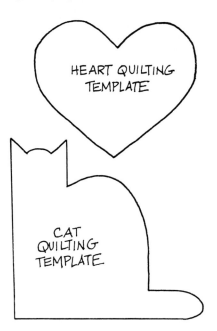

HEART QUILTING TEMPLATE

CAT QUILTING TEMPLATE

# Scrap Cats

Finished Quilt: 35 × 34 inches
Finished Block: 6 × 8 inches

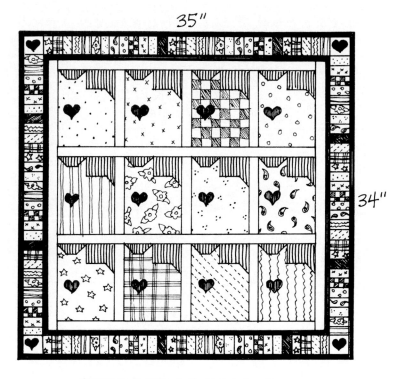

SCRAP CATS QUILT LAYOUT

## Materials

Obvious directional prints are not recommended.

**FABRIC A** (cats, scrap border, hearts)

¼ yard each of twelve fabrics

**FABRIC B** (block background, lattice, scrap border, corner squares)

| | |
|---|---|
| Blocks and Scrap Border | ½ yard |
| Lattice | ⅓ yard |
| Corner Squares | ⅛ yard |
| TOTAL | 1 yard |

**FABRIC C** (border, binding)

| | |
|---|---|
| Half-Inch Border | ¼ yard |
| Binding | ½ yard |
| TOTAL | ¾ yard |

**BACKING**     1⅛ yards

**BATTING**     1⅛ yards
or crib-size package
(45 × 60 inches)

**Tear-away paper** (for machine appliqué only)

## Before You Begin

Many of the assembly techniques for Scrap Cats are the same as those given earlier for Four-Patch Cats. Throughout these directions you will be referred back to Four-Patch Cats for steps that are identical. Specific assembly directions needed for Scrap Cats are given in detail here.

## Cutting Directions

Prewash and press all of your fabrics. Using a rotary cutter, see-through ruler, and cutting mat, prepare the strips as described in the first column in the chart below. Then from those strips, cut the pieces listed in the second column. Some portions of the quilt need to be cut only once, so no additional cutting information will appear in the second column.

## Speedy Triangles

**STEP 1.** Refer to Speedy Triangle directions on page 11 for how to mark, sew, and cut.

**STEP 2.** Use twelve $4 \times 6$-inch pieces each of Fabrics A and B.

| | FIRST CUT | | SECOND CUT | |
|---|---|---|---|---|
| | **NO. OF STRIPS** | **DIMENSIONS** | **NO. OF PIECES** | **DIMENSIONS** |
| **FABRIC A** | CAT BLOCKS: from *each* of the *twelve* cat fabrics, cut the following pieces | | | |
| | 1 | $1\frac{1}{2} \times 3\frac{1}{2}$-inch piece | | |
| | 1 | $1\frac{1}{2} \times 5\frac{1}{2}$-inch piece | | |
| | 1 | $5\frac{1}{2} \times 6\frac{1}{2}$-inch piece | | |
| | 1 | $4 \times 6$-inch piece | | |
| | SCRAP BORDER: from *each* of the *twelve* fabrics, cut the following strip | | | |
| | 1 | $1\frac{1}{2} \times 24$-inch strip | | |
| **FABRIC B** | CAT BLOCKS | | | |
| | 1 | $1\frac{1}{2} \times 44$-inch strip | 12 | $1\frac{1}{2} \times 1\frac{1}{2}$-inch pieces |
| | 1 | $2\frac{1}{2} \times 44$-inch strip | 12 | $2\frac{1}{2} \times 3\frac{1}{2}$-inch pieces |
| | 2 | $4 \times 44$-inch strips | 12 | $4 \times 6$-inch pieces |
| | LATTICE | | | |
| | **Before You Cut:** From two of the 44-inch strips, cut the pieces as directed in the second column. The remaining six 44-inch strips require no further cutting. | | | |
| | 8 | $1\frac{1}{2} \times 44$-inch strips | 9 | $1\frac{1}{2} \times 8\frac{1}{2}$-inch pieces |
| | SCRAP BORDER | | | |
| | 2 | $1\frac{1}{2} \times 24$-inch strips | | |
| | CORNER SQUARES | | | |
| | 4 | $2\frac{1}{2} \times 2\frac{1}{2}$-inch squares | | |
| **FABRIC C** | HALF-INCH BORDER | | | |
| | 4 | $1 \times 44$-inch strips | | |
| | BINDING | | | |
| | 4 | $2\frac{3}{4} \times 44$-inch strips | | |

Position one piece of Fabric A with one piece of Fabric B, right sides together. Repeat for a total of twelve sets. On each set mark a 1⅞-inch grid of two squares. See **Diagram 13**.

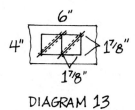

DIAGRAM 13

**STEP 3.** After sewing and cutting are complete, press seam allowances toward Fabric A. You will make four triangle sets per 4 × 6-inch rectangle. You will use only three of those sets.

### Assembling the Blocks

Follow all the steps for assembling Section One, Section Two, and Section Three under Four-Patch Cats beginning on page 51. Remember that each Scrap Cat block has a different Fabric A. As you assemble the block sections, match up the same Fabric A for each cat.

### The Hearts

Machine or hand appliqué hearts to the chest of each cat using the **Heart Appliqué Pattern** provided at right. (Refer to Machine or Hand Appliqué on page 19.) Use leftover scraps of Fabric A for the hearts, and mix and match the colors among the different cat blocks.

### The Lattice

Using the Fabric B strips, follow Steps 1 through 3 under The Lattice for Four-Patch Cats beginning on page 52.

### Inner Border

For the solid inner border, sew 1 × 44-inch strips of Fabric C to the quilt top and bottom. Trim the excess and press all seams toward the border. Sew the remaining strips to the quilt sides. Trim excess and press.

### Scrap Border

**STEP 1.** In addition to the fourteen 1½ × 24-inch strips you cut of Fabrics A and B, cut one extra 1½ × 24-inch strip of your favorite Fabric A.

**STEP 2.** Arrange the fifteen strips in a pleasing order and sew right sides together to make a 15½ × 24-inch strip set. As you add each strip, press the seams in the same direction. See **Diagram 14**.

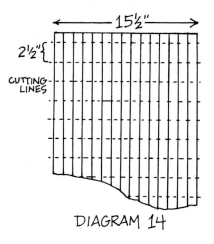

DIAGRAM 14

**STEP 3.** Cut eight 2½ × 15½-inch strips from the strip set following the cutting lines in **Diagram 14**.

**STEP 4.** Sew two of those strips together end to end to make a 2½ × 30½-inch strip. Repeat with the remaining strips to make a total of four scrap border strips.

**STEP 5.** If you wish, appliqué a heart cut from leftover scraps onto each corner square of Fabric B. (Refer to Machine or Hand Appliqué on page 19.) Use the **Heart Quilting Template** on page 53 to cut out these appliqué pieces (the **Heart Appliqué Pattern** is too large to fit within the corner squares).

**STEP 6.** Fit and sew the scrap borders to the top and bottom of the quilt. Press toward the border. Compare the remaining scrap borders to the sides of the quilt (not including top and bottom borders). If the side borders don't fit, see Hints on Fitting a Scrap Border on page 28 to make the necessary adjustments. Sew the corner squares to each end of the borders. Press seams toward the border. Pin border strips with corner squares to the sides of the quilt; sew, and press toward the border.

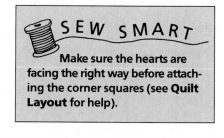

**S E W   S M A R T**

Make sure the hearts are facing the right way before attaching the corner squares (see **Quilt Layout** for help).

### Completing the Quilt

Refer to Layering the Quilt on page 32 and Binding the Quilt on page 33.

### The Finishing Stitches

Outline your cats and hearts by quilting in the ditch or ¼ inch from the seam lines. For the background, stitch a 1-inch diagonal grid.

HEART APPLIQUÉ PATTERN

# Flock of Sheep

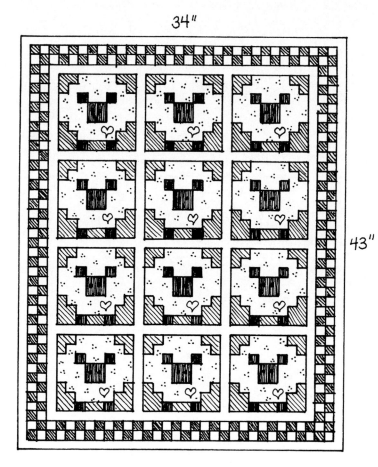

34"

43"

QUILT LAYOUT

**I**t looks as if Mary's little lamb has found a whole flock of buddies. This wallhanging is a suitable gift for anyone who is allergic to wool, since it's guaranteed to be itch-free! As you're selecting fabrics, make sure the one you choose for the head and legs contrasts with the fabrics used for the bodies and background.

Finished Quilt: 34 × 43 inches
Finished Block: 8 × 8 inches

## Materials

Directional prints may be used for Fabrics A and B; they are not recommended for Fabrics C or D.

**FABRIC A** *(sheep body, checkerboard)*

| | |
|---|---|
| Blocks | ¾ yard |
| Checkerboard | ⅓ yard |
| TOTAL | 1⅛ yards |
| | (1¼ yards if directional print is used) |

**FABRIC B** *(block background, checkerboard)*

| | |
|---|---|
| Blocks | ½ yard |
| Checkerboard | ⅓ yard |
| TOTAL | ⅞ yard |
| | (1¼ yards if directional print is used) |

**FABRIC C** *(head, legs)*

| | |
|---|---|
| Blocks | ⅙ yard (6 inches) |

**FABRIC D** *(lattice, binding)*

| | |
|---|---|
| Lattice | ½ yard |
| Binding | ⅔ yard |
| TOTAL | 1¼ yards |

**BACKING** — 1⅜ yards

**BATTING** — 1⅜ yards or crib-size package (45 × 60 inches)

## Cutting Directions

Prewash and press all of your fabrics. Using a rotary cutter, see-through ruler, and cutting mat, prepare the strips as described in the first column in the chart below. Then from those strips, cut the pieces listed in the second column. Some portions of the quilt need to be cut only once, so no additional cutting information will appear in the second column.

**SEW SMART**

If you're using directional prints for Fabrics A and B, cut all strips so the direction of the print is parallel to the length of the strip.

GUIDE FOR
CUTTING STRIPS
OF DIRECTIONAL
FABRIC

| | FIRST CUT | | SECOND CUT | |
|---|---|---|---|---|
| | **NO. OF STRIPS** | **DIMENSIONS** | **NO. OF PIECES** | **DIMENSIONS** |
| **FABRIC A** | **SHEEP BODY** | | | |
| | 2 | 2½ × 44-inch strips | 3 | 2½ × 22-inch strips |
| | 2 | 3½ × 44-inch strips | | |
| | 1 | 4½ × 44-inch strip | | |
| | 1 | 6½ × 44-inch strip | | |
| | **CHECKERBOARD BORDER** | | | |
| | 7 | 1½ × 44-inch strips | | |
| **FABRIC B** | **BACKGROUND** | | | |
| | 2 | 1½ × 44-inch strips | | |
| | **Before You Cut:** From two of the 44-inch strips, cut the pieces as directed in the second column. The remaining two 44-inch strips require no further cutting. | | | |
| | 4 | 2½ × 44-inch strips | 3 | 2½ × 22-inch strips |
| | **CHECKERBOARD BORDER** | | | |
| | 7 | 1½ × 44-inch strips | | |
| **FABRIC C** | **HEAD AND LEGS** | | | |
| | 2 | 1½ × 44-inch strips | 4 | 1½ × 22-inch strips |
| | 1 | 2½ × 44-inch strip | | |
| **FABRIC D** | **LATTICE** | | | |
| | **Before You Cut:** From two of the 44-inch strips, cut the pieces as directed in the second column. The remaining seven 44-inch strips require no further cutting. | | | |
| | 9 | 1½ × 44-inch strips | 8 | 1½ × 8½-inch pieces |
| | **BINDING** | | | |
| | 4 | 5½ × 44-inch strips | | |

## Sewing the Strip Sets

Sew the strips together following **Diagrams 1 through 7.** Use accurate ¼-inch seam allowances. Be sure to press seams as you go following the directions given in the individual steps. Refer to the Fabric Key for fabric identification. All finished strip sets will be 8½ inches wide.

FABRIC KEY   FABRIC A
FABRIC B
FABRIC C

**STRIP SET 1.** Strip Sets 1 and 6 are identical and you will be making both at the same time. Use two 2½ × 44-inch strips of Fabric B and one 4½ × 44-inch strip of Fabric A. Press seams to Fabric B. Cut this strip set in half to make two 8½ × 22-inch units for Strip Sets 1 and 6. See **Diagram 1.**

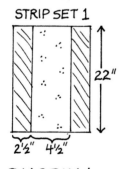

STRIP SET 1

22"

2½"   4½"

DIAGRAM 1

**STRIP SET 2.** Strip Sets 2 and 5 are also identical. Use two 1½ × 44-inch strips of Fabric B and one 6½ × 44-inch strip of Fabric A. Press seams to Fabric A. Cut this strip set in half to make Strip Sets 2 and 5. See **Diagram 2.**

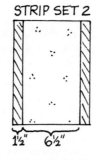

STRIP SET 2

1½"   6½"

DIAGRAM 2

**STRIP SET 3.** Use three 2½ × 22-inch strips of Fabric A and two 1½ × 22-inch strips of Fabric C. Press seams to Fabric A. See **Diagram 3.**

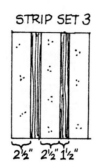

STRIP SET 3

2½"  2½" 1½"

DIAGRAM 3

**STRIP SET 4.** Use two 3½ × 44-inch strips of Fabric A and one 2½ × 44-inch strip of Fabric C. Press seams to Fabric C. This strip set will remain 44 inches long. See **Diagram 4.**

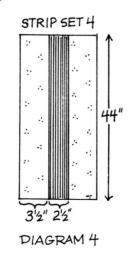

STRIP SET 4

44"

3½"   2½"

DIAGRAM 4

**STRIP SET 5.** Made earlier with Strip Set 2. See **Diagram 5.**

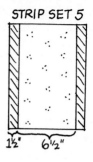

STRIP SET 5

1½"   6½"

DIAGRAM 5

**STRIP SET 6.** Made earlier with Strip Set 1. See **Diagram 6.**

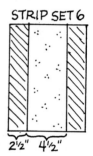

STRIP SET 6

2½"   4½"

DIAGRAM 6

**STRIP SET 7.** Use three 2½ × 22-inch strips of Fabric B and two 1½ × 22-inch strips of Fabric C. Press seams to Fabric C. See **Diagram 7.**

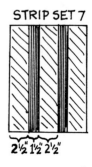

STRIP SET 7

2½" 1½" 2½"

DIAGRAM 7

## Stacking and Cutting the Strip Sets

**STEP 1.** Stack the strip sets in order, with Strip Set 7 on the bottom and Strip Set 1 on the top of the pile. Do not include Strip Set 4 in this pile. This is the only 44-inch strip set, and it is cut separately in a later step.

**STEP 2.** Take the bottom half of your stack (Strip Sets 5 through 7) and cut twelve 1½ × 8½-inch strips. Cut through all three layers at once. Repeat with the top half of your stack (Strip Sets 1 through 3), cutting twelve 1½ × 8½-inch strips. See **Diagram 8.**

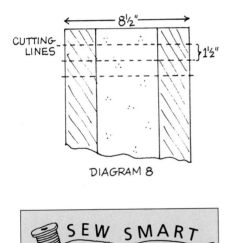

DIAGRAM 8

**STEP 3.** From Strip Set 4, cut twelve 2½ × 8½-inch strips.

**STEP 4.** After all the strips are cut, make twelve piles of seven strips. Each pile will need one strip from each strip set, stacked in sequence, starting with Strip 7 on the bottom and ending with Strip 1 on the top of the pile. Each of these piles will be one block.

## Making the Blocks

**STEP 1.** Lay out the twelve piles of strips next to your sewing machine.

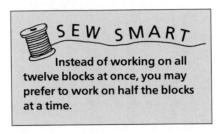

**STEP 2.** From the first pile, sew one Strip 1 to one Strip 2 (right sides together). From the second pile, again sew one Strip 1 to one Strip 2. Repeat until you have sewn together all Strips 1 and 2 in all twelve piles. Butt all strips behind one another and sew together in a Continuous Seam. Do not backstitch and do not cut threads. See **Diagram 9.** Press seams to Strip 2. You will end up with twelve joined pieces that look like those in **Diagram 10.** Resist the temptation to cut them apart!

**STEP 3.** Sew all Strip 3 pieces from all twelve piles to the units made from Strips 1 and 2. Again, do not cut threads. Press seams to Strip 3. See **Diagram 11.**

**STEP 4.** Sew all Strip 4 pieces to the units made from Strips 1, 2, and 3. Press seams to Strip 4.

**STEP 5.** Sew all the remaining strips together using the same method. Be sure to add your strips in sequence, and do not cut threads. Press all seams in the direction of the piece you have just added. Once all the strips have been sewn together, you can cut the threads that join your blocks. Your sheep blocks are now complete.

## The Lattice

**STEP 1.** Sew the 1½ × 8½-inch Fabric D lattice strips to each side of four sheep blocks. Press all seams to the lattice. See **Diagram 12.**

**STEP 2.** Sew a block to each side of those lattice strips to make a row of three sheep. Press. Repeat for the remaining three rows. See **Diagram 13.**

STRIP 1
STRIP 2

DIAGRAM 9

STRIP 1
STRIP 2

DIAGRAM 10

STRIP 1
STRIP 2
STRIP 3

DIAGRAM 11

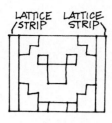

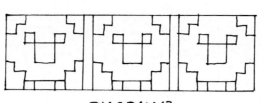

DIAGRAM 12          DIAGRAM 13

**STEP 3.** Sew a 1½ × 44-inch lattice strip below each row of blocks. On just one row of blocks, also sew a lattice strip across the top; this will be the top row of the quilt. Trim excess and press.

**STEP 4.** Sew together the four rows of blocks, making sure the row with the two lattice strips is positioned at the top. Press.

**STEP 5.** Sew the remaining lattice strips to the quilt sides. Trim and press.

## Checkerboard Border

**STEP 1.** Sew together the seven 1½ × 44-inch strips of Fabrics A and B, alternating fabrics as shown in **Diagram 14.** Press all seams toward Fabric A as you go.

**STEP 2.** Cut this strip set into thirds as shown in **Diagram 14.** The sections will be approximately 14 inches long. Resew the thirds together to make a 42½ × 14-inch strip set as shown in **Diagram 15.**

**STEP 3.** From the strip set created in Step 2, cut eight 1½ × 42½-inch strips, referring to the cutting lines in **Diagram 15.** Rematch two strips so they form a checkerboard and stitch together. Make four 2½ × 42½-inch checkerboard sets like the one shown in **Diagram 16.**

**STEP 4.** Fit and sew checkerboard borders to the quilt top and bottom first, then the sides. See Hints on Fitting a Checkerboard Border on page 29. Press all seams to the lattice.

## Layering the Quilt

Arrange and baste the backing, batting, and top together following directions for Layering the Quilt on page 32. Trim batting and backing to ¾ inch from the raw edge of the quilt top.

## Binding the Quilt

Using strips of Fabric D, follow the directions on page 33 for Binding the Quilt. Bind the sides first, then the top and bottom.

## The Finishing Stitches

Outline your sheep by quilting either in the ditch or ¼ inch from the seam line. For an extra special touch, quilt a small heart on their chests in a contrasting thread color. See **Diagram 17.**

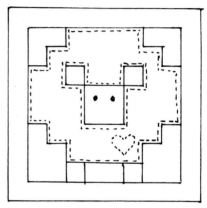

DIAGRAM 17

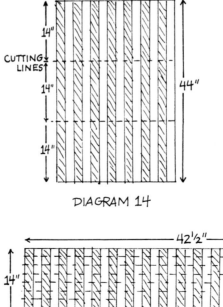

DIAGRAM 14

DIAGRAM 15

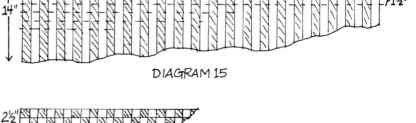

DIAGRAM 16

# The Goose Quilt

40"

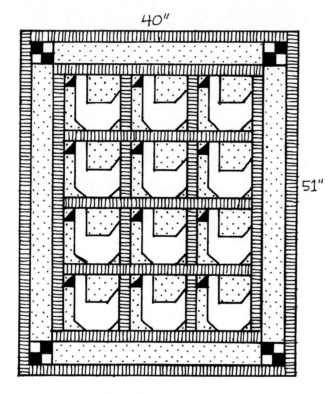

51"

QUILT LAYOUT

Great goosefeathers! It's a gaggle of good-natured geese! The soft shades of peach, green, and cream in the quilt shown at the left create a definite feeling of springtime. If you'd rather have a Christmas goose, just add an appliquéd wreath in appropriately seasonal fabric as shown on page 67.

Finished Quilt: 40 × 51 inches
Finished Block: 10 × 10 inches

## Materials

Obvious directional prints are not recommended.

**FABRIC A** *(geese, four-patch corners)*

| | |
|---|---|
| Blocks and Four-Patch | 1 yard |

**FABRIC B** *(block background, border)*

| | |
|---|---|
| Blocks | 1 yard |
| Two-Inch Border | ½ yard |
| TOTAL | 1½ yards |

**FABRIC C** *(beak, four-patch corners)*

| | |
|---|---|
| Blocks and Four-Patch | ¼ yard |

**FABRIC D** *(lattice, binding)*

| | |
|---|---|
| Lattice | ½ yard |
| Binding | 1 yard |
| TOTAL | 1½ yards |

| | |
|---|---|
| **BACKING** | 1½ yards |

| | |
|---|---|
| **BATTING** | 1½ yards or crib-size package (45 × 60 inches) |

**Tear-away paper** *(for machine appliqué only)*

## Cutting Directions

Prewash and press all of your fabrics. Using a rotary cutter, see-through ruler, and cutting mat, prepare the strips as described in the first column in the chart below. Then from those strips, cut the pieces listed in the second column.

Some portions of the quilt need to be cut only once, so no additional cutting information will appear in the second column.

| | FIRST CUT | | SECOND CUT | |
| --- | --- | --- | --- | --- |
| | NO. OF STRIPS | DIMENSIONS | NO. OF PIECES | DIMENSIONS |
| **FABRIC A** | **GEESE** | | | |
| | 2 | 2½ × 44-inch strips | 12 | 2½ × 2½-inch pieces |
| | | | 12 | 2½ × 4½-inch pieces |
| | 4 | 3½ × 44-inch strips | 12 | 3½ × 2½-inch pieces |
| | | | 12 | 3½ × 8½-inch pieces |
| | 1 | 9 × 30-inch strip | | |
| | **FOUR-PATCH CORNER SQUARES** | | | |
| | 1 | 1½ × 15-inch strip | | |
| **FABRIC B** | **BACKGROUND** | | | |
| | 2 | 2½ × 44-inch strips | 12 | 2½ × 4½-inch pieces |
| | | | 2 | 2½ × 8½-inch pieces |
| | 1 | 8½ × 44-inch strip | 10 | 8½ × 2½-inch pieces |
| | | | 1 | 8½ × 14-inch piece |
| | 2 | 3½ × 44-inch strips | 12 | 3½ × 6½-inch pieces |
| | 1 | 9 × 30-inch strip | | |
| | **BORDER** | | | |
| | 5 | 2½ × 44-inch strips | | |
| **FABRIC C** | **BEAK** | | | |
| | 1 | 8½ × 14-inch strip | | |
| | **FOUR-PATCH CORNER SQUARES** | | | |
| | 1 | 1½ × 15-inch strip | | |
| **FABRIC D** | **LATTICE** | | | |
| | **Before You Cut:** From two of the 44-inch strips, cut the pieces as directed in the second column. The remaining eight strips require no further cutting. | | | |
| | 10 | 1½ × 44-inch strips | 8 | 1½ × 10½-inch pieces |
| | **BINDING** | | | |
| | 5 | 5½ × 44-inch strips | | |

## Speedy Triangles

**STEP 1.** Refer to Speedy Triangle directions on page 11 for how to mark, sew, and cut.

**STEP 2.** Position the 8½ × 14-inch pieces of Fabrics B and C with right sides together. Mark a 2⅞-inch grid of six squares. See **Diagram 1**.

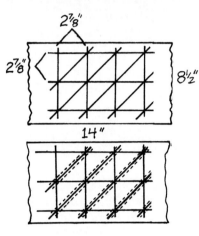

DIAGRAM 1

**STEP 3.** After sewing and cutting are complete, press seam allowances toward Fabric B. You will have made a total of twelve triangle sets of Fabrics B/C.

**STEP 4.** For the second set of triangle sets, position the 9 × 30-inch strips of Fabrics A and B with right sides together. Mark a 2⅞-inch grid of eighteen squares. Press seam allowances toward Fabric B. You will have made a total of thirty-six triangle sets of Fabrics A/B.

## Assembling the Blocks

Throughout this section, refer to the Fabric Key to identify the fabric placements in the diagrams. Also, it's a good idea to review Assembly Line Piecing on page 13 before you get started. It's more efficient to do the same step for each block at the same time than to piece one entire block

together at a time. Be sure to press as you go, and follow the arrows for pressing direction.

FABRIC KEY    FABRIC A ☐
FABRIC B ▦
FABRIC C ■

### SECTION ONE

**STEP 1.** Sew twelve 6½ × 3½-inch pieces of Fabric B to twelve 2½ × 3½-inch pieces of Fabric A as shown in **Diagram 2**. Position them right sides together and line up next to your sewing machine. Stitch the first set together, then butt the next set directly behind it and continue sewing each set without breaking your seam. Press seams toward Fabric B and cut the joining threads.

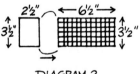

DIAGRAM 2

In each of the remaining steps, use the same Continuous Seam method. You will be making a total of twelve blocks.

**STEP 2.** Sew twelve 4½ × 2½-inch pieces of Fabric B to twelve 2½ × 2½-inch pieces of Fabric A. Press toward Fabric A. See **Diagram 3**.

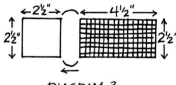

DIAGRAM 3

**STEP 3.** Sew twelve Fabric A/B triangle sets to the right ends of units from Step 2. Press toward Step 2 units. See **Diagram 4**.

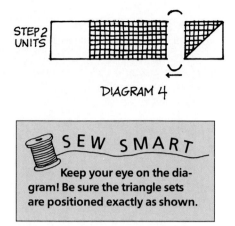

DIAGRAM 4

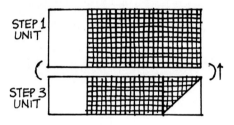
S E W  S M A R T
Keep your eye on the diagram! Be sure the triangle sets are positioned exactly as shown.

**STEP 4.** Sew units from Step 1 to units from Step 3. Press toward the Step 1 units. See **Diagram 5**.

DIAGRAM 5

### SECTION TWO

The second section is the 3½ × 8½-inch piece of Fabric A as shown in **Diagram 6**. Section Two is complete as is! Now that was easy!

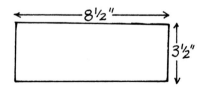

DIAGRAM 6

### SECTION THREE

**STEP 1.** Sew twelve 4½ × 2½-inch pieces of Fabric A to twelve Fabric A/B triangle sets. Press toward Fabric A. See **Diagram 7**.

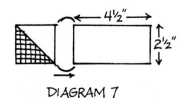

DIAGRAM 7

**STEP 2.** Sew twelve Fabric A/B triangle sets to the right end of the unit from Step 1. Make sure you place the triangle sets correctly. Press toward the Step 1 unit. See **Diagram 8.**

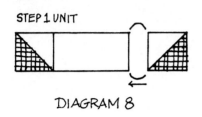

DIAGRAM 8

### SECTION FOUR

Sew twelve 8½ × 2½-inch pieces of Fabric B to twelve Fabric B/C triangle sets. Press toward Fabric B. See **Diagram 9.**

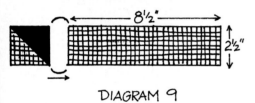

DIAGRAM 9

### SECTION ASSEMBLY

**STEP 1.** Sew the units from Section Two to the units from Section Three. Press toward Section Three. See **Diagram 10.**

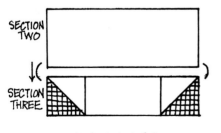

DIAGRAM 10

**STEP 2.** Sew the units from Section One to the units from Step 1 above. Press toward Sections Two and Three. See **Diagram 11.**

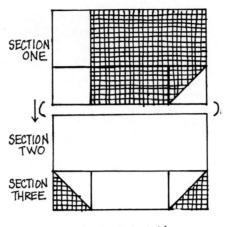

DIAGRAM 11

**STEP 3.** Sew the units from Section Four to the left side of the units from Step 2 above, referring to **Diagram 12.** Press toward Section Four.

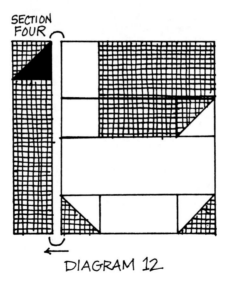

DIAGRAM 12

### The Lattice

**STEP 1.** Sew the 1½ × 10½-inch strips of Fabric D to each side of four goose blocks as shown in **Diagram 13.** Press all seams toward the lattice.

DIAGRAM 13

**STEP 2.** Sew a goose block to each side of those lattice strips to make a row of three geese. See **Diagram 14.** Repeat for the remaining three rows.

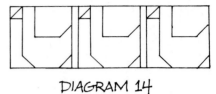

DIAGRAM 14

**STEP 3.** Sew 1½ × 44-inch lattice strips between each row of geese to join the rows together. Trim the excess and press.

**STEP 4.** Sew lattice strips to the quilt top and bottom. Trim and press.

**STEP 5.** The side lattice strips need to be pieced. Cut one strip in half. Sew one half to each of the side strips. Sew the strips to the quilt sides. Trim the excess and press.

### The Border with Four-Patch Corner Squares

**STEP 1.** Sew together 1½ × 15-inch strips of Fabrics A and C. Press toward Fabric C. See **Diagram 15.**

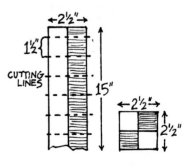

DIAGRAM 15

**STEP 2.** Cut eight 1½ × 2½-inch strips, referring to the cutting lines in **Diagram 15.**

**STEP 3.** Rematch two strips to form a four-patch and sew together. Repeat to make a total of four 2½-inch four-patch squares.

**STEP 4.** Sew 2½ × 44-inch border strips to the quilt sides. Trim the excess and press all seams to the border.

**STEP 5.** Compare border strips to the top and bottom edges and fit to the correct length. Measure up to but do not include the borders you just added to the quilt sides. Then add ¼ inch to each end of the strips before trimming so they will fit correctly after the corner squares are added.

**STEP 6.** Sew a four-patch corner square to each end of the top and bottom border strips. Press toward the border. Pin in position and sew to the quilt top and bottom. Press.

### Layering the Quilt

Arrange and baste the backing, batting, and top together following directions for Layering the Quilt on page 32. Trim backing and batting to ¾ inch from the raw edge of the quilt top.

### Binding the Quilt

Using the strips cut from Fabric D, follow directions for Binding the Quilt on page 33. Cut the fifth strip in half and sew one half to each side binding strip.

### The Finishing Stitches

Outline your geese by quilting in the ditch or ¼ inch from the seam lines. Give them each a "heart" by quilting one on their chests, using the **Heart Quilting Template** below. In the background, quilt a scallop design as shown in **Diagram 16**.

# Christmas Geese

To create a quilt with a holiday feel, choose fabrics in Christmas colors and prints and follow all the directions given above. Before you layer the quilt, appliqué the wreaths to the necks of a few select geese. Cut out the wreaths using the **Christmas Wreath**

**Appliqué Pattern** below. See Machine Appliqué directions on page 19.

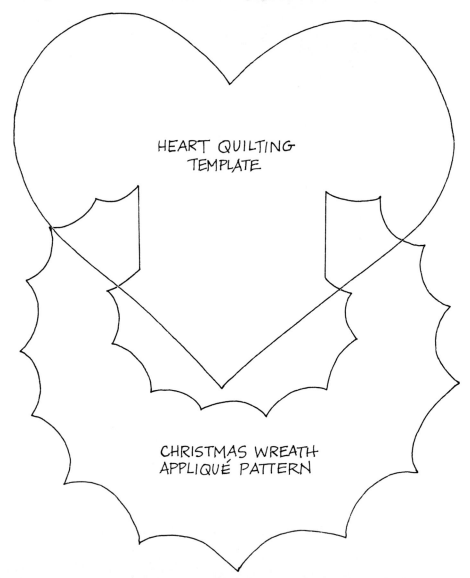

HEART QUILTING TEMPLATE

CHRISTMAS WREATH APPLIQUÉ PATTERN

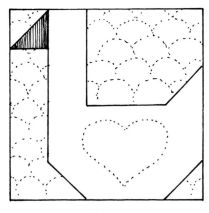

DIAGRAM 16

# Elsie & Co.

39½"

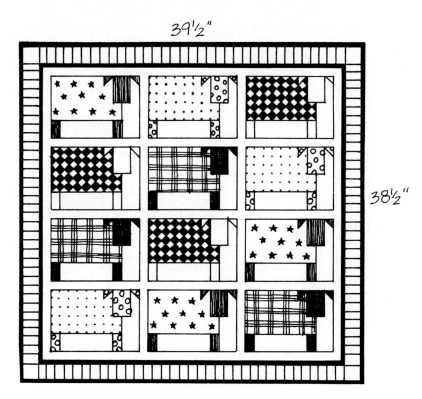

38½"

QUILT LAYOUT

$\mathbf{Y}$ou'll be in good company with Elsie and her corral of country cows. Choose your favorite herd size—four cows or twelve. For an especially lovable bevy of bovines, appliqué hearts on their sides (see the quilt displayed on the wall in the photograph). As always, you'll be "udderly" thrilled with the speed and ease with which these quilts go together.

# Twelve-Cow Quilt

Finished Quilt: 39½ × 38½ inches
Finished Block: 10 × 7 inches

**Materials**

Obvious directional prints are not recommended.

**FABRIC A** *(cows, scrap border)*
Use four fabrics.
Blocks and Border      ⅓ yard
                     *each* of *four* fabrics

**FABRIC B** *(block background, lattice, scrap border)*
Blocks                      ½ yard
Lattice and Scrap
    Border              ⅝ yard
    TOTAL          1⅛ yards

**FABRIC C** *(heads, feet, corner squares, hearts)*
Use four fabrics.
Blocks and Corner
    Squares            ¼ yard
               *each* of *four* fabrics
               (increase to ⅓ yard
               each if you decide to
               use appliqué hearts)

**FABRIC D** *(binding, border)*
Binding                ⅞ yard
Half-Inch Border      ⅛ yard
    TOTAL            1 yard

**BACKING**          1¼ yards

**BATTING**          1¼ yards
        or crib-size package
        (45 × 60 inches)

**Tear-away paper** *(for machine appliqué only)*

## Cutting Directions

Prewash and press all of your fabrics. Using a rotary cutter, see-through ruler, and cutting mat, prepare the strips as described in the first column in the chart below. Then from those strips, cut the pieces listed in the second column. Some portions of the quilt need to be cut only once, so no additional cutting information will appear in the second column.

| | FIRST CUT | | SECOND CUT | |
|---|---|---|---|---|
| | **NO. OF STRIPS** | **DIMENSIONS** | **NO. OF PIECES** | **DIMENSIONS** |
| **FABRIC A** | COWS: from *each* of the *four* fabrics, cut the following | | | |
| | 1 | 4 × 44-inch strip | 1 | 4 × 6-inch piece |
| | | | 3 | 3½ × 6½-inch pieces |
| | 1 | 2½ × 44-inch strip | 3 | 2½ × 1½-inch pieces |
| | | | 3 | 2½ × 8½-inch pieces |
| | SCRAP BORDER: from *each* of the *four* fabrics, cut the following | | | |
| | 1 | 1½ × 44-inch strip | | |
| **FABRIC B** | BACKGROUND | | | |
| | 1 | 4 × 44-inch strip | 4 | 4 × 6-inch pieces |
| | 4 | 2½ × 44-inch strips | 12 | 2½ × 1½-inch pieces |
| | | | 24 | 2½ × 2½-inch pieces |
| | | | 12 | 2½ × 6½-inch pieces |
| | SCRAP BORDER | | | |
| | 2 | 1½ × 44-inch strips | | |
| | LATTICE | | | |
| | **Before You Cut:** From two of the 44-inch strips, cut the pieces as directed in the second column. The remaining seven strips require no further cutting. | | | |
| | 9 | 1½ × 44-inch strips | 8 | 1½ × 7½-inch pieces |
| **FABRIC C** | HEADS AND FEET: from *each* of the *four* fabrics, cut the following | | | |
| | 1 | 4 × 44-inch strip | 2 | 4 × 6-inch pieces |
| | | | 3 | 2½ × 3½-inch pieces |
| | | | 6 | 2½ × 1½-inch pieces |
| | SCRAP BORDER: from *each* of the *four* fabrics, cut the following | | | |
| | 1 | 1½ × 44-inch strip | | |
| | CORNER SQUARES (choose one Fabric C) | | | |
| | 4 | 2¼ × 2¼-inch squares | | |

| FIRST CUT | | SECOND CUT | |
|---|---|---|---|
| NO. OF STRIPS | DIMENSIONS | NO. OF PIECES | DIMENSIONS |
| **FABRIC D** | HALF-INCH BORDER | | |
| 4 | 1 × 44-inch strips | | |
| | BINDING | | |
| 4 | 2¾ × 44-inch strips | | |

## Speedy Triangles

**STEP 1.** Refer to Speedy Triangle directions on page 11 for how to mark, sew, and cut.

**STEP 2.** You are going to make three cows each of four different Fabric A and C color combinations for a total of twelve cow blocks. Determine your four color combinations.

**STEP 3.** Use a 4 × 6-inch piece of Fabric A (cow color #1) and a 4 × 6-inch piece of Fabric C (head color #1) for your first color combination. Position the rectangles with right sides together. Mark a 1⅞-inch grid of two squares. See **Diagram 1**.

**STEP 4.** After sewing and cutting are complete, press seam allowances toward Fabric C. You will have made four triangle sets. You will only be using three of the triangle sets in the quilt.

**STEP 5.** Continue making triangle sets by matching the three remaining 4 × 6-inch pieces each of

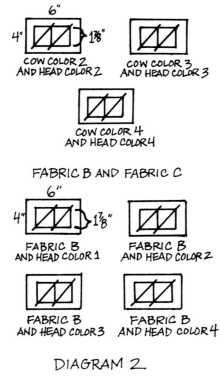

DIAGRAM 2

Fabrics A and C and four 4 × 6-inch pieces each of Fabrics B and C. For each set, mark a 1⅞-inch grid of two squares as you did in Step 3. Press all seam allowances toward Fabric C. To make it easier for you to pair the different colors, refer to **Diagram 2** and the descriptions that follow.

Match Fabric A (cow color #2) with Fabric C (head color #2).

Match Fabric A (cow color #3) with Fabric C (head color #3).

Match Fabric A (cow color #4) with Fabric C (head color #4).

Match Fabric B (background) with Fabric C (head color #1).

Match Fabric B (background) with Fabric C (head color #2).

Match Fabric B (background) with Fabric C (head color #3).

Match Fabric B (background) with Fabric C (head color #4).

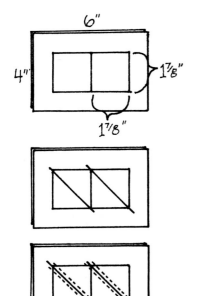

DIAGRAM 1

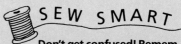

**SEW SMART**

**Don't get confused!** Remember that you will be making three blocks each of the four different cow/head color combinations. Keep track of your combinations so you don't intermix them.

## Assembling the Blocks

Throughout this section, refer to the Fabric Key to identify the fabric placements in the diagrams. Also, it's a good idea to review Assembly Line Piecing on page 13 before you get started. It is more efficient to do the same step for each block at the same time than to piece one entire block together at a time. Be sure to press as you go, and follow the arrows for pressing direction.

FABRIC KEY   FABRIC A (COWS)
FABRIC B (BACKGROUND)
FABRIC C (HEADS, FEET)

### SECTION ONE

**STEP 1.** Sew twelve Fabric A/C triangle sets to twelve 1½ × 2½-inch pieces of Fabric A. Position them right sides together and line up next to your sewing machine. Stitch the first set together, then butt the next set directly behind them and continue sewing each set without breaking your seam. Press toward Fabric A and cut the joining threads. Pay close attention that the triangle sets are positioned the same way as shown in **Diagram 3**.

DIAGRAM 3

In each of the remaining steps, use the same Continuous Seam method. You will be making three each of the four different cow/head color combinations for a total of twelve blocks.

**STEP 2.** Sew twelve Fabric B/C triangle sets to twelve 1½ × 2½-inch pieces of Fabric B. Press toward Fabric B as shown in **Diagram 4**.

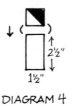

DIAGRAM 4

**STEP 3.** Sew twelve 2½ × 3½-inch pieces of Fabric C to the units from Step 1. Press toward Fabric C. See **Diagram 5**.

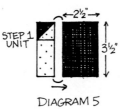

DIAGRAM 5

**STEP 4.** Sew the units from Step 2 to the units from Step 3. Press toward the Step 3 units as shown in **Diagram 6**.

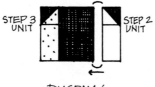

DIAGRAM 6

**STEP 5.** Sew the units from Step 4 to twelve 6½ × 3½-inch pieces of Fabric A as shown in **Diagram 7**. Press toward Fabric A.

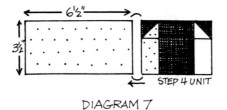

DIAGRAM 7

### SECTION TWO

**STEP 1.** Sew twelve 2½ × 2½-inch pieces of Fabric B to twelve 8½ × 2½-inch pieces of Fabric A. Press toward Fabric A. See **Diagram 8**.

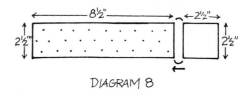

DIAGRAM 8

**STEP 2.** Sew twelve 6½ × 2½-inch pieces of Fabric B to twelve 1½ × 2½-inch pieces of Fabric C as shown in **Diagram 9**. Press toward Fabric C.

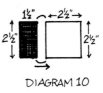

DIAGRAM 9

**STEP 3.** Sew twelve 2½ × 2½-inch pieces of Fabric B to twelve 1½ × 2½-inch pieces of Fabric C. Press toward Fabric B. See **Diagram 10**.

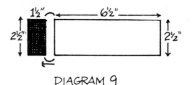

DIAGRAM 10

**STEP 4.** Sew the units from Step 2 to the units from Step 3. Press toward the Step 3 units. See **Diagram 11**.

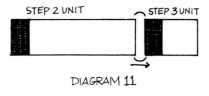

DIAGRAM 11

**STEP 5.** Sew the units from Step 1 to the units from Step 4. Press toward the Step 1 unit as shown in **Diagram 12.**

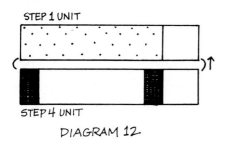

DIAGRAM 12

### SECTION ASSEMBLY

Sew the units from Section One to the units from Section Two as shown in **Diagram 13.** Press toward Section Two. Those cows should look like they're ready to moo!

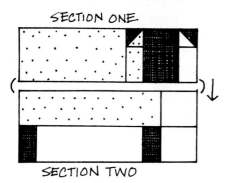

DIAGRAM 13

### The Lattice

**STEP 1.** Lay out your cow blocks in a pleasing arrangement, with four rows of three cows each (refer to the **Quilt Layout**). Keep track of your layout while sewing on the lattice.

**STEP 2.** Sew the 7½-inch lattice strips to each side of the four center blocks from each row. See **Diagram 14.** Press all seams toward the lattice.

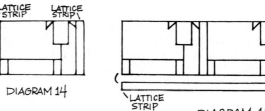

DIAGRAM 14

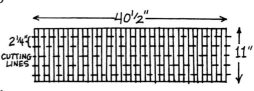

DIAGRAM 15

**STEP 3.** Sew a block to each side of those lattice strips to make a row of three cows as shown in **Diagram 15.** Repeat for the three remaining rows. Press.

**STEP 4.** Sew 1½ × 44-inch lattice strips to the bottom of all four rows as shown in **Diagram 15.** Trim the excess and press. Stitch the four rows together. Press.

**STEP 5.** Sew a 44-inch lattice strip to the top edge of the quilt. Trim and press.

**STEP 6.** Sew 44-inch lattice strips to the quilt sides. Trim and press.

### Half-Inch Border

**STEP 1.** Sew 1 × 44-inch strips of Fabric D to the quilt top and bottom. Trim the excess and press all seams toward the border.

**STEP 2.** Sew remaining Fabric D borders to the quilt sides. Trim and press.

### The Scrap Border

**STEP 1.** Take the ten 1½ × 44-inch strips of Fabrics A, B, and C and arrange them in a pleasing order. Sew the strips together to make a 10½ × approximately 44-inch strip set. See **Diagram 16.** Press all the seams in the same direction as you go.

**STEP 2.** Cut this strip set in half widthwise, referring to the cutting line in **Diagram 16.** Resew the halves together to make a 20½ × 22-inch strip set. See **Diagram 17.**

**STEP 3.** Cut the 20½-inch strip set in half, referring to the cutting line in **Diagram 17.** Resew the halves together to make a 40½ × 11-inch strip set. See **Diagram 18.**

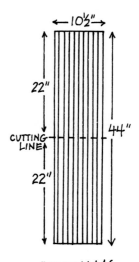

DIAGRAM 16

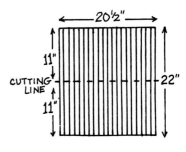

DIAGRAM 17

DIAGRAM 18

**STEP 4.** Cut four 2¼ × 40½-inch strips from the strip set created in Step 3. Refer to **Diagram 18** on page 73 for cutting lines. These four strips are the borders.

**STEP 5.** See Hints on Fitting a Scrap Border on page 28 for details on how to fit a scrap border to the quilt. Sew the borders to the top and bottom edges of the quilt.

**STEP 6.** Compare the remaining two borders to the quilt sides and fit to the correct length. Measure up to the outside seam line of the half-inch border (do not include the scrap borders you just added to the top and bottom). Then add ¼ inch to the ends of each strip so they will fit correctly after the corner squares are added.

**STEP 7.** Sew the 2¼-inch corner squares cut from Fabric C to each end of a side border strip. Pin in position and sew the border strips to the sides of the quilt.

## Optional Appliquéd Hearts

For extra-lovable cows, you may want to hand or machine appliqué a heart to the middle of each body. Cut the hearts from leftovers of Fabrics A and C, using the **Heart Appliqué Pattern** on page 77. Refer to Machine or Hand Appliqué on page 19 for directions on how to appliqué.

## Layering the Quilt

Arrange and baste the backing, batting, and top together following directions for Layering the Quilt on page 32. Trim batting and backing to ¼ inch from the raw edge of the quilt top.

## Binding the Quilt

Using the strips cut from Fabric D, follow directions for Binding the Quilt on page 33.

## The Finishing Stitches

Outline the bodies, ears, heads, and feet of your cows in quilting. If you didn't appliqué hearts, you may want to quilt a heart on the cows. Use the **Heart Quilting Template** on page 77.

# Four-Cow Quilt

Finished Quilt: 28½ × 22½ inches
Finished Block: 10 × 7 inches

## Materials

**FABRIC A** *(cows)*
Use four fabrics.
Blocks                              ⅛ yard
                    *each* of *four* fabrics

**FABRIC B** *(block background, lattice)*
Blocks                              ⅓ yard
Lattice                             ¼ yard
  TOTAL                             ⅔ yard

**FABRIC C** *(heads, feet, corner squares)*
Use four fabrics.
Blocks                              ⅛ yard
                    *each* of *four* fabrics

**FABRIC D** *(border, binding)*
Half-Inch Border
  and Binding                       ½ yard

**SCRAPS** *(border)*
Use eight fabrics.
Scrap Border                        ⅛ yard
                    *each* of *eight* fabrics
                    (or one 1½ × 33-inch
                        strip of each)

**BACKING**                         ¾ yard

**BATTING**                         ¾ yard

## Before You Begin

Many of the assembly techniques for the Four-Cow Quilt are the same as those given earlier for the Twelve-Cow Quilt. Throughout these directions, you will be referred back to the Twelve-Cow Quilt for steps that are identical. Specific assembly directions needed for the Four-Cow Quilt are given in detail here.

## Cutting Directions

Prewash and press all of your fabrics. Using a rotary cutter, see-through ruler, and cutting mat, prepare the strips as described in the first column in the chart below.

Then from those strips, cut the pieces listed in the second column. Some portions of the quilt need to be cut only once, so no additional cutting information will appear in the second column.

| | FIRST CUT | | SECOND CUT | |
|---|---|---|---|---|
| | **NO. OF STRIPS** | **DIMENSIONS** | **NO. OF PIECES** | **DIMENSIONS** |
| **FABRIC A** | **COWS:** from *each* of the *four* fabrics, cut the following | | | |
| | 1 | 4 × 44-inch strip | 1 | 4 × 4-inch piece |
| | | | 1 | 3½ × 6½-inch piece |
| | | | 1 | 2½ × 8½-inch piece |
| | | | 1 | 2½ × 1½-inch piece |
| **FABRIC B** | **BACKGROUND** | | | |
| | 1 | 4 × 44-inch strip | 4 | 4 × 4-inch pieces |
| | 2 | 2½ × 44-inch strips | 4 | 2½ × 6½-inch pieces |
| | | | 8 | 2½ × 2½-inch pieces |
| | | | 4 | 2½ × 1½-inch pieces |
| | **LATTICE** | | | |
| | **Before You Cut:** From one of the 44-inch strips, cut the pieces listed in the second column. Save the remainder of that strip to use as lattice between the rows. The remaining two 44-inch strips require no further cutting. | | | |
| | 3 | 1½ × 44-inch strips | 2 | 1½ × 7½-inch pieces |
| **FABRIC C** | **HEADS AND FEET:** from *each* of the *four* fabrics, cut the following | | | |
| | 1 | 4 × 44-inch strip | 2 | 4 × 4-inch pieces |
| | | | 1 | 2½ × 3½-inch piece |
| | | | 2 | 2½ × 1½-inch pieces |
| | **CORNER SQUARES** (choose one Fabric C) | | | |
| | 4 | 2¼ × 2¼-inch squares | | |
| **FABRIC D** | **HALF-INCH BORDER** | | | |
| | 3 | 1 × 44-inch strips | | |
| **SCRAPS** | **SCRAP BORDER** | | | |
| | **Before You Cut:** Cut *one* from each of the eight scrap fabrics plus one strip from Fabric B. | | | |
| | 9 | 1½ × 33-inch strips | | |

## Speedy Triangles

**STEP 1.** Refer to Speedy Triangle directions on page 11 for how to mark, sew, and cut.

**STEP 2.** You are going to make each cow a different cow/head color combination for a total of four cow blocks. Determine your four color combinations.

**STEP 3.** Use a 4 × 4-inch piece of Fabric A (cow color #1) and a 4 × 4-inch piece of Fabric C (head color #1) for your first color combination. Position the squares with right sides together. Mark with one 1⅞-inch square. See **Diagram 19**.

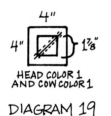

HEAD COLOR 1
AND COW COLOR 1

DIAGRAM 19

**STEP 4.** After sewing and cutting are complete, press seam allowances toward Fabric C. You will have made two triangle sets. Only one set will be used.

**STEP 5.** Continue making triangle sets by matching the remaining pieces of Fabrics A, B, and C. For each set, mark one 1⅞-inch square as you did in Step 3. Press all seam allowances toward Fabric C. To make it easier for you to pair the different colors, refer to **Diagram 20** and the descriptions that follow.

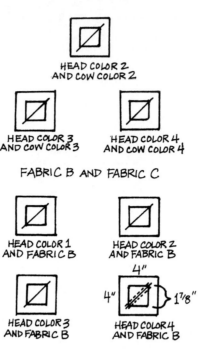

FABRIC A AND FABRIC C

HEAD COLOR 2
AND COW COLOR 2

HEAD COLOR 3
AND COW COLOR 3

HEAD COLOR 4
AND COW COLOR 4

FABRIC B AND FABRIC C

HEAD COLOR 1
AND FABRIC B

HEAD COLOR 2
AND FABRIC B

HEAD COLOR 3
AND FABRIC B

HEAD COLOR 4
AND FABRIC B

DIAGRAM 20

Match Fabric C (head color #2) with Fabric A (cow color #2).

Match Fabric C (head color #3) with Fabric A (cow color #3).

Match Fabric C (head color #4) with Fabric A (cow color #4).

Match Fabric C (head color #1) with Fabric B (background).

Match Fabric C (head color #2) with Fabric B (background).

Match Fabric C (head color #3) with Fabric B (background).

Match Fabric C (head color #4) with Fabric B (background).

## Assembling the Blocks

Follow all steps for Section One, Section Two, and Section Assembly under Twelve-Cow Quilt beginning on page 72. You will be making one block each of the four different cow/head color combinations instead of twelve total blocks.

## The Lattice

**STEP 1.** Lay out your cow blocks in a pleasing arrangement, with two rows of two cows each. Keep track of your layout while sewing on the lattice.

**STEP 2.** Sew a 1½ × 7½-inch lattice strip between each set of blocks. Press all seams toward the lattice.

**STEP 3.** Use the remainder of that first lattice strip to sew between the two rows of cows. Trim excess and press.

**STEP 4.** Sew 1½ × 44-inch lattice strips to the top and bottom edges of the quilt. Trim and press. Save the excess lattice.

**STEP 5.** Use excess lattice from Step 4 to sew to the quilt sides. Trim and press.

### Half-Inch Border

Refer to Steps 1 and 2 on page 73 under Half-Inch Border for the Twelve-Cow Quilt.

### Scrap Border

**STEP 1.** Arrange the nine 1½ × 33-inch strips in a pleasing order and sew right sides together to make a 9½ × 33-inch strip set. As you add each strip, press the seams in the same direction.

**STEP 2.** Cut the strip set into thirds. Resew the thirds together end to end to make a 27½ × 11-inch strip set.

**STEP 3.** Cut four 2¼ × 27½-inch strips from the 27½ × 11-inch strip set. These strips are the borders.

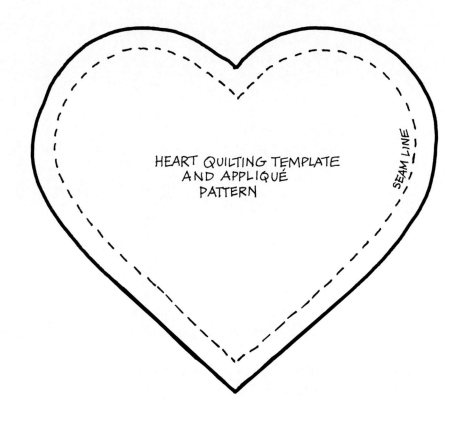

**STEP 4.** See Hints on Fitting a Scrap Border on page 28 for guidelines on how to fit your scrap border to the quilt. Sew the borders to the top and bottom edges of the quilt.

**STEP 5.** Compare the remaining two borders to the quilt sides and fit to the correct length. Measure up to the outside seam line of the half-inch border. Do not include the scrap borders you just added to the top and bottom. Then add ¼ inch to the ends of each strip so they will fit correctly after the corner squares are added. Attach a corner square cut from Fabric C to each end of a side border strip. Sew the border strips to the sides of the quilt.

### Completing the Quilt

Refer to instructions from Layering the Quilt through The Finishing Stitches under the Twelve-Cow Quilt on page 74.

HEART QUILTING TEMPLATE
AND APPLIQUÉ
PATTERN

SEAM LINE

# Heart's Content

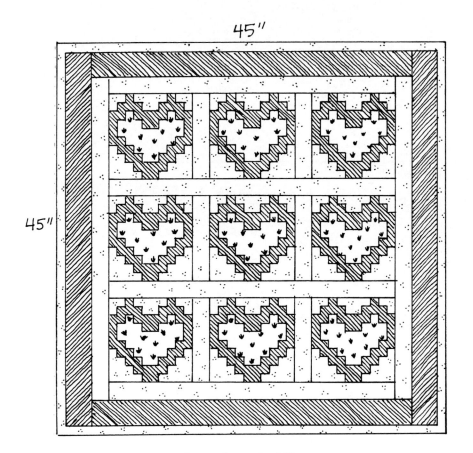

45"

45"

QUILT LAYOUT

It's easy to give away a piece of your heart—
just make someone you love this
speedy-quick quilt. This sentimental favorite
uses nine blocks, but there is enough
extra fabric to make a dozen. Turn those
three extra blocks into heartfelt gifts such as
pillows or even a miniature banner.

Finished Quilt: 45 × 45 inches
Finished Block: 10 × 10 inches

## Materials

Directional prints may be used for
Fabrics A and C; they are not
recommended for Fabric B.

**FABRIC A** *(outer heart, border)*

| | |
|---|---|
| Blocks | ¾ yard |
| | (1¼ yards if directional |
| | print is used) |
| Border | ½ yard |
| TOTAL | 1¼ yards |
| | (1¾ yards if directional |
| | print is used) |

**FABRIC B** *(block background, lattice, binding)*

| | |
|---|---|
| Blocks | ⅔ yard |
| Lattice | ⅔ yard |
| Binding | 1 yard |
| TOTAL | 2⅓ yards |

**FABRIC C** *(inner heart)*

| | |
|---|---|
| Blocks | ⅝ yard |
| | (yardage remains the |
| | same for directional |
| | print) |

| | |
|---|---|
| **BACKING** | 2 yards |
| **BATTING** | 2 yards |

## Cutting Directions

Prewash and press all of your fabrics. Using a rotary cutter, see-through ruler, and cutting mat, prepare the strips as described in the two charts below. The first chart tells you how to cut the strips for the heart blocks. The second chart explains how to cut pieces for the rest of the quilt.

### CUTTING THE STRIPS

Refer to the fabric requirements for blocks *only*. Cut the block yardage in half lengthwise (on the fold) so you will have two approximately 22-inch-wide pieces. Do this for Fabrics A, B, and C. It is very important to remember this cutting applies to block yardages only.

**SEW SMART**

If you are using directional prints, turn the fabric so the direction of the print is parallel to the length of the strip.

GUIDE FOR CUTTING STRIPS OF DIRECTIONAL FABRIC

| CUTTING THE STRIPS | FIRST CUT | | SECOND CUT | |
|---|---|---|---|---|
| | NO. OF STRIPS | DIMENSIONS | NO. OF PIECES | DIMENSIONS |
| **FABRIC A** | OUTER HEARTS | | | |
| | 2 | 4½ × 22-inch strips | | |
| | 2 | 3½ × 22-inch strips | | |
| | 10 | 2½ × 22-inch strips | | |
| | 6 | 1½ × 22-inch strips | | |
| **FABRIC B** | BACKGROUND | | | |
| | 3 | 4½ × 22-inch strips | | |
| | 2 | 3½ × 22-inch strips | | |
| | 5 | 2½ × 22-inch strips | | |
| | 4 | 1½ × 22-inch strips | | |
| **FABRIC C** | INNER HEARTS | | | |
| | 1 | 8½ × 22-inch strip | | |
| | 1 | 6½ × 22-inch strip | | |
| | 1 | 4½ × 22-inch strip | | |
| | 2 | 3½ × 22-inch strips | | |
| | 1 | 2½ × 22-inch strip | | |
| | 2 | 1½ × 22-inch strips | | |

## CUTTING THE OTHER QUILT PIECES

| | FIRST CUT | | SECOND CUT | |
|---|---|---|---|---|
| | NO. OF STRIPS | DIMENSIONS | NO. OF PIECES | DIMENSIONS |
| **FABRIC A** | BORDER | | | |
| | 5 | 3 × 44-inch strips | | |
| **FABRIC B** | LATTICE | | | |
| | **Before You Cut:** From two of the 44-inch strips, cut the pieces as directed in the second column. The remaining six 44-inch strips require no further cutting. | | | |
| | 8 | 2½ × 44-inch strips | 6 | 2½ × 10½-inch pieces |
| | BINDING | | | |
| | 5 | 5½ × 44-inch strips | | |

## Sewing the Strip Sets

Sew the strips together following **Diagrams 1 through 10.** Use accurate ¼-inch seam allowances. Press as you go, with all seams facing toward Fabric A except in Strip Set 5, where you should press seams to Fabric C. Refer to the Fabric Key for fabric identification. All finished strip sets will be 10½ inches wide × 22 inches long. As a reminder if you are using a directional print, keep the pattern running in the same direction for all the strip sets.

FABRIC KEY    FABRIC A ▨
              FABRIC B ▢
              FABRIC C ▨

**STRIP SET 1.** Use two 1½-inch strips of Fabric A and two 2½-inch strips and one 4½-inch strip of Fabric B. See **Diagram 1.**

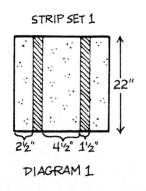

STRIP SET 1

2½"  4½"  1½"

DIAGRAM 1

**STRIP SET 2.** Use two 3½-inch strips of Fabric A and two 1½-inch strips and one 2½-inch strip of Fabric B. See **Diagram 2.**

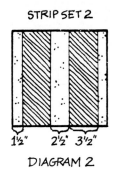

STRIP SET 2

1½"  2½"  3½"

DIAGRAM 2

**STRIP SET 3.** Use two 2½-inch strips and one 4½-inch strip of Fabric A and two 1½-inch strips of Fabric C. See **Diagram 3.**

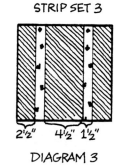

STRIP SET 3

2½"  4½"  1½"

DIAGRAM 3

**STRIP SET 4.** Use two 1½-inch strips and one 2½-inch strip of Fabric A and two 3½-inch strips of Fabric C. See **Diagram 4.**

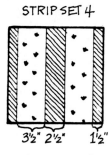

STRIP SET 4

3½"  2½"  1½"

DIAGRAM 4

**STRIP SET 5.** Use two 1½-inch strips of Fabric A and one 8½-inch strip of Fabric C. Press seams toward Fabric C. See **Diagram 5.**

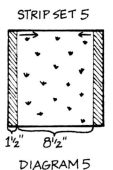

STRIP SET 5

1½"  8½"

DIAGRAM 5

**STRIP SET 6.** Use two 2½-inch strips of Fabric A and one 6½-inch strip of Fabric C. See **Diagram 6.**

STRIP SET 6

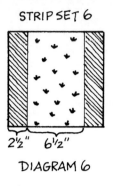

2½″  6½″

DIAGRAM 6

**STRIP SET 7.** Use two 2½-inch strips of Fabric A, two 1½-inch strips of Fabric B, and one 4½-inch strip of Fabric C. See **Diagram 7.**

STRIP SET 7

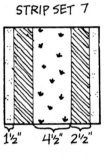

1½″  4½″  2½″

DIAGRAM 7

**STRIP SET 8.** Use two 2½-inch strips of Fabric A, two 2½-inch strips of Fabric B, and one 2½-inch strip of Fabric C. See **Diagram 8.**

STRIP SET 8

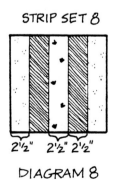

2½″  2½″  2½″

DIAGRAM 8

**STRIP SET 9.** Use one 4½-inch strip of Fabric A and two 3½-inch strips of Fabric B. See **Diagram 9.**

STRIP SET 9

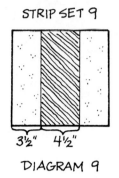

3½″  4½″

DIAGRAM 9

**STRIP SET 10.** Use one 2½-inch strip of Fabric A and two 4½-inch strips of Fabric B. See **Diagram 10.**

STRIP SET 10

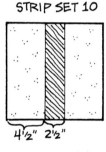

4½″  2½″

DIAGRAM 10

## Stacking and Cutting the Strip Sets

**STEP 1.** Stack the strip sets in order, with Strip Set 10 on the bottom and Strip Set 1 on the top of the pile.

**STEP 2.** Take the bottom half of your pile (Sets 6 through 10) and cut nine 1½-inch strips. Cut through all the layers at once. Now take the top half of your pile (Sets 1 through 5) and cut nine 1½-inch strips. See **Diagram 11.**

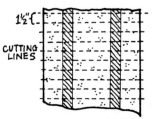

1½″{

CUTTING
LINES

DIAGRAM 11

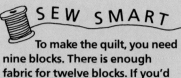

**STEP 3.** After all the strips are cut, put them back in order. You will make nine piles and each pile will have one strip from each of the ten strip sets. They must be in sequence, with Strip Set 10 on the bottom and Strip Set 1 on the top of each pile.

### Making the Blocks

**STEP 1.** Line up the nine piles of 1½-inch strips next to your sewing machine.

**STEP 2.** From the first pile, sew one Strip 1 to one Strip 2 (right sides together). From the second pile, again sew one Strip 1 to one Strip 2. Repeat until you have sewn all Strips 1 and 2 together in all nine piles. Butt all strips behind one another and sew together in a Continuous Seam. Do not back-stitch or cut threads. See **Diagram 12.** Press seams to Strip 2. You will end up with nine joined pieces that look like those in **Diagram 13.** Resist the temptation to cut them apart!

STRIP 1
STRIP 2

DIAGRAM 12

DIAGRAM 13

STRIP 1
STRIP 2
STRIP 3

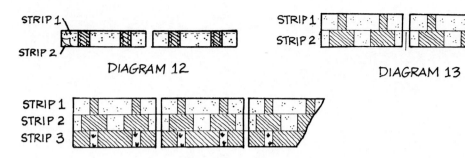

DIAGRAM 14

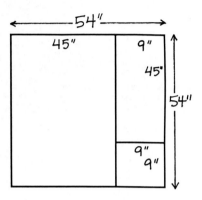

DIAGRAM 17

**STEP 3.** Sew all Strip 3 pieces to the units made from Strips 1 and 2. Remember, do not cut the connecting threads. Press seams to Strip 3. See **Diagram 14.**

**STEP 4.** Sew all Strip 4 pieces to the units made from Strips 1, 2, and 3. Press seams to Strip 4.

**STEP 5.** Sew all the remaining strips together through Strip 10 using the same method. Be sure to add your strips in sequence, and do not cut threads. Press all seams in the direction of the piece you have just added. Once all the strips have been sewn together, you can cut the threads that join your completed heart blocks.

## The Lattice

**STEP 1.** Sew the 2½ × 10½-inch strips of Fabric B to both sides of three blocks. See **Diagram 15.** Press all seams toward the lattice.

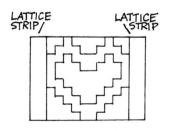

DIAGRAM 15

**STEP 2.** Sew a block to each side of those 10½-inch lattice strips to make a row of three hearts. Press. Repeat for the remaining two rows.

**STEP 3.** Sew a 2½ × 44-inch lattice strip below each row of blocks. On just one row of blocks, also sew a lattice strip across the top; this will be the top row of the quilt. Trim the excess and press. See **Diagram 16.**

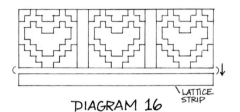

DIAGRAM 16

**STEP 4.** Sew lattice strips to the quilt sides. Trim and press.

## The Border

**STEP 1.** Sew strips cut from Fabric A to the quilt top and bottom. Trim the excess and press all seams toward the border.

**STEP 2.** The 3 × 44-inch strips will not be long enough to fit the sides of the quilt. Cut the fifth strip in half and sew one half to each of the side strips. Sew the lengthened strips to the quilt sides. Trim any excess and press.

## Layering the Quilt

Before you layer the quilt, the backing needs to be pieced. Follow the piecing layout shown in **Diagram 17.** Then arrange and baste the backing, batting, and top

together following the directions for Layering the Quilt on page 32. Trim batting and backing to ¾ inch from the raw edge of the quilt top.

## Binding the Quilt

**STEP 1.** Two of the binding strips will need to be lengthened to fit along the sides of the quilt. Cut the fifth strip in half and sew one half to each of the 44-inch side strips.

**STEP 2.** Follow the directions on page 33 for Binding the Quilt.

## The Finishing Stitches

Outline the inner and outer hearts by quilting in the ditch or ¼ inch from the seam line. See **Diagram 18** for reference. Stitch a 2-inch diagonal grid in the background.

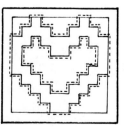

DIAGRAM 18

# An Apple a Day

37"

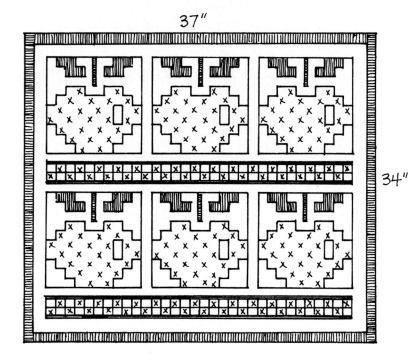

34"

QUILT LAYOUT

**A**n apple a day will keep the sewing blues away! With the Speedy Strip technique, you can create this fun, fresh fruit design in not much more time than it takes to say "apple pie." Variations on the red and green theme can also work well, if you want to match your kitchen or dining room colors. Apples come in all sorts of delicious shades of yellow, green, and red!

Finished Quilt: 37 × 34 inches
Finished Block: 10 × 10 inches

## Materials

Directional print may be used for Fabric A only; it is not recommended for Fabrics B or C.

**FABRIC A** *(apples, checkerboard)*
| | |
|---|---|
| Blocks | ⅝ yard |
| Checkerboard | ¼ yard |
| TOTAL | 1 yard |
| | (1¼ yards if directional print is used) |

**FABRIC B** *(block background, checkerboard, lattice, border)*
| | |
|---|---|
| Blocks | ½ yard |
| Checkerboard | ¼ yard |
| Lattice | ¼ yard |
| One-and-a-Half-Inch Border | ¼ yard |
| TOTAL | 1¼ yards |

**FABRIC C** *(leaves, stem, border, binding)*
| | |
|---|---|
| Blocks | ⅙ yard (6 inches) |
| Half-Inch Border on Checkerboard | ⅛ yard |
| Binding | ⅔ yard |
| TOTAL | 1 yard |

**BACKING**     1⅛ yards

**BATTING**     1⅛ yards

## Cutting Directions

Prewash and press all of your fabrics. Using a rotary cutter, see-through ruler, and cutting mat, prepare the strips as described in the two charts below. The first chart tells you how to cut the strips for the apple blocks. The second chart explains how to cut pieces for the rest of the quilt.

### CUTTING THE STRIPS

Refer to the fabric requirements for blocks *only*. Cut the block yardage in half lengthwise (on the fold) so you will have two approximately 22-inch-wide pieces. Do this for Fabrics A, B, and C. It is very important to remember this cutting applies to block yardages only.

Referring to the lists of strips to be cut, cut the 22-inch-long strips of Fabrics A, B, and C first. When all the 22-inch strips have been cut, cut the remaining block fabric in half again. For each 22-inch-wide piece, this means you will now have two 11-inch-wide pieces. From the 11-inch-wide pieces, now cut the 11-inch strips of Fabrics A, B, and C.

S E W   S M A R T

When using a directional print, cut all the strips so the direction of the print is parallel to the length of the strip.

| CUTTING THE STRIPS | \multicolumn{2}{FIRST CUT} | | \multicolumn{2}{SECOND CUT} | |
|---|---|---|---|---|
| | NO. OF STRIPS | DIMENSIONS | NO. OF PIECES | DIMENSIONS |
| **FABRIC A** | APPLE BLOCK | | | |
| | 1 | 7½ × 22-inch strip | | |
| | 1 | 2½ × 22-inch strip | | |
| | 2 | 2½ × 11-inch strips | | |
| | 1 | 4½ × 11-inch strip | | |
| | 1 | 6½ × 11-inch strip | | |
| | 2 | 8½ × 11-inch strips | | |
| **FABRIC B** | BACKGROUND | | | |
| | 1 | 1½ × 22-inch strip | | |
| | 6 | 1½ × 11-inch strips | | |
| | 8 | 2½ × 11-inch strips | | |
| | 2 | 3½ × 11-inch strips | | |
| | 1 | 4½ × 11-inch strip | | |
| | 1 | 10½ × 11-inch strip | | |
| **FABRIC C** | LEAVES | | | |
| | 4 | 2½ × 11-inch strips | | |
| | STEMS | | | |
| | 2 | 1 × 22-inch strips | 6 | 1 × 3½-inch pieces |

GUIDE FOR CUTTING STRIPS OF DIRECTIONAL FABRIC

## CUTTING THE OTHER QUILT PIECES

| | FIRST CUT | | SECOND CUT | |
|---|---|---|---|---|
| | NO. OF STRIPS | DIMENSIONS | NO. OF PIECES | DIMENSIONS |
| **FABRIC A** | CHECKERBOARD ROWS | | | |
| | 3 | 1½ × 44-inch strips | | |
| **FABRIC B** | LATTICE | | | |
| | **Before You Cut:** From one of the 44-inch strips, cut the pieces as directed in the second column. The remaining three 44-inch strips require no further cutting. | | | |
| | 4 | 1½ × 44-inch strips | 4 | 1½ × 10½-inch pieces |
| | CHECKERBOARD ROWS | | | |
| | 3 | 1½ × 44-inch strips | | |
| | ONE-AND-A-HALF-INCH BORDER | | | |
| | 4 | 2 × 44-inch strips | | |
| **FABRIC C** | HALF-INCH BORDER ON CHECKERBOARD | | | |
| | 4 | 1 × 44-inch strips | | |
| | BINDING | | | |
| | 4 | 5½ × 44-inch strips | | |

### Sewing the Strip Sets

Sew the strips together following **Diagrams 1 through 9.** Use accurate ¼-inch seam allowances. Be sure to press all seams as you go, as directed in each individual step. Refer to the Fabric Key for fabric identification. All finished strip sets will be 10½ inches wide.

FABRIC KEY  FABRIC A ▨
FABRIC B □
FABRIC C ▤

**STRIP SET 1.** Use two 1½ × 11-inch and one 4½ × 11-inch strips of Fabric B and two 2½ × 11-inch strips of Fabric C. Press seams to Fabric C. See **Diagram 1.**

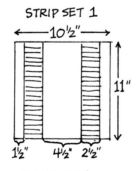

STRIP SET 1
DIAGRAM 1

**STRIP SET 2.** Use three 2½ × 11-inch strips of Fabric B and two 2½ × 11-inch strips of Fabric C. Press seams to Fabric C. See **Diagram 2.**

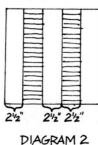

STRIP SET 2
DIAGRAM 2

**STRIP SET 3.** Use the 10½ × 11-inch piece of Fabric B. No sewing here! See **Diagram 3.**

**STRIP SET 4.** Use two 2½ × 11-inch strips of Fabric A and three 2½ × 11-inch strips of Fabric B. Press seams to Fabric A. See **Diagram 4.**

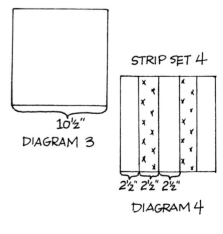

STRIP SET 3
DIAGRAM 3

STRIP SET 4
DIAGRAM 4

**STRIP SET 5.** Use one 8½ × 11-inch strip of Fabric A and two 1½ × 11-inch strips of Fabric B. Press seams to Fabric A. See **Diagram 5.**

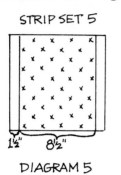

STRIP SET 5

1½"   8½"

DIAGRAM 5

**STRIP SET 6.** Use one 2½ × 22-inch and one 7½ × 22-inch strip of Fabric A and one 1½ × 22-inch strip of Fabric B. Press seams to Fabric A. See **Diagram 6.**

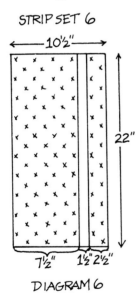

STRIP SET 6

← 10½" →

22"

7½"   1½" 2½"

DIAGRAM 6

**STRIP SET 7.** Use one 8½ × 11-inch strip of Fabric A and two 1½ × 11-inch strips of Fabric B. Press seams to Fabric A. See **Diagram 7.**

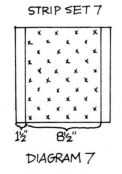

STRIP SET 7

1½"   8½"

DIAGRAM 7

**STRIP SET 8.** Use one 6½ × 11-inch strip of Fabric A and two 2½ × 11-inch strips of Fabric B. Press seams to Fabric A. See **Diagram 8.**

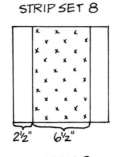

STRIP SET 8

2½"   6½"

DIAGRAM 8

**STRIP SET 9.** Use one 4½ × 11-inch strip of Fabric A and two 3½ × 11-inch strips of Fabric B. Press seams to Fabric A. See **Diagram 9.**

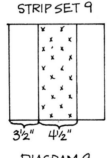

STRIP SET 9

3½"   4½"

DIAGRAM 9

## Stacking and Cutting the Strip Sets

**STEP 1.** Stack the strip sets in order, starting with Strip 9 on the bottom and ending with Strip 1 on the top of the pile.

**STEP 2.** Remove Strip Set 6 from this pile (this is the only 22-inch-long strip set). From Strip Set 6, cut six 2½ × 10½-inch strips. Set aside.

**STEP 3.** Take the bottom half of your stack (Strip Sets 5 through 9, minus 6) and cut six 1½ × 10½-inch strips. Cut through all four layers at once. Now take the top half of your stack (Strip Sets 1 through 4) and cut six 1½ × 10½-inch strips.

**STEP 4.** After all the strips are cut, make six piles, each pile containing one each of the nine strips. Stack the strips in sequence, starting with Strip 9 on the bottom and ending with Strip 1 on the top. Each pile, when sewn together, will make one block.

## Making the Blocks

For the time being, set aside all Strips 1, 2, and 3 from your piles. Those are the leaves and will be added at a later step.

### THE APPLES

**STEP 1.** Lay out the six piles of strips next to your sewing machine, keeping them in order (Strips 4 through 9).

**STEP 2.** From the first pile, sew one Strip 4 to one Strip 5 (right sides together). Repeat until you have sewn all Strips 4 and 5 together in all six piles. Butt all strips behind one another and sew together in a Continuous Seam. Do not backstitch or cut threads. See **Diagram 10.** Press seams to Strip 5. You will end up with six joined pieces that look like those in **Diagram 11.** Resist the temptation to cut them apart!

**STEP 3.** Sew all Strip 6 pieces to the units made from Strips 4 and 5. Again, do not cut the connecting threads. Press seams to Strip 6. See **Diagram 12.**

**STEP 4.** Sew all Strip 7 pieces to the units made from Strips 4, 5, and 6. Press seams to Strip 7.

**STEP 5.** Sew all the remaining strips together through Strip 9 using the same method. Be sure to add your strips in sequence, and do not cut threads. Press all seams in the direction of the piece you have just added. Once all the strips have been sewn together,

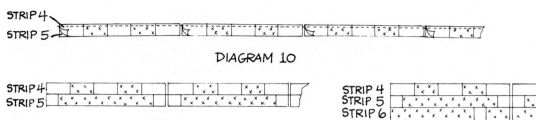

STRIP 4
STRIP 5

DIAGRAM 10

STRIP 4
STRIP 5

DIAGRAM 11

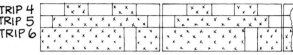

STRIP 4
STRIP 5
STRIP 6

DIAGRAM 12

you can cut the threads that join your completed apple sections.

## THE LEAVES

**STEP 1.** Using the same Continuous Seam method you used for the apple sections, stitch together Strips 1 through 3.

**STEP 2.** Use a see-through ruler to find the center of each leaf section (Strips 1 through 3). Mark the center, then cut along the line. (See the dotted line in **Diagram 13**.)

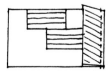

DIAGRAM 13

**STEP 3.** Sew a 1 × 3½-inch stem strip to the left side of a leaf section, right sides together. See **Diagram 14**. Press all seams toward the stem. Now sew the right side of the leaf section to the stem. Press. Repeat for all six blocks. The finished leaf sections should look like the one shown in **Diagram 15**.

DIAGRAM 14

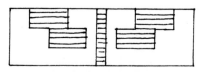

DIAGRAM 15

## Assembling the Apple Blocks

Stitch the apple sections to the leaf sections using the Continuous Seam method, placing right sides together. Make sure the leaf section is positioned so the leaves will point upward in the finished block. Press seams to apple sections. See **Diagrams 16 and 17**.

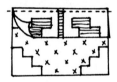

DIAGRAM 16

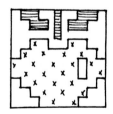

DIAGRAM 17

## The Lattice

**STEP 1.** Sew the 1½ × 10½-inch strips of Fabric B to each side of two blocks. Press all seams toward the lattice.

**STEP 2.** Make a row of three apples by sewing one block without lattice on each side of the block with lattice strips. See **Diagram 18**. Press. Repeat to make a second row of three apples.

**STEP 3.** On one row of apples, sew a 44-inch-long lattice strip to the bottom. On the second row, sew a 44-inch-long lattice strip to both the top and bottom of the row. This row with two lattices will be the bottom row of apples in the finished wallhanging. Trim and press all the lattice strips.

LATTICE STRIP         LATTICE STRIP

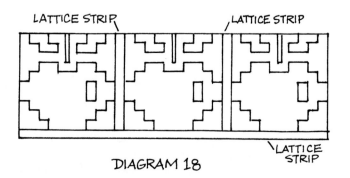

DIAGRAM 18

LATTICE STRIP

## Checkerboard Rows

**STEP 1.** Sew together six 1½ × 44-inch strips of Fabrics A and B, alternating the fabrics. Press all seams toward Fabric A as you go. See **Diagram 19.**

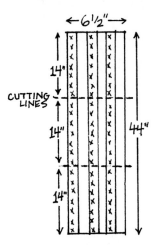

DIAGRAM 19

**STEP 2.** Cut the strip set in thirds as shown in **Diagram 19.** Each third will be approximately 14 inches. Resew those thirds together to make an 18½ × 14-inch strip set as shown in **Diagram 20.**

**STEP 3.** Cut the 18½ × 14-inch strip set in half as shown in **Diagram 20.** Resew those halves together to make a 36½ × 7-inch strip set like the one shown in **Diagram 21.**

**STEP 4.** From this 36½-inch strip set cut four 1½ × 36½-inch strips, referring to the cutting lines in **Diagram 21.** Rematch the strips so they form a checkerboard and stitch them together. Make two 2½ × 36½-inch checkerboard sets that look like the one shown in **Diagram 22.**

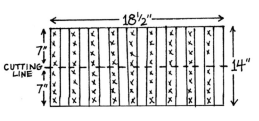

DIAGRAM 20

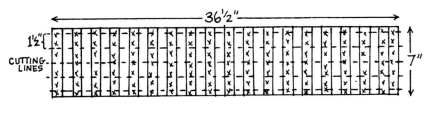

DIAGRAM 21

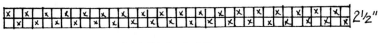

DIAGRAM 22

## Putting It All Together

Use the **Quilt Layout** on page 79 as a visual guide for putting your quilt top together.

**STEP 1.** Sew one 1 × 44-inch strip of Fabric C to the bottom of each row of apples. Trim the excess and press all seams toward Fabric C.

**STEP 2.** Attach a checkerboard border to each of the apple rows. See Hints on Fitting a Checkerboard Border on page 29 for details on how to fit the checkerboard. Press.

**STEP 3.** Below the checkerboard rows, sew another 1 × 44-inch accent strip of Fabric C. Trim and press.

**STEP 4.** Stitch together the two rows of apples.

## The One-and-a-Half-Inch Border

**STEP 1.** Sew 2 × 44-inch strips of Fabric B to the quilt top and bottom. Trim the excess and press all seams toward the border.

**STEP 2.** Sew the remaining two strips to the quilt sides. Trim and press.

## Layering the Quilt

Arrange and baste the backing, batting, and top together following directions for Layering the Quilt on page 32. Trim the batting and backing to ¾ inch from the raw edge of the quilt top.

## Binding the Quilt

Using the strips cut from Fabric C, follow directions on page 33 for Binding the Quilt.

## The Finishing Stitches

Outline the apples and leaves by quilting either in the ditch or ¼ inch from the seam line. For extra detailing, you may want to stitch a 1-inch grid in the background or some vertical or even curved lines on the apples. Another option is to quilt diagonal lines through the checkerboard. See **Diagram 23** for suggested quilting patterns.

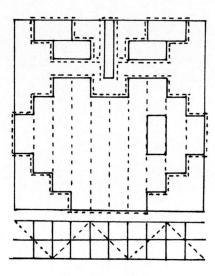

DIAGRAM 23

# Watermelon Patch

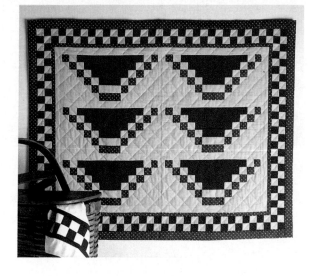

W̲hat's a picnic without watermelon? These watermelons are a fresh fruit delight—fast, fun, and easy to make! The Watermelon Quilt and the Placemats use the Speedy Strip technique that will get you out of the house in no time. The Tablecloth and Napkins repeat the checkerboard pattern, and the tablecloth has the added touch of appliquéd watermelons. So whether you're picnicking in your kitchen or beside a shady stream, pack this set into your basket and get ready for fun!

## Watermelon Quilt

Finished Quilt: 37 × 30 inches
Finished Block: 13 × 6 inches

### Materials

Directional print may be used for Fabric A only; it is not recommended for Fabrics B or C.

**FABRIC A** *(melons, checkerboard)*

| | |
|---|---|
| Blocks | ⅓ yard |
| Checkerboard | ⅓ yard |
| TOTAL | ⅔ yard |
| | (1¼ yards if directional fabric is used) |

**FABRIC B** *(block background, checkerboard, lattice)*

| | |
|---|---|
| Blocks | ½ yard |
| Checkerboard | ⅓ yard |
| Lattice | ⅓ yard |
| TOTAL | 1¼ yards |

**FABRIC C** *(rind, border, binding)*

| | |
|---|---|
| Blocks | ⅜ yard |
| Half-Inch Border | ⅛ yard |
| Binding | ⅝ yard |
| TOTAL | 1⅛ yards |

**BACKING** 1 yard

**BATTING** 1 yard

## Cutting Directions

Prewash and press your fabrics. Using a rotary cutter, see-through ruler, and cutting mat, prepare the strips as described in the charts below. The first chart tells you how to cut the strips for the watermelon blocks. The second chart explains how to cut the pieces for the rest of the quilt.

### CUTTING THE STRIPS

Refer to the fabric requirements for blocks *only.* Cut the block yardage in half lengthwise (on the fold) so you will have two approximately 22-inch-wide pieces. Then cut each of those pieces in half again, making each piece approximately 11 inches wide. From the 11-inch-wide pieces, cut the following strips of Fabrics A, B, and C.

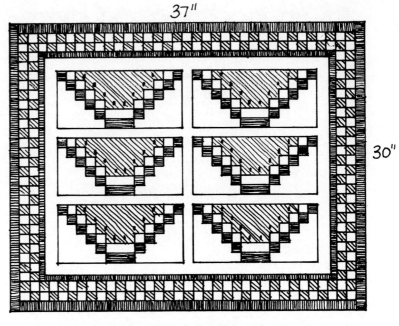

37"

30"

QUILT LAYOUT

| CUTTING THE STRIPS | FIRST CUT | | SECOND CUT | |
|---|---|---|---|---|
| | NO. OF STRIPS | DIMENSIONS | NO. OF PIECES | DIMENSIONS |
| **FABRIC A** | MELON | | | |
| | 1 | 9½ × 11-inch strip | | |
| | 1 | 7½ × 11-inch strip | | |
| | 1 | 5½ × 11-inch strip | | |
| | 1 | 3½ × 11-inch strip | | |
| **FABRIC B** | BACKGROUND | | | |
| | 2 | 5½ × 11-inch strips | | |
| | 2 | 4½ × 11-inch strips | | |
| | 3 | 3½ × 11-inch strips | | |
| | 2 | 2½ × 11-inch strips | | |
| | 10 | 1½ × 11-inch strips | | |
| **FABRIC C** | RIND | | | |
| | 10 | 1½ × 11-inch strips | | |
| | 1 | 3½ × 11-inch strip | | |

## CUTTING THE OTHER QUILT PIECES

| | FIRST CUT | | SECOND CUT | |
|---|---|---|---|---|
| | NO. OF STRIPS | DIMENSIONS | NO. OF PIECES | DIMENSIONS |
| **FABRIC A** | CHECKERBOARD | | | |
| | 6 | 1½ × 44-inch strips | | |
| **FABRIC B** | CHECKERBOARD | | | |
| | 6 | 1½ × 44-inch strips | | |
| | LATTICE | | | |
| | **Before You Cut:** From one of the 44-inch strips, cut the pieces as directed in the second column. The remaining six 44-inch strips require no further cutting. | | | |
| | 7 | 1½ × 44-inch strips | 3 | 1½ × 6½-inch pieces |
| **FABRIC C** | HALF-INCH BORDER | | | |
| | 4 | 1 × 44-inch strips | | |
| | BINDING | | | |
| | 4 | 5½ × 44-inch strips | | |

## Sewing the Strip Sets

Sew the strips together following **Diagrams 1 through 6.** Use accurate ¼-inch seam allowances. All the strips used for the blocks are 11 inches long. Be sure to press as you go, turning all seams away from Fabric B. Do not press the seams open. Refer to the Fabric Key for fabric identification. All finished strip sets will be 13½ inches wide × 11 inches long.

**SEW SMART**

Alternate the sewing direction each time you piece one strip to another. This will help avoid the warpage that occurs when sewing strips.

FABRIC KEY   FABRIC A 
FABRIC B 
FABRIC C 

**STRIP SET 1.** Use one 9½-inch strip of Fabric A, two 1½-inch strips of Fabric B and two 1½-inch strips of Fabric C. See **Diagram 1.**

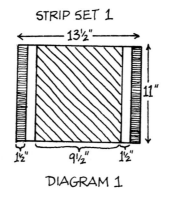

STRIP SET 1

13½"

11"

1½"    9½"    1½"

DIAGRAM 1

**STRIP SET 2.** Use one 7½-inch strip of Fabric A, four 1½-inch strips of Fabric B and two 1½-inch strips of Fabric C. See **Diagram 2.**

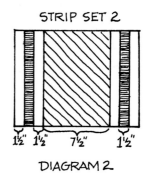

STRIP SET 2

1½" 1½"    7½"    1½"

DIAGRAM 2

**STRIP SET 3.** Use one 5½-inch strip of Fabric A, two 1½-inch and two 2½-inch strips of Fabric B and two 1½-inch strips of Fabric C. See **Diagram 3.**

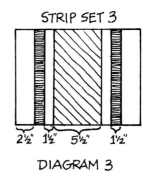

STRIP SET 3

2½"  1½"   5½"   1½"

DIAGRAM 3

**STRIP SET 4.** Use one 3½-inch strip of Fabric A, two 1½-inch and two 3½-inch strips of Fabric B and two 1½-inch strips of Fabric C. See **Diagram 4.**

STRIP SET 4

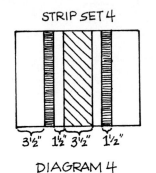

3½"  1½"  3½"  1½"

DIAGRAM 4

**STRIP SET 5.** Use one 3½-inch and two 4½-inch strips of Fabric B and two 1½-inch strips of Fabric C. See **Diagram 5.**

STRIP SET 5

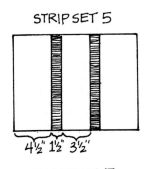

4½"  1½"  3½"

DIAGRAM 5

**STRIP SET 6.** Use one 3½-inch strip of Fabric C and two 5½-inch strips of Fabric B. See **Diagram 6.**

STRIP SET 6

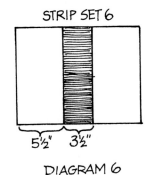

5½"  3½"

DIAGRAM 6

## Stacking and Cutting the Strip Sets

**STEP 1.** Stack the strip sets in sequence, starting with Strip 6 on the bottom and Strip 1 on the top of the pile.

**STEP 2.** Take the bottom half of your stack (Strip Sets 4 through 6) and cut six 1½ × 13½-inch strips, referring to the cutting lines in **Diagram 7.** Cut through all three layers at once. Now take the top half of your stack (Strip Sets 1 through 3) and cut six 1½ × 13½-inch strips.

**STEP 3.** After all the strips are cut, make six piles, each pile containing one each of the six strips. Stack the strips in sequence, starting with Strip 6 on the bottom and ending with Strip 1 on the top. Each pile, when sewn together, will make one block.

## Making the Blocks

**STEP 1.** Lay out the six piles of strips next to your sewing machine, keeping them in order.

**STEP 2.** From the first pile, sew Strip 1 to Strip 2 (right sides together). Repeat until you have sewn all Strips 1 and 2 together from all six piles. Butt all strips behind one another and sew together in a Continuous Seam. Do not backstitch or cut joining threads. See **Diagram 8.** Press seams to Strip 2. You will end up with six joined pieces that look like those in **Diagram 9.**

**STEP 3.** Sew all Strip 3 pieces to the units made from Strips 1 and 2. Remember, do not cut the connecting threads. Press seams to Strip 3. See **Diagram 10.**

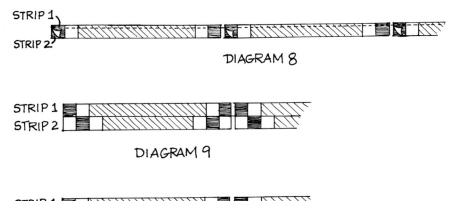

DIAGRAM 7

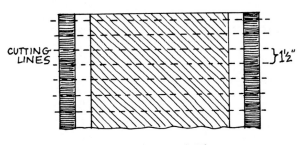

DIAGRAM 8

DIAGRAM 9

DIAGRAM 10

**STEP 4.** Sew all the remaining strips together through Strip 6 using the same method. Be sure to add your strips in sequence, and do not cut threads. Press all seams in the direction of the piece you have just added. Once all the strips have been added, you can cut the threads that join your completed watermelon blocks.

## The Seeds

Before you begin, refer to Machine Appliqué on page 19 for general directions. Set your sewing machine for an appliqué/satin stitch, and practice this technique several times on scrap fabrics before trying it on your watermelon blocks. Start with the stitch width at zero. Do a few stitches to tack in place, and gradually increase your stitch width to the widest setting as you sew. Then gradually return to zero again. The seeds should look like the one in **Diagram 11**. Some machines have a stitch in this seed shape. You could also embroider the seeds by hand using a satin stitch. Use **Diagram 16** as a guide for placement of the seeds.

DIAGRAM 11

## The Lattice

**STEP 1.** Sew one 1½ × 6½-inch Fabric B lattice strip between two blocks to make a row of two watermelons. Repeat for the other two rows. Press all seams toward the lattice. See **Diagram 12**.

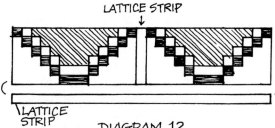

DIAGRAM 12

**STEP 2.** Sew a 1½ × 44-inch lattice strip below each row of watermelons and across the top of the top row of watermelons. Trim excess and press. Refer to **Diagram 12**.

**STEP 3.** Stitch the melon rows together.

**STEP 4.** Sew the remaining lattice strips to the quilt sides. Trim the excess and press.

## Half-Inch Border

**STEP 1.** Sew two 1 × 44-inch strips of Fabric C to the quilt top and bottom. Trim the excess and press all seams toward the border.

**STEP 2.** Sew the remaining two strips to the quilt sides. Trim and press.

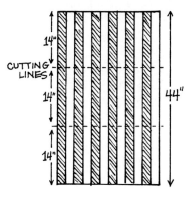

DIAGRAM 13

## Checkerboard Border

**STEP 1.** Sew together the twelve 1½ × 44-inch strips of Fabrics A and B, alternating the fabrics. Press all seams toward Fabric A as you go. See **Diagram 13**.

**STEP 2.** Cut the strip set in thirds as shown in **Diagram 13**. Each third will measure approximately 14 inches. Resew those thirds together to make a 36½ × 14-inch strip set like the one shown in **Diagram 14**.

**STEP 3.** From this 36½-inch strip set, cut eight 1½ × 36½-inch strips, referring to the cutting lines in **Diagram 14**. Rematch the strips so they form a checkerboard and stitch them together. See **Diagram 15**. Make four 2½ × 36½-inch checkerboard sets.

**STEP 4.** Fit the checkerboard border to the quilt top and bottom first. See Hints on Fitting a Checkerboard Border on page 29 for details on how to achieve a perfect fit of the checkerboard to the quilt. Press.

**STEP 5.** Fit and sew the checkerboard to the quilt sides. Press.

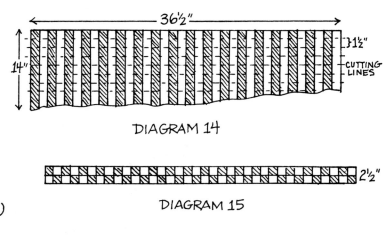

DIAGRAM 14

DIAGRAM 15

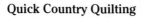

## Layering the Quilt

Arrange and baste the backing, batting, and top together following directions for Layering the Quilt on page 32. Trim the batting and backing to ¾ inch from the raw edge of the quilt top.

## Binding the Quilt

Using the 5½ × 44-inch strips cut from Fabric C, follow directions on page 33 for Binding the Quilt.

## The Finishing Stitches

For the finishing touch, outline the rind in quilting and stitch a heart in the center of each melon using the **Heart Quilting Template** on page 103. For the background, stitch hearts or a diagonal grid. See **Diagram 16** for suggested quilting patterns.

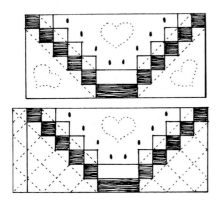

DIAGRAM 16

# Watermelon Placemats

(shown on top of the tablecloth in the photo on page 92)

Finished Size: Makes six placemats, each 16 × 11½ inches

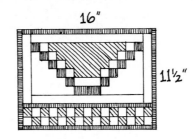

WATERMELON PLACEMAT
LAYOUT

## Materials

**FABRIC A** (melons, checkerboard)

| | |
|---|---|
| Blocks | ⅓ yard |
| Checkerboard | ¼ yard |
| TOTAL | ⅝ yard |

**FABRIC B** (block background, checkerboard, lattice)

| | |
|---|---|
| Blocks | ½ yard |
| Checkerboard | ¼ yard |
| Lattice | ⅓ yard |
| TOTAL | 1⅛ yards |

**FABRIC C** (rind, border, binding)

| | |
|---|---|
| Blocks | ¼ yard |
| Border and Binding | ⅜ yard |
| TOTAL | ⅔ yard |

| | |
|---|---|
| **BACKING** | 1⅛ yards |
| **LIGHTWEIGHT BATTING** | 1⅛ yards |

**SEW SMART**
**Use Scotchgard on your placemats to protect the fabric and keep them looking great!**

## Cutting Directions

Prewash and press all of your fabrics. Using a rotary cutter, see-through ruler, and cutting mat, prepare the strips for the watermelon blocks as described in Cutting the Strips for the Watermelon Quilt on page 94. Use the yardages given for the blocks in the Materials list above. Refer to the chart on the opposite page for directions on cutting the pieces for the rest of the placemat. First, prepare the strips as described in the first column. Then from those strips, cut the pieces listed in the second column.

## Making the Watermelon Blocks

Follow the directions that begin on page 95 for Sewing the Strip Sets, Stacking and Cutting the Strip Sets, and Making the Blocks for the Watermelon Quilt. You will end up with six watermelon blocks to use for the placemats.

## The Seeds

To add these details to the watermelon blocks, refer to The Seeds for the Watermelon Quilt on page 97.

## The Checkerboard

**STEP 1.** Sew together the eight 1½ × 44-inch strips of Fabrics A and B, alternating the fabrics. See **Diagram 17**. Press all seams toward Fabric A as you go.

**STEP 2.** Cut the strip set in half as shown in **Diagram 17**. Each half will measure approximately 22 inches. Resew those halves together to make a 16½ × 22-inch strip set like the one shown in **Diagram 18**.

**STEP 3.** From this 22-inch strip set, cut twelve 1½ × 16½-inch strips, referring to the cutting lines in **Diagram 18**. Rematch the strips so

## CUTTING THE OTHER PLACEMAT PIECES

| | FIRST CUT | | SECOND CUT | |
|---|---|---|---|---|
| | **NO. OF STRIPS** | **DIMENSIONS** | **NO. OF PIECES** | **DIMENSIONS** |
| **FABRIC A** | CHECKERBOARD | | | |
| | 4 | 1½ × 44-inch strips | | |
| **FABRIC B** | CHECKERBOARD | | | |
| | 4 | 1½ × 44-inch strips | | |
| | LATTICE | | | |
| | 7 | 1½ × 44-inch strips | 12 | 1½ × 13½-inch pieces |
| | | | 12 | 1½ × 8½-inch pieces |
| **FABRIC C** | BORDER AND BINDING | | | |
| | 13 | 1 × 44-inch strips | 18 | 1 × 15½-inch pieces |
| | | | 12 | 1 × 12-inch pieces |
| **BACKING AND BATTING** | BACKING AND BATTING | | | |
| | 6 | 12½ × 17-inch pieces | | |

they form a checkerboard, and stitch them together. See **Diagram 19.** Make six 2½ × 16½-inch checkerboard sets.

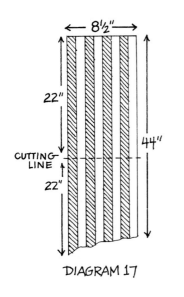

DIAGRAM 17

### Putting It All Together

**STEP 1.** Use the **Watermelon Placemat Layout** on the opposite page as a visual guide when putting your placemats together. Sew the 1½ × 13½-inch Fabric B lattice strips to the block top and bottom. Press all seams toward the lattice. Repeat each step for each of the six placemats.

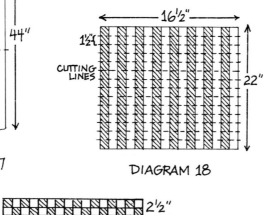

DIAGRAM 18

🍉 2½"

DIAGRAM 19

**STEP 2.** Sew the 1½ × 8½-inch lattice strips to the sides. Press.

**STEP 3.** Sew one of the 1 × 15½-inch Fabric C border strips to the top and bottom of each block. Press seams toward the border.

**STEP 4.** Fit and sew the checkerboard to the bottom of the block. See Hints on Fitting a Checkerboard Border on page 29. Press seams toward the Fabric C border.

### Binding the Placemats

**STEP 1.** Sew the remaining 1 × 15½-inch Fabric C binding strips to the bottom of the placemats. Press all seams toward the binding.

**STEP 2.** Sew the 1 × 12-inch Fabric C strips to the sides. Press.

## Finishing

**STEP 1.**  Position the placemat top and the 12½ × 17-inch backing piece right sides together. Trim the backing piece to the same size as the top. Lay both pieces on top of the batting and pin all three layers together. Sew, leaving a 3- to 4-inch opening for turning. Repeat each step for all six placemats.

**STEP 2.**  Turn right side out and handstitch the opening. Press.

**STEP 3.**  Machine or hand quilt in the ditch around the watermelon and along the borders and binding.

# Watermelon Tablecloth

(shown spread on the grass in the photo on page 92)

Finished Size: 43 × 43 inches

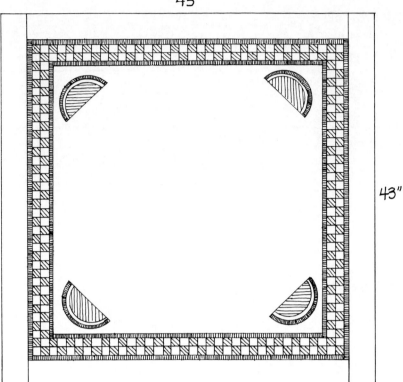

WATERMELON TABLECLOTH LAYOUT

## Materials and Cutting

Prewash and press all of your fabrics. Using a rotary cutter, see-through ruler, and cutting mat, prepare the pieces as directed in the chart below.

| MATERIALS AND CUTTING | YARDAGE | CUTTING | |
|---|---|---|---|
| | | **NO. OF PIECES** | **DIMENSIONS** |
| **Fabric A** | | | |
| Checkerboard | ⅓ yard | 6 | 1½ × 44-inch strips |
| **Fabric B** | | | |
| Main Tablecloth Pieces | 1½ yards | 1 | 31½ × 31½-inch piece |
| | | 2 | 3½ × 37½-inch strips |
| | | 3 | 3½ × 44-inch strips |
| Checkerboard | ⅓ yard | 6 | 1½ × 44-inch strips |
| **Fabric C** | | | |
| Half-Inch Border | ¼ yard | 2 | 1 × 31½-in strips |
| | | 2 | 1 × 32½-inch strips |
| | | 2 | 1 × 36½-inch strips |
| | | 2 | 1 × 37½-inch strips |
| **Appliqué Pieces** | ⅛ yard each of Fabrics A, B, and C | | |
| **Tear-away paper (for machine appliqué only)** | | | |

## The Checkerboard

**STEP 1.** Sew together the twelve 1½ × 44-inch strips of Fabrics A and B, alternating the fabrics. Press all seams toward the darkest fabric as you go. See **Diagram 20**.

**STEP 2.** Cut this strip set into thirds as shown in **Diagram 20**. Each third will measure approximately 14 inches. Resew those thirds together to make a 36½ × 14-inch strip set like the one shown in **Diagram 21**.

**STEP 3.** From this 36½-inch strip set, cut eight 1½ × 36½-inch strips, referring to the cutting lines in **Diagram 21**. Rematch the strips so they form a checkerboard, and stitch them together. Make two 2½ × 36½-inch-long sets and two 2½ × 32½-inch-long sets that look like the one in **Diagram 22**. Use a seam ripper to remove the excess checkerboard for the shorter rows.

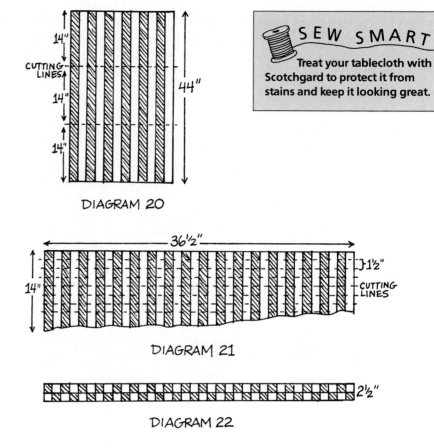

DIAGRAM 20

DIAGRAM 21

DIAGRAM 22

**SEW SMART**
Treat your tablecloth with Scotchgard to protect it from stains and keep it looking great.

## Half-Inch Border

**STEP 1.** Sew the two 1 × 31½-inch Fabric C border strips to the top and bottom of the 31½ × 31½-inch main piece. Press all seams toward the borders.

**STEP 2.** Sew the two 1 × 32½-inch border strips to the sides. Press.

## Putting It All Together

**STEP 1.** Attach the 2½ × 32½-inch checkerboard border to the top and bottom. See Hints on Fitting a Checkerboard Border on page 29 for details on how to achieve a perfect fit. Press all seams to the half-inch border.

**STEP 2.** Fit and sew the 2½ × 36½-inch checkerboard border to the sides. Press.

**STEP 3.** Sew the 1 × 36½-inch border strips to the top and bottom.

Press all seams toward the half-inch border.

**STEP 4.** Sew the 1 × 37½-inch border strips to the sides. Press.

**STEP 5.** Sew the 3½ × 37½-inch strips of Fabric B to the top and bottom. Press all seams to the half-inch border.

**STEP 6.** Sew the 3½ × 44-inch strips of Fabric B to the sides. If the side strips aren't long enough, cut the third strip in half and add one half to each side to achieve the needed length. Press.

## The Hem

Turn under ¼ inch on the outside edge of the tablecloth top. Press in position. Turn under another ¼ inch to hide all raw edges. Press in position and topstitch in place.

## The Watermelon Appliqués

**STEP 1.** Refer to Machine Appliqué on page 19 for details on this technique. Using the **Watermelon Appliqué Pattern** on page 103, trace and cut appliqué designs for four watermelon wedges. Cut the entire wedge for each piece: the watermelon, rind, and white piece.

**STEP 2.** Machine appliqué one watermelon to each of the four corners of the tablecloth. Referring to the **Watermelon Tablecloth Layout** for placement, position them about 3 inches from the inside corner of the half-inch border and about 1 inch from both sides. Appliqué the green rind in position first, then add the white part and the red center.

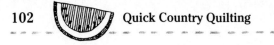

# Four Napkins

(shown tucked into the basket in the photos on pages 92 and 93)

Finished Size: 16 × 16 inches

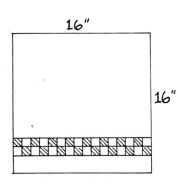

WATERMELON NAPKIN LAYOUT

## Materials and Cutting

Prewash and press all of your fabrics. Using a rotary cutter, see-through ruler, and cutting mat, prepare the pieces as directed in the chart below.

## The Checkerboard

**STEP 1.** Sew together the six 1½ × 44-inch strips of Fabrics A and B, alternating the fabrics. See **Diagram 23**. Press all seams toward the darkest fabric as you go.

**STEP 2.** Cut the strip set into thirds as shown in **Diagram 23**. Each third will measure approximately 14 inches. Resew those thirds together to make an 18½ × 14-inch strip set like the one shown in **Diagram 24**. From this set, cut eight 1½ × 18½-inch strips, referring to the cutting lines in **Diagram 24**.

**STEP 3.** Rematch the strips to form a checkerboard, and stitch them together. Make four 2½ × 16½-inch checkerboard sets that look like the one shown in **Diagram 25**. Use a seam ripper to remove excess checkerboard.

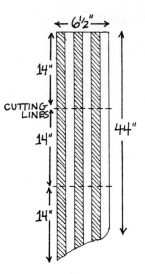

DIAGRAM 23

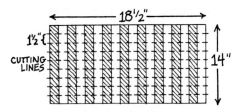

DIAGRAM 24

DIAGRAM 25

| MATERIALS AND CUTTING | YARDAGE | CUTTING | |
|---|---|---|---|
| | | NO. OF PIECES | DIMENSIONS |
| **Fabric A** | | | |
| Checkerboard | ⅛ yard (6 inches) | 3 | 1½ × 44-inch strips |
| **Fabric B** | | | |
| Main Napkin Pieces | 2 yards | 4 | 17 × 12½-inch pieces |
| | | 4 | 17 × 2½-inch pieces |
| | | 4 | 17½ × 17½-inch pieces |
| Checkerboard | ⅛ yard (6 inches) | 3 | 1½ × 44-inch strips |

## Putting It All Together

> **SEW SMART**
>
> I added an optional, half-inch border to the napkins shown in the photograph. To make this border, you will need ¼ yard of fabric. Cut two 1 × 16½-inch strips for each napkin. Sew one strip to each side of the checkerboard border before adding the checkerboard to the main piece. Press toward the half-inch border.

**STEP 1.** See Hints on Fitting a Checkerboard Border on page 29. Sew a 2½ × 17-inch napkin piece to one of the checkerboard borders. The napkin pieces are cut slightly oversized to make for easy fitting to the checkerboard. Trim the napkin piece to the same width as the checkerboard. Press seams toward the napkin piece. Repeat each step for the other three napkins.

**STEP 2.** Sew the 17 × 12½-inch napkin piece to the other side of the checkerboard border. Trim the napkin piece to same width as the checkerboard and the first napkin piece. The napkin front is now completed.

## The Backing

With right sides together, pin the napkin front to the 17½ × 17½-inch backing piece. Trim the backing piece to the same size as the napkin front. Sew all the way around the outside edge, leaving a 3- to 4-inch opening for turning. Turn right side out, press, and handstitch the opening.

## Finishing

Topstitch ¼ inch from the outside edge of the napkin, and machine quilt in the ditch on both sides of the checkerboard.

HEART QUILTING TEMPLATE

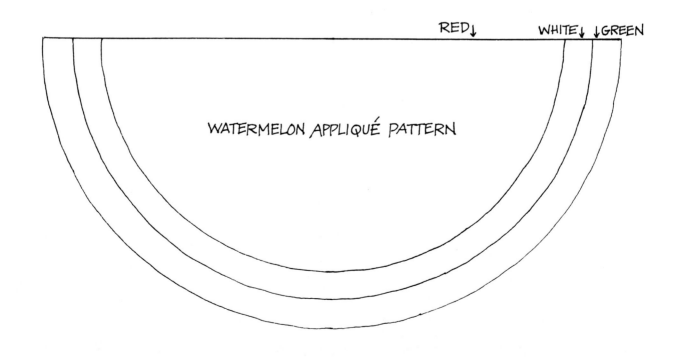

RED↓    WHITE↓  ↓GREEN

WATERMELON APPLIQUÉ PATTERN

# Checkerboard Crossing

Here's a new approach to an old favorite. The familiar house block takes on a new shape in this template-free design. Use traditional Amish colors or make a scrap version. Make your blocks all one fabric, or mix and match the roofs and houses for some real variety. The choices are yours; the speedy techniques used here make it easy to be as creative as you like!

## Amish Version

Finished Quilt: 43 × 43 inches
Finished Block: 8 × 8 inches

**Materials**

Obvious directional prints are not recommended.

**FABRIC A** *(houses, corner squares, checkerboard)*

Use four fabrics.

| | |
|---|---|
| Blocks and Corner Squares | ⅜ yard |
| Checkerboard | ⅛ yard |
| TOTAL | ½ yard |
| | *each* of *four* fabrics |

**FABRIC B** *(block background, lattice, checkerboard, binding)*

| | |
|---|---|
| Blocks | ½ yard |
| Lattice | ⅝ yard |
| Checkerboard | ⅜ yard |
| Binding | ⅞ yard |
| TOTAL | 2⅜ yards |

| | |
|---|---|
| **TWO-INCH BORDER** | ⅜ yard |
| | (choose one Fabric A) |

| | |
|---|---|
| **BACKING** | 1⅞ yards |

| | |
|---|---|
| **BATTING** | 1⅞ yards |

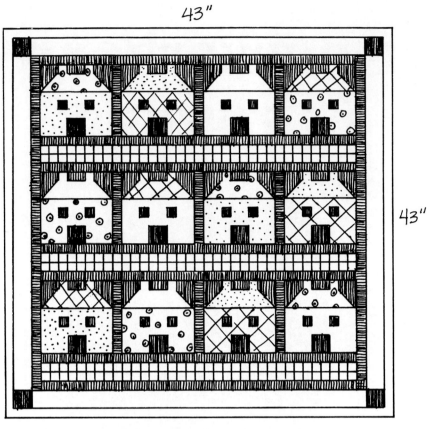

43"

43"

QUILT LAYOUT

## Cutting Directions

Prewash and press all of your fabrics. Using a rotary cutter, see-through ruler, and cutting mat, prepare the strips as described in the first column in the chart below. Then from those strips, cut the pieces listed in the second column. Some portions of the quilt need to be cut only once, so no additional cutting information will appear in the second column.

|  | FIRST CUT | | SECOND CUT | |
|---|---|---|---|---|
|  | NO. OF STRIPS | DIMENSIONS | NO. OF PIECES | DIMENSIONS |
| **FABRIC A** | **HOUSES:** from *each* of the *four* fabrics, cut the following | | | |
|  | 1 | 2½ × 44-inch strip | 3 | 2½ × 4½-inch pieces |
|  |  |  | 6 | 2½ × 3½-inch pieces |
|  | 2 | 1½ × 44-inch strips | 6 | 1½ × 8½-inch pieces |
|  |  |  | 9 | 1½ × 2½-inch pieces |
|  |  |  | 6 | 1½ × 1½-inch pieces |
|  | 1 | 5 × 11-inch piece |  |  |
|  | **CHECKERBOARD:** from *each* of the *four* fabrics, cut the following | | | |
|  | 2 | 1½ × 44-inch strips |  |  |
|  | **CORNER SQUARES** (choose one Fabric A) | | | |
|  | 4 | 2½ × 2½-inch squares |  |  |
|  | **TWO-INCH BORDER** (choose one Fabric A) | | | |
|  | 4 | 2½ × 44-inch strips |  |  |

| FABRIC B | FIRST CUT | | SECOND CUT | |
|---|---|---|---|---|
| | **NO. OF STRIPS** | **DIMENSIONS** | **NO. OF PIECES** | **DIMENSIONS** |
| | **BACKGROUND** | | | |
| | 1 | 2½ × 44-inch strip | 12 | 2½ × 2½-inch pieces |
| | 3 | 1½ × 44-inch strips | 24 | 1½ × 1½-inch pieces |
| | | | 36 | 1½ × 2½-inch pieces |
| | 1 | 5 × 44-inch strip | 4 | 5 × 11-inch pieces |
| | **LATTICE** | | | |
| | **Before You Cut:** From three of the 44-inch strips, cut the pieces as directed in the second column. The remaining nine strips require no further cutting. | | | |
| | 12 | 1½ × 44-inch strips | 9 | 1½ × 8½-inch pieces |
| | **CHECKERBOARD** | | | |
| | 8 | 1½ × 44-inch strips | | |
| | **BINDING** | | | |
| | 5 | 5½ × 44-inch strips | | |

FABRIC KEY

FABRIC A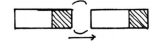

FABRIC B

## Speedy Triangles

**STEP 1.** Refer to Speedy Triangle directions on page 11 for how to mark, sew, and cut.

**STEP 2.** Position the 5 × 11-inch pieces of Fabrics A and B with right sides together. You will have four sets. On each set draw a 2⅞-inch grid of three squares. See **Diagram 1**.

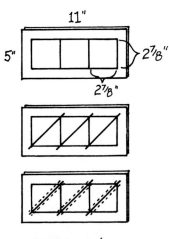

DIAGRAM 1

**STEP 3.** After sewing and cutting are complete, press seam allowances toward Fabric A. You will have made a total of twenty-four triangle sets, six of each house fabric.

## Assembling the Blocks

Throughout this section, refer to the Fabric Key to identify the fabric placements in the diagrams. Also, it's a good idea to review Assembly Line Piecing on page 13 before you get started. It's more efficient to do the same step for each block at the same time than to piece one entire block together at a time. Be sure to press as you go, and follow the arrows for pressing direction.

### SECTION ONE (Roof)

**STEP 1.** Sew twenty-four 1½ × 2½-inch pieces of Fabric B to twenty-four 1½ × 1½-inch squares of Fabric A as shown in **Diagram 2**. Use six squares of each Fabric A. Position them right sides together

and line them up next to your sewing machine. Use the Continuous Seam technique described on page 14 to join all twenty-four sets together. Press seams toward Fabric B and cut joining threads.

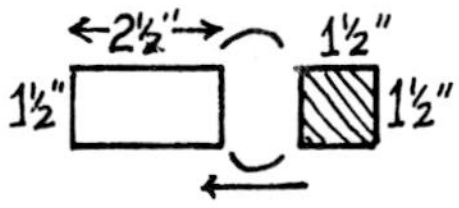

DIAGRAM 2

In each of the remaining steps, use the same Continuous Seam technique. You will be making a total of twelve blocks, three each of the four different Fabric A's.

**STEP 2.** Sew the Step 1 units together in pairs. Make sure the units are positioned as shown in **Diagram 3** and the Fabric A's match. Press. You should have a total of twelve units.

DIAGRAM 3

**STEP 3.** Sew twelve 1½ × 2½-inch pieces of Fabric B to the units made in Step 2. See **Diagram 4.** Press toward Fabric B.

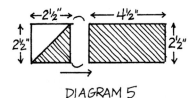

DIAGRAM 4

**STEP 4.** Sew twelve 2½ × 4½-inch pieces of Fabric A to twelve 2½-inch triangle sets. Press toward Fabric A. See **Diagram 5.**

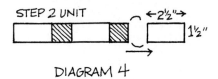

DIAGRAM 5

**STEP 5.** Sew the remaining twelve triangle sets to the right sides of the Step 4 units as shown in **Diagram 6.** Press toward the Step 4 unit.

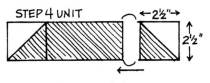

DIAGRAM 6

**STEP 6.** Sew the Step 3 units to the Step 5 units. Press toward the Step 5 unit. Your roof sections should look like the one in **Diagram 7** with two chimneys on the top.

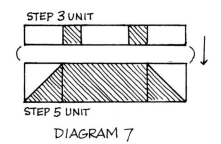

DIAGRAM 7

**SECTION TWO (House)**

**STEP 1.** Sew twenty-four 1½ × 1½-inch pieces of Fabric B to

twenty-four 1½ × 2½-inch pieces of Fabric A, using six pieces of each Fabric A. See **Diagram 8.** Press toward Fabric B.

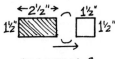

DIAGRAM 8

**STEP 2.** Sew the Step 1 units together in pairs paying close attention to the position of Fabric B shown in **Diagram 9.** Make twelve pairs. Press.

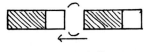

DIAGRAM 9

**STEP 3.** Sew twelve 1½ × 2½-inch pieces of Fabric A to the right side of the Step 2 units, using three pieces of each Fabric A. See **Diagram 10.** Press toward the Step 2 units.

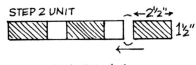

DIAGRAM 10

**STEP 4.** Sew twelve 1½ × 8½-inch strips of Fabric A to the Step 3 units, using three strips of each Fabric A. See **Diagram 11.** Press toward Fabric A.

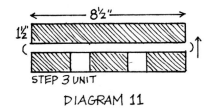

DIAGRAM 11

**STEP 5.** Sew the twelve 2½ × 2½-inch squares of Fabric B to twelve 2½ × 3½-inch pieces of Fabric A, using three pieces of each Fabric A. See **Diagram 12.** Press toward Fabric B.

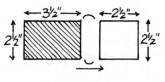

DIAGRAM 12

**STEP 6.** Sew the remaining twelve 2½ × 3½-inch pieces of Fabric A to the right side of the Step 5 units as shown in **Diagram 13.** Press toward the Step 5 units.

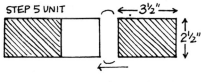

DIAGRAM 13

**STEP 7.** Sew twelve 1½ × 8½-inch strips of Fabric A to the Step 6 units as shown in **Diagram 14.** Press toward Fabric A.

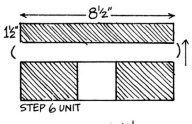

DIAGRAM 14

**STEP 8.** Sew the Step 4 units to the Step 7 units as shown in **Diagram 15.** Press toward the Step 7 unit.

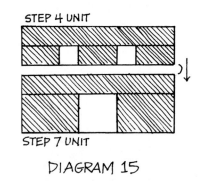

DIAGRAM 15

**HOUSE ASSEMBLY**

Lay out your houses and roofs in a pleasing arrangement. Play around with the layout, matching different roof fabrics with different house fabrics. When you're satisfied with the arrangement, stitch the Section One roof units to the Section Two house units as shown in **Diagram 16**. Keep track of your layout while sewing on the lattice.

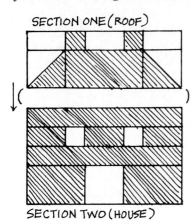

SECTION ONE (ROOF)

SECTION TWO (HOUSE)

DIAGRAM 16

## The Lattice

**STEP 1.** Sew the 1½ × 8½-inch Fabric B lattice strips to the right side of nine house blocks as shown in **Diagram 17**. The last block on the right end of each row will not have lattice on the right. Press all seams toward the lattice.

**STEP 2.** Sew three of the Step 1 units plus the end block together to make a row, making sure the blocks are in the desired order. See **Diagram 18**. Press. Repeat for the remaining two rows.

**STEP 3.** Sew a 1½ × 44-inch Fabric B lattice strip to the top and bottom of each row of houses. Trim excess and press. Set aside the remaining three strips.

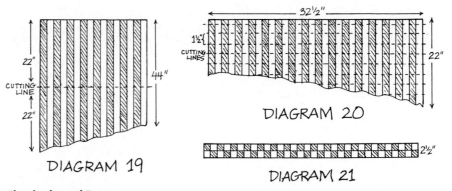

DIAGRAM 19

DIAGRAM 20

DIAGRAM 21

## Checkerboard Rows

**STEP 1.** Sew together the sixteen 1½ × 44-inch strips of Fabrics A and B, alternating the fabrics. See **Diagram 19**. Press as you go, facing all seams toward Fabric B.

**STEP 2.** Cut the strip set in half as shown in **Diagram 19**. Each half will be approximately 22 inches. Resew those halves together to make a 32½ × 22-inch strip set. See **Diagram 20**.

**STEP 3.** From this strip set, cut seven 1½ × 32½-inch strips, referring to the cutting lines in **Diagram 20**. Rematch the strips so they form a checkerboard, and stitch them together. Make three 2½ × 32½-inch sets that look like the one shown in **Diagram 21**. Set aside the seventh strip.

## Putting It All Together

Use the **Quilt Layout** as a visual guide for putting your quilt top together.

**STEP 1.** Fit the checkerboard to the bottom of each row of houses. See Hints on Fitting a Checkerboard Border on page 29. Use the seventh

1½-inch strip to add extra needed checkerboard squares. Pin in position and sew. Press all seams toward the lattice.

**STEP 2.** Stitch together the three rows of houses. Press.

**STEP 3.** Add a 1½ × 44-inch strip of Fabric B lattice to the bottom of the quilt, below the checkerboard. Trim excess and press.

**STEP 4.** Add Fabric B lattice strips to the quilt sides. Trim excess and press.

## The Two-Inch Border

**STEP 1.** Attach 2½ × 44-inch Fabric A border strips to the top and bottom of the quilt. Trim the excess and press seams toward border.

**STEP 2.** Compare the side border strips to the quilt sides and fit to the correct length. Measure up to but do not include the borders you just added to the top and bottom. Then add ¼ inch on the ends of each strip before trimming so they will fit correctly after the corner squares are added.

**STEP 3.** Sew a Fabric A corner square to the ends of both side strips. Press toward the border. Pin in position and sew to the sides of the quilt. Press seams toward border. See **Quilt Layout** for reference.

DIAGRAM 17

DIAGRAM 18

## Layering the Quilt

Arrange and baste the backing, batting, and top together following the directions for Layering the Quilt on page 32. Trim batting and backing to ¾ inch from the raw edge of the quilt top.

## Binding the Quilt

Using the strips cut from Fabric B, follow the directions on page 33 for Binding the Quilt. Cut the fifth strip in half and add one half to each of the side binding strips to achieve the needed length.

## The Finishing Stitches

Outline the houses, windows, doors, and checkerboard in quilting, and stitch a 1- to 2-inch diagonal grid in the background. You can also quilt a design in the borders if you like.

# Scrap Version

## Materials

**FABRIC A** (houses, corner squares, checkerboard)
Use six fabrics.

| | |
|---|---|
| Blocks and Corner Squares | ⅜ yard |
| Checkerboard | ⅛ yard |
| TOTAL | ½ yard |
| | each of six fabrics |

**FABRIC B** (block background, lattice, checkerboard)

| | |
|---|---|
| Blocks | ½ yard |
| Lattice | ⅝ yard |
| Checkerboard | ⅜ yard |
| TOTAL | 1½ yards |

**FABRIC C**

| | |
|---|---|
| Binding | ⅞ yard |

| | |
|---|---|
| **TWO-INCH BORDER** | ⅜ yard |
| (choose one Fabric A) | |
| **BACKING** | 1⅞ yards |
| **BATTING** | 1⅞ yards |

## Before You Begin

Many of the assembly techniques for the Scrap Version are the same as those given earlier for the Amish Version. Throughout these directions, you will be referred back to the Amish Version for steps that are identical. Specific assembly directions needed for the Scrap Version are given in detail here.

## Cutting Directions

Prewash and press all of your fabrics. Using a rotary cutter, see-through ruler, and cutting mat, prepare the strips as described in the first column in the chart below. Then from those strips, cut the pieces listed in the second column. Some portions of the quilt need to be cut only once, so no additional cutting information will appear in the second column.

| | FIRST CUT | | SECOND CUT | |
|---|---|---|---|---|
| | **NO. OF STRIPS** | **DIMENSIONS** | **NO. OF PIECES** | **DIMENSIONS** |
| **FABRIC A** | HOUSES: from *each* of the *six* fabrics, cut the following | | | |
| | 1 | 2½ × 44-inch strip | 2 | 2½ × 4½-inch pieces |
| | | | 4 | 2½ × 3½-inch pieces |
| | 2 | 1½ × 44-inch strips | 4 | 1½ × 8½-inch pieces |
| | | | 6 | 1½ × 2½-inch pieces |
| | | | 4 | 1½ × 1½-inch pieces |
| | 1 | 5 × 7-inch piece | | |
| | CHECKERBOARD: from *each* of the *six* fabrics, cut the following | | | |
| | **Before You Cut:** You will need two additional 1½ × 44-inch strips, for a total of eight. Cut these from your two favorite Fabric A's. | | | |
| | 1 | 1½ × 44-inch strip | | |

*(continued on next page)*

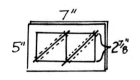

| | FIRST CUT | | SECOND CUT | |
|---|---|---|---|---|
| | NO. OF STRIPS | DIMENSIONS | NO. OF PIECES | DIMENSIONS |
| **FABRIC A,** *continued* | CORNER SQUARES (choose one Fabric A) | | | |
| | 4 | 2½ × 2½-inch squares | | |
| | TWO-INCH BORDER (choose one Fabric A) | | | |
| | 4 | 2½ × 44-inch strips | | |
| **FABRIC B** | BACKGROUND | | | |
| | 1 | 2½ × 44-inch strip | 12 | 2½ × 2½-inch pieces |
| | 3 | 1½ × 44-inch strips | 24 | 1½ × 1½-inch pieces |
| | | | 36 | 1½ × 2½-inch pieces |
| | 1 | 5 × 44-inch strip | 6 | 5 × 7-inch pieces |
| | LATTICE | | | |
| | **Before You Cut:** From three of the 44-inch strips, cut the strips as directed in the second column. The remaining nine strips require no further cutting. | | | |
| | 12 | 1½ × 44-inch strips | 9 | 1½ × 8½-inch pieces |
| | CHECKERBOARD | | | |
| | 8 | 1½ × 44-inch strips | | |
| **FABRIC C** | BINDING | | | |
| | 5 | 5½ × 44-inch strips | | |

## Speedy Triangles

**STEP 1.** Refer to Speedy Triangle directions on page 11 for how to mark, sew, and cut.

**STEP 2.** Position the 5 × 7-inch pieces of Fabrics A and B with right sides together. You will have six sets. On each set, mark a 2⅞-inch grid of two squares as shown in **Diagram 22**.

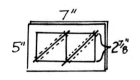

DIAGRAM 22

**STEP 3.** After sewing and cutting are complete, press seam allowances toward Fabric A. You will have made a total of twenty-four triangle sets, four of each Fabric A.

## Assembling the Blocks

Follow all steps for assembly in Section One, Section Two, and the House Assembly of the Amish Version beginning on page 107. You will be making two blocks each of the six different house fabrics, for a total of twelve blocks.

## The Lattice

To attach the lattice, follow the directions on page 109 under the Amish Version.

## Checkerboard Rows

Arrange the sixteen 1½ × 44-inch Fabric A and B strips in a pleasing order, alternating the fabrics and adding the two extra Fabric A's at the end of the strip set. Sew together and press toward Fabric B. To complete the checkerboard, refer to Steps 2 and 3 under Checkerboard Rows for the Amish Version on page 109.

## Completing the Quilt

Refer to Putting It All Together through The Finishing Stitches under the Amish Version beginning on page 109.

# All Sewed Up

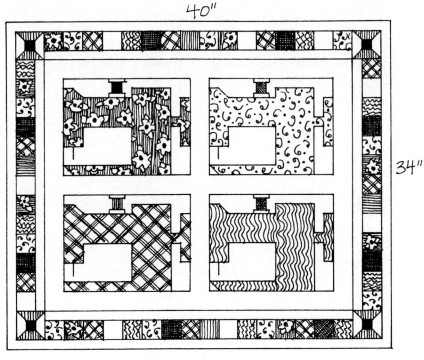

40″

34″

QUILT LAYOUT

If your sewing machine is your favorite household appliance, then this wall quilt is for you! In no time flat you can put together a colorful wallhanging to brighten your sewing room. What better form of inspiration does a quilter need?

Finished Quilt: 40 × 34 inches
Finished Block: 13 × 10 inches

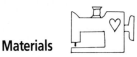

**Materials**

Obvious directional prints are not recommended.

**FABRIC A** *(sewing machines)*
Use four fabrics.　　　　⅓ yard
　　　　　　*each* of *four* fabrics

**FABRIC B** *(block background, lattice)*
Blocks　　　　　　½ yard
Lattice　　　　　　½ yard
　TOTAL　　　　　1 yard

**FABRIC C** *(thread, scrap border)*
Use four fabrics.　　　　⅛ yard
　　　　　　*each* of *four* fabrics

**FABRIC D** *(border, binding)*
One-Inch Border
　and Binding　　　　⅞ yard

**FABRIC E** *(appliquéd spool ends)*
Fabric Scraps

**OPTIONAL SPOOL CORNER SQUARES**
Use leftover scraps of:
　Fabric B (background)
　Fabric C (thread)
　One Fabric A (spool)

**BACKING**　　　　　1⅛ yards

**BATTING**　　　　　1⅛ yards

## Cutting Directions

Prewash and press all of your fabrics. Using a rotary cutter, see-through ruler, and cutting mat, prepare the strips as described in the first column in the chart below. Then from those strips, cut the pieces listed in the second column. Some portions of the quilt need to be cut only once, so no additional cutting information will appear in the second column.

| | FIRST CUT | | SECOND CUT | |
| | NO. OF STRIPS | DIMENSIONS | NO. OF PIECES | DIMENSIONS |
|---|---|---|---|---|
| **FABRIC A** | **SEWING MACHINES:** from *each* of the *four* fabrics, cut the following | | | |
| | 1 | 1½ × 44-inch strip | 2 | 1½ × 1½-inch pieces |
| | | | 1 | 1½ × 5½-inch piece |
| | | | 1 | 1½ × 6½-inch piece |
| | 1 | 4½ × 44-inch strip | 1 | 4½ × 9½-inch piece |
| | | | 1 | 4½ × 4½-inch piece |
| | | | 1 | 3½ × 7½-inch piece |
| | | | 1 | 2½ × 2½-inch piece |
| | **SCRAP BORDER:** from *each* of the *four* fabrics, cut the following | | | |
| | 1 | 2½ × 44-inch strip | 1 | 2½ × 22-inch strip |
| **FABRIC B** | **BACKGROUND** | | | |
| | 1 | 1½ × 44-inch strip | 16 | 1½ × 2½-inch pieces |
| | 3 | 2½ × 44-inch strips | 4 | 2½ × 2½-inch pieces |
| | | | 8 | 2½ × 3½-inch pieces |
| | | | 4 | 2½ × 5½-inch pieces |
| | | | 4 | 2½ × 7½-inch pieces |
| | 1 | 4½ × 44-inch strip | 4 | 4½ × 1½-inch pieces |
| | | | 4 | 4½ × 4½-inch pieces |
| | **LATTICE** | | | |
| | **Before You Cut:** From one of the 44-inch strips, cut the pieces as directed in the second column. The remaining five strips require no further cutting. | | | |
| | 6 | 2½ × 44-inch strips | 2 | 2½ × 10½-inch pieces |
| | **SCRAP BORDER** | | | |
| | 1 | 2½ × 44-inch strip | 2 | 2½ × 22-inch strips |
| **FABRIC C** | **THREAD AND SCRAP BORDER:** from *each* of the *four* fabrics, cut the following | | | |
| | 1 | 2½ × 44-inch strip | 1 | 2½ × 1½-inch piece |
| | | | 1 | 2½ × 22-inch piece |

| | FIRST CUT | | SECOND CUT | |
|---|---|---|---|---|
| | **NO. OF STRIPS** | **DIMENSIONS** | **NO. OF PIECES** | **DIMENSIONS** |
| **FABRIC D** | **ONE-INCH BORDER** | | | |
| | 4 | 1½ × 44-inch strips | | |
| | **BINDING** | | | |
| | 4 | 5½ × 44-inch strips | | |
| **FABRIC E** | **APPLIQUÉD SPOOL ENDS** | | | |
| | 8 | ⅞ × 2¼-inch pieces | | |
| **Optional Spool Corner Squares** | **FABRIC A (spool)** | | | |
| | 1 | 6 × 10-inch piece | 8 | 1½ × 1½-inch pieces |
| | **FABRIC B (background)** | | | |
| | 1 | 6 × 10-inch piece | 8 | 1½ × 1½-inch pieces |
| | **FABRIC C (thread):** from *each* of the *four* fabrics, cut the following | | | |
| | 1 | 1½ × 1½-inch piece | | |

## Speedy Triangles

**STEP 1.** Refer to Speedy Triangle directions on page 11 for how to mark, sew, and cut.

**STEP 2.** Position the 4½ × 4½-inch pieces of Fabrics A and B with right sides together. Repeat for four sets. On each set, mark a 1⅞-inch square. See **Diagram 1**.

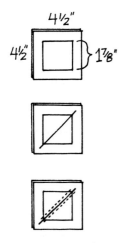

DIAGRAM 1

**STEP 3.** After sewing and cutting are complete, press seam allowances toward Fabric A. You will have made a total of eight 1½-inch triangle sets.

## Assembling the Blocks

Throughout this section, refer to the Fabric Key to identify the fabric placements in the diagrams. Also, it's a good idea to review Assembly Line Piecing on page 13 before you get started. It is more efficient to do the same step for each block at the same time than to piece one entire block together at a time. Be sure to press as you go, and follow the arrows for pressing direction.

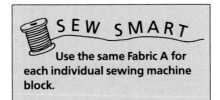

SEW SMART

**Use the same Fabric A for each individual sewing machine block.**

FABRIC KEY    FABRIC A ▦

FABRIC B ☐

FABRIC C ▩

## SECTION ONE

**STEP 1.** Sew four 1½ × 1½-inch pieces of Fabric A to four 1½-inch triangle sets. (Use one each of the four different Fabric A's.) Position them right sides together and line up next to your sewing machine. Stitch the first set together, then butt the next set directly behind them and continue sewing each set without breaking your seam. Be sure to position the triangle sets as shown in **Diagram 2**. Press seams to Fabric A and cut the joining threads.

DIAGRAM 2

In each of the remaining steps, use the same Continuous Seam method. You will be making four sewing machine blocks.

**STEP 2.** Sew four 1½ × 2½-inch pieces of Fabric B to the units from Step 1. Press seams to Fabric B. See **Diagram 3.**

DIAGRAM 3

**STEP 3.** Sew the units from Step 2 to four 3½ × 2½-inch pieces of Fabric B. Press seams to Fabric B. See **Diagram 4.**

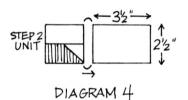

DIAGRAM 4

**STEP 4.** Sew four 1½ × 2½-inch pieces of Fabric C to four 1½ × 2½-inch pieces of Fabric B. Press seams to Fabric C. See **Diagram 5.**

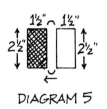

DIAGRAM 5

**STEP 5.** Sew the units from Step 3 to the units from Step 4. Press seams to the Step 4 unit. See **Diagram 6.**

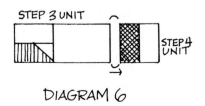

DIAGRAM 6

**STEP 6.** Sew the units from Step 5 to four 7½ × 3½-inch pieces of Fabric A. Press seams to Fabric A. See **Diagram 7.**

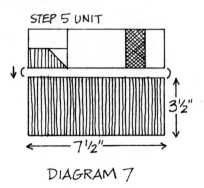

DIAGRAM 7

## SECTION TWO

**STEP 1.** Sew four 2½ × 2½-inch pieces of Fabric A to four 5½ × 2½-inch pieces of Fabric B. Press seams to Fabric A. See **Diagram 8.**

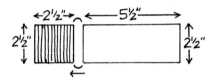

DIAGRAM 8

**STEP 2.** Sew the units from Step 1 to four 7½ × 2½-inch pieces of Fabric B. Press seams to Fabric B. See **Diagram 9.**

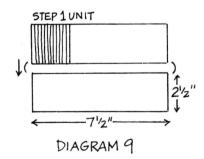

DIAGRAM 9

**STEP 3.** Sew four 1½-inch triangle sets to four 6½ × 1½-inch pieces of Fabric A. Press seams to Fabric A. See **Diagram 10.**

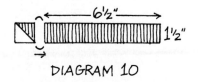

DIAGRAM 10

**STEP 4.** Sew the units from Step 2 to the units from Step 3. Press seams to the Step 2 unit. See Diagram 11.

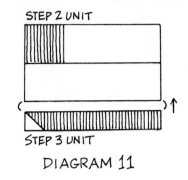

DIAGRAM 11

## SECTION THREE

**STEP 1.** Sew four 1½ × 2½-inch pieces of Fabric B to four 1½ × 1½-inch pieces of Fabric A. Press seams to Fabric A. See **Diagram 12.**

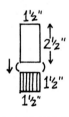

DIAGRAM 12

**STEP 2.** Sew the units from Step 1 to four 1½ × 2½-inch pieces of Fabric B. Press seams to the Step 1 unit. See **Diagram 13.**

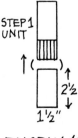

DIAGRAM 13

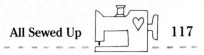

**STEP 3.** Sew the units from Step 2 to four 1½ × 5½-inch pieces of Fabric A. Press seams to Fabric A. See **Diagram 14**.

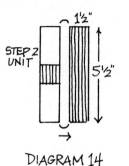

DIAGRAM 14

**STEP 4.** Sew four 2½ × 2½-inch pieces of Fabric B to the units from Step 3. Press seams to Fabric B. See **Diagram 15**.

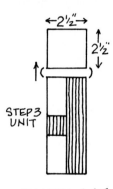

DIAGRAM 15

**STEP 5.** Sew the units from Step 4 to four 2½ × 3½-inch pieces of Fabric B. Press seams to Fabric B. See **Diagram 16**.

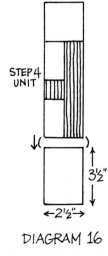

DIAGRAM 16

**STEP 6.** Sew four 4½ × 1½-inch pieces of Fabric B to four 4½ × 9½-inch pieces of Fabric A. Press seams to Fabric A. See **Diagram 17**.

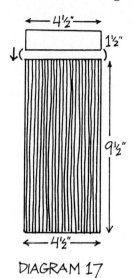

DIAGRAM 17

**STEP 7.** Sew the units from Step 6 to the units from Step 5. Press seams to the Step 6 unit. See **Diagram 18**.

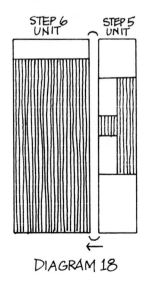

DIAGRAM 18

**SECTION ASSEMBLY**

**STEP 1.** Sew the units from Section One to the units from Section Two as shown in **Diagram 19**. Press seams to the Section One unit.

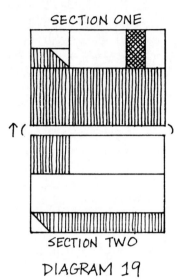

DIAGRAM 19

**STEP 2.** Sew the units from Step 1 to the units from Section Three as shown in **Diagram 20**. Press seams to Section Three. You should have four sewing machines that look ready to plug in!

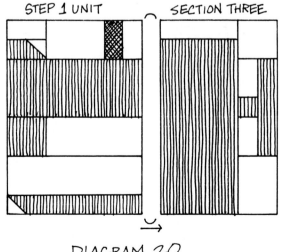

DIAGRAM 20

## The Lattice

**STEP 1.** Sew the 2½ × 10½-inch strips of Fabric B lattice to the right side of the two blocks that will be positioned on the left side of the quilt. Press all seams to the lattice. Sew the right-side blocks to the lattice to make two rows of two blocks. See **Diagram 21**. Press.

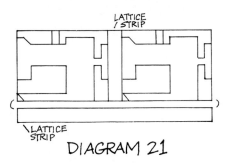

DIAGRAM 21

**STEP 2.** Sew 2½ × 44-inch lattice strips to the bottom of both rows. Trim excess and press. Pin and sew the two rows together. Press.

**STEP 3.** Sew a lattice strip to the quilt top. Trim and press. Sew lattice strips to the quilt sides. Trim and press.

## The Borders

### SCRAP BORDER

**STEP 1.** Take the ten 2½ × 22-inch strips of Fabrics A, B, and C, and arrange them in a pleasing order.

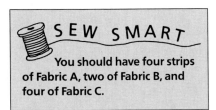

**SEW SMART**

You should have four strips of Fabric A, two of Fabric B, and four of Fabric C.

**STEP 2.** Sew the strips together to make a 20½ × 22-inch strip set as shown in **Diagram 22**.

**STEP 3.** Cut this strip set in half widthwise, referring to the cutting

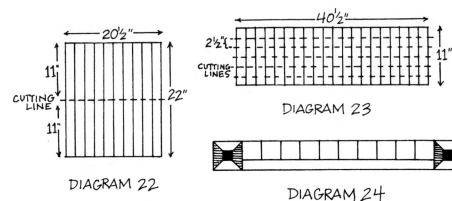

DIAGRAM 22

line in **Diagram 22**. Resew the halves together to make a 40½ × 11-inch strip set. From this strip set cut four 2½ × 40½-inch strips, referring to the cutting lines in **Diagram 23**.

**STEP 4.** See Hints on Fitting a Scrap Border on page 28. Fit the border to the top and bottom and the sides of the quilt top to the correct length. Measure up to the outside seam line of the lattice. Do not sew the borders to the quilt top at this time; they will be attached at a later step.

### ONE-INCH BORDER

**STEP 1.** Sew one 1½ × 44-inch strip of Fabric D to each strip of scrap border. Trim the excess so they are the same length. Press seams to the one-inch border.

**STEP 2.** Sew scrap border/one-inch border strips to the top and bottom of the quilt top. Be sure to position the strips so the one-inch border is on the inside and the scrap border is on the outside. Press.

**STEP 3.** For corner squares, you may use the 3-inch spool block (as described in the next section) or cut four 3½ × 3½-inch squares of plain fabric. Sew the corner squares of your choice to the ends of the side border strips as shown in **Diagram 24**. Pin in position and sew to the sides. Press.

DIAGRAM 23

DIAGRAM 24

## Optional Spool Corner Squares

**STEP 1.** Use scraps of the four thread (Fabric C) fabrics for the thread, and choose one Fabric A to use for the spools. The thread fabrics will be different in each of the corner squares, but the spool ends will be the same among those four blocks. Cut a 6 × 10-inch piece each of the spool (Fabric A) and background (Fabric B) fabrics.

**STEP 2.** Using the Speedy Triangle method described on page 11, draw a grid of eight 1⅞-inch squares to make a total of sixteen 1½-inch triangle sets. See **Diagram 25**.

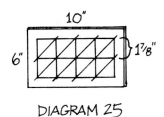

DIAGRAM 25

**STEP 3.** After sewing and cutting are complete, press seam allowances toward Fabric A. You will have made a total of sixteen 1½-inch triangle sets.

### ASSEMBLING THE SPOOL BLOCKS

Use Assembly Line Piecing described on page 13 to piece the spool blocks. Refer to the **Spool Block Fabric Key** to identify the different fabrics.

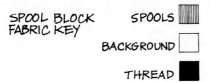

SPOOL BLOCK FABRIC KEY    SPOOLS ▥    BACKGROUND ☐    THREAD ■

**STEP 1.** Sew four 1½-inch triangle sets to four 1½ × 1½-inch pieces of spool fabric. Press seams to spool fabric as shown in **Diagram 26**.

DIAGRAM 26

**STEP 2.** Sew the units from Step 1 to four 1½-inch triangle sets. Press seams to the Step 1 units. See **Diagram 27**.

DIAGRAM 27

**STEP 3.** Sew four 1½ × 1½-inch pieces of background to four 1½ × 1½-inch thread pieces. Press seams to background. See **Diagram 28**.

DIAGRAM 28

**STEP 4.** Sew the units from Step 3 to four 1½ × 1½-inch pieces of background fabric. Press seams to background. See **Diagram 29**.

DIAGRAM 29

**STEP 5.** Sew the units from Step 2 to the units from Step 4. Press seams to the Step 4 units. See **Diagram 30**.

DIAGRAM 30

**STEP 6.** Sew four 1½-inch triangle sets to four 1½ × 1½-inch pieces of spool fabric. Press seams to spool fabric as shown in **Diagram 31**.

DIAGRAM 31

**STEP 7.** Sew the units from Step 6 to four 1½-inch triangle sets. Press seams to the Step 6 units. See **Diagram 32**.

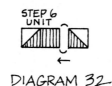

DIAGRAM 32

**STEP 8.** Sew the units from Step 5 to the units from Step 7. Press seams to the Step 5 units. See **Diagram 33**. The spool blocks are done and ready to add to the end of the border strips, as described in Step 3 under One-Inch Border.

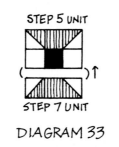

DIAGRAM 33

## The Needle

Using the backstitch or stem stitch, embroider a 1¼-inch-long needle on each of the sewing machines. Refer to Stitches for Special Touches on page 16 for instructions on embroidery stitches.

## Layering the Quilt

Arrange and baste the backing, batting, and top together following directions for Layering the Quilt on page 32. Trim batting and backing to ¾ inch from the raw edge of the quilt top.

## Binding the Quilt

Using the strips cut from Fabric D, follow directions for Binding the Quilt on page 33.

## The Finishing Stitches

**STEP 1.** Use the eight ⅞ × 2¼-inch pieces of Fabric E for the thread spools. Turn and press raw edges under ¼ inch all the way around. Pin in position on the top and bottom of the thread sections on the sewing machines, and hand appliqué in place. See **Diagram 34** to help with positioning the spool ends.

DIAGRAM 34

**STEP 2.** Outline your sewing machine by quilting in the ditch or ¼ inch from the seam allowance. Quilt a 2-inch diagonal grid in the background. For an extra touch, quilt a thread leading from the spool to the needle as shown in **Diagram 35**. Use quilting thread or embroidery floss that matches the color of the thread on the spool.

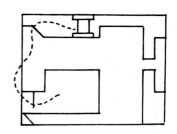

DIAGRAM 35

# Country Cousins

36"

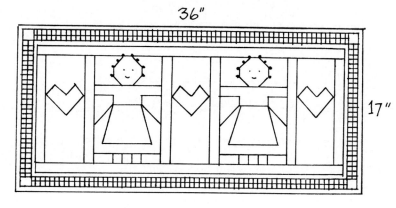

17"

QUILT LAYOUT

If it's an authentic country look you're after, these dolls are just the thing. This wallhanging is a nice shape and size to fit above or below a shelf in your kitchen or anywhere else in your house that could use a touch of country. Make sure your background fabric is dark enough to provide a contrast with the fabrics you've chosen for the dolls' faces and feet.

Finished Quilt: 36 × 17 inches
Finished Block: 7 × 11 inches

## Materials

Obvious directional prints are not recommended.

**FABRIC A** *(hearts, corner squares)*

| | |
|---|---|
| Hearts and Corner Squares | ⅛ yard |

**FABRIC B** *(block background, lattice, checkerboard)*

| | |
|---|---|
| Blocks | ⅓ yard |
| Lattice | ¼ yard |
| Checkerboard | ¼ yard |
| TOTAL | ⅞ yard |

**FABRIC C** *(heads, feet)*

| | |
|---|---|
| For *each* doll | ⅛ yard |

**FABRIC D** *(dresses, checkerboard)*

| | |
|---|---|
| For *each* doll | ¼ yard |
| Checkerboard | ¼ yard |
| | of *one* dress fabric |

**FABRIC E** *(border, binding)*

| | |
|---|---|
| Half-Inch Border | ⅛ yard |
| Binding | ⅓ yard |
| TOTAL | ½ yard |

**FABRIC F** *(aprons)*

| | |
|---|---|
| For *each* doll | ⅛ yard |

| | |
|---|---|
| **BACKING** | ⅝ yard |

| | |
|---|---|
| **BATTING** | ⅝ yard |

## Cutting Directions

Prewash and press all of your fabrics. Using a rotary cutter, see-through ruler, and cutting mat, prepare the strips as described in the first column in the chart below.

Then from those strips, cut the pieces listed in the second column. Some portions of the quilt need to be cut only once, so no additional cutting information will appear in the second column.

| | FIRST CUT | | SECOND CUT | |
| --- | --- | --- | --- | --- |
| | **NO. OF STRIPS** | **DIMENSIONS** | **NO. OF PIECES** | **DIMENSIONS** |
| **FABRIC A** | **HEARTS** | | | |
| | 2 | $12 \times 4\frac{1}{2}$-inch pieces | | |
| | **CORNER SQUARES** | | | |
| | 4 | $1\frac{1}{2} \times 1\frac{1}{2}$-inch squares | | |
| **FABRIC B** | **BACKGROUND** | | | |
| | **Before You Cut:** Refer to the **Fabric B Cutting Diagram** for the most efficient way to cut the pieces listed below. | | | |
| | 8 | $1\frac{1}{2} \times 2\frac{1}{2}$-inch pieces | | |
| | 2 | $1\frac{1}{2} \times 1\frac{1}{2}$-inch pieces | | |
| | 3 | $3\frac{1}{2} \times 4\frac{1}{2}$-inch pieces | | |
| | 4 | $3\frac{1}{2} \times 2\frac{1}{2}$-inch pieces | | |
| | 3 | $5\frac{1}{2} \times 4\frac{1}{2}$-inch pieces | | |
| | 2 | $5 \times 6$-inch pieces | | |
| | 2 | $4\frac{1}{2} \times 4\frac{1}{2}$-inch pieces | | |
| | 2 | $4\frac{1}{2} \times 12$-inch pieces | | |
| | **LATTICE** | | | |
| | 4 | $1\frac{1}{2} \times 44$-inch strips | | |
| | **CHECKERBOARD BORDER** | | | |
| | 6 | $1 \times 44$-inch strips | | |
| **FABRIC C** | **HEADS AND FEET** | | | |
| | **Before You Cut:** Cut the following for *both* Fabric C's, referring to the **Fabric C Cutting Diagram** for the most efficient way to cut the pieces listed below. | | | |
| | 4 | $1\frac{1}{2} \times 1\frac{1}{2}$-inch pieces | | |
| | 1 | $1\frac{1}{2} \times 3\frac{1}{2}$-inch piece | | |
| | 1 | $4\frac{1}{2} \times 4\frac{1}{2}$-inch piece | | |

| | FIRST CUT | | SECOND CUT | |
|---|---|---|---|---|
| | **NO. OF STRIPS** | **DIMENSIONS** | **NO. OF PIECES** | **DIMENSIONS** |
| **FABRIC D** | **DRESSES** | | | |
| | *Before You Cut:* Cut the following for *both* Fabric D's, referring to the **Fabric D Cutting Diagram** for the most efficient way to cut the pieces listed below. | | | |
| | 1 | 3½ × 7½-inch piece | | |
| | 2 | 2½ × 3½-inch pieces | | |
| | 2 | 1½ × 2½-inch pieces | | |
| | 1 | 5 × 6-inch piece | | |
| | **CHECKERBOARD BORDER** | | | |
| | 6 | 1 × 44-inch strips | | |
| **FABRIC E** | **HALF-INCH BORDER** | | | |
| | 3 | 1 × 44-inch strips | | |
| | **BINDING** | | | |
| | 4 | 2¾ × 44-inch strips | | |

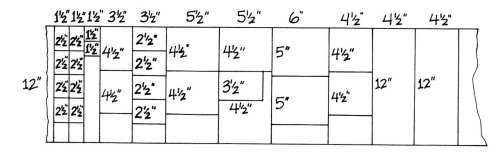

FABRIC B CUTTING DIAGRAM

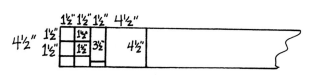

FABRIC C CUTTING DIAGRAM

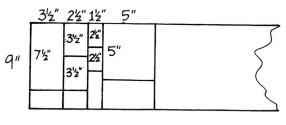

FABRIC D CUTTING DIAGRAM

## Speedy Triangles

**STEP 1.** Refer to the Speedy Triangle directions on page 11 for how to mark, sew, and cut.

**STEP 2.** For the heart tops, position the 4½ × 12-inch pieces of Fabrics A and B with right sides together. Mark a 1⅞-inch grid of six squares. See **Diagram 1**.

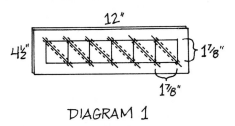

DIAGRAM 1

**STEP 3.** After sewing and cutting are complete, press half the seam allowances to Fabric A and the other half to Fabric B. You will have made a total of twelve 1½-inch Fabric A/B triangle sets.

**STEP 4.** For the heads, use the two 4½ × 4½-inch pieces of Fabric C with two 4½ × 4½-inch pieces of Fabric B. Position the pieces of Fabrics B and C with right sides together. On both sets, mark a 1⅞-inch grid of two squares. Press seams to Fabric B. You will have made a total of eight triangle sets, four of each Fabric C.

**STEP 5.** For the dresses, use two 5 × 6-inch pieces each of Fabrics B and D. Position the pieces with right sides together, and on both sets mark one 2⅞-inch square. Press seams to Fabric B. You will have made a total of four triangle sets, two of each Fabric D.

**STEP 6.** For the heart bases, position the 4½ × 12-inch pieces of Fabrics A and B with right sides together. Mark a 2⅞-inch grid of three squares. You will have made a total of six triangle sets. Press three of the seams to Fabric A and the other three to Fabric B.

## Assembling the Blocks

Throughout this section, refer to the Fabric Key to identify the fabric placements in the diagrams. Also, it's a good idea to review Assembly Line Piecing on page 13 before you get started. It's more efficient to do the same step for each block at the same time when piecing the heart blocks. Piece the doll blocks one at a time. Be sure to press as you go, and follow the arrows for pressing direction.

FABRIC KEY    FABRIC A ⬛
              FABRIC B ⬛
              FABRIC C ☐
              FABRIC D ⬛

### SECTION ONE (Doll's Head)

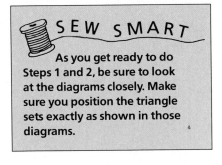

**SEW SMART**

As you get ready to do Steps 1 and 2, be sure to look at the diagrams closely. Make sure you position the triangle sets exactly as shown in those diagrams.

**STEP 1.** Sew 1½-inch Fabric B/C triangle sets to each side of a 1½ × 1½-inch piece of Fabric C. Press both seams to Fabric C. See **Diagram 2**.

DIAGRAM 2

**STEP 2.** Sew a 1½-inch Fabric B/C triangle set to each side of a 1½ × 1½-inch piece of Fabric C. Press both seams to Fabric C. See **Diagram 3**.

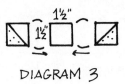

DIAGRAM 3

**STEP 3.** Sew the unit from Step 1 to the top of a 3½ × 1½-inch piece of Fabric C. Sew the unit from Step 2 to the bottom of that same piece of Fabric C. Press both seams to Fabric C. See **Diagram 4**.

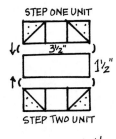

DIAGRAM 4

**STEP 4.** Sew a 2½ × 3½-inch piece of Fabric B to each side of the unit from Step 3. Press both seams to Fabric B. See **Diagram 5**.

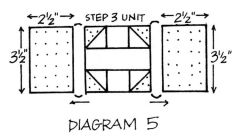

DIAGRAM 5

### SECTION TWO (Arms)

**STEP 1.** Sew two 2½ × 1½-inch pieces of Fabric D to two 2½ × 1½-inch pieces of Fabric B. Press both seams to Fabric D. See **Diagram 6**.

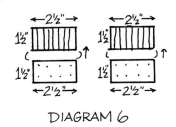

DIAGRAM 6

**STEP 2.** Sew units from Step 1 to each side of a 3½ × 2½-inch piece of Fabric D. Press both seams to the Step 1 units. See **Diagram 7**.

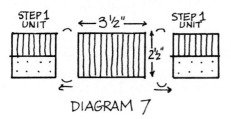

DIAGRAM 7

### SECTION THREE (Skirt)

Sew a 2½-inch Fabric B/D triangle set to each side of a 3½ × 2½-inch piece of Fabric D. Press both seams to Fabric D. See **Diagram 8**.

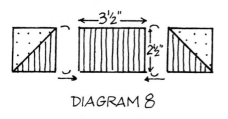

DIAGRAM 8

### SECTION FOUR (Skirt)

Section Four is a 7½ × 3½-inch piece of Fabric D and is complete as it is. No sewing here! See **Diagram 9**.

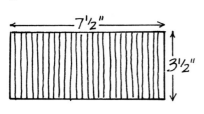

DIAGRAM 9

### SECTION FIVE (Feet)

**STEP 1.** Sew a 1½ × 1½-inch piece of Fabric C to the right side of a 2½ × 1½-inch piece of Fabric B. Sew another 1½ × 1½-inch piece of Fabric C to a 1½ × 1½-inch piece of Fabric B. Press both seams to Fabric C. Sew those units together, referring to **Diagram 10** for their placement. Press to Fabric C.

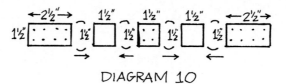

DIAGRAM 10

**STEP 2.** Sew a 2½ × 1½-inch piece of Fabric B to the right side of the unit from Step 2, referring to **Diagram 10**. Press to Fabric C.

### SECTION ASSEMBLY

Sew the five sections together in sequence, referring to **Diagram 11**. Follow arrows for pressing direction.

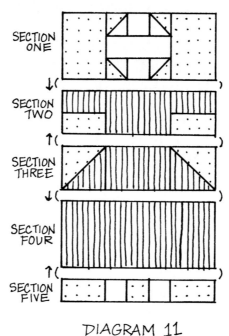

DIAGRAM 11

Repeat instructions from Section One through Section Assembly for the second doll.

## The Hearts

In the following steps, the position of the seam allowances on the triangle sets is very important. Pay close attention to the directions and refer to the diagrams, in which the seam allowances are visible.

**STEP 1.** Sew six 1½-inch Fabric A/B triangle sets (pressed to Fabric B) to six 1½-inch Fabric A/B triangle sets (pressed to Fabric A). Make sure the joined sets look like those in **Diagram 12**. Press toward triangle sets pressed to Fabric A.

DIAGRAM 12

**STEP 2.** Sew two of the units from Step 1 together as shown in **Diagram 13** to create the heart top section. Press seams to the units on the left. Repeat for a total of three heart top sections.

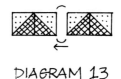

DIAGRAM 13

**STEP 3.** For the heart bases, sew three 2½-inch Fabric A/B triangle sets (pressed to Fabric B) to three 2½-inch Fabric A/B triangle sets (pressed to Fabric A). Press toward triangle sets pressed to Fabric A. See **Diagram 14**.

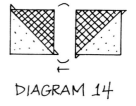

DIAGRAM 14

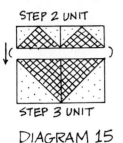

**STEP 4.** Sew units from Step 2 (heart tops) to units from Step 3 (heart bases). Press toward heart bases. Your finished hearts should look like the one in **Diagram 15**.

STEP 2 UNIT

↓(          )

STEP 3 UNIT

DIAGRAM 15

### The Aprons

Using the **Apron Appliqué Pattern** on the opposite page, cut out two aprons from Fabric F. Hand appliqué an apron to each doll, referring to Hand Appliqué directions on page 19. For this design you may prefer to use just one layer of fabric and turn the edges in ¼ inch before appliquéing. Appliqué around the top and sides of the apron, and leave the bottom open. This gives you the option of fringing the bottom edges of the aprons.

### Face and Hair

Bring a smile to the faces of these dolls by embroidering one, using the stem or outline stitch. Use French knots for their eyes and hair. Choose embroidery floss in colors that complement the fabrics used in each doll.

### Putting It All Together

**STEP 1.** For the heart sections, sew three 4½ × 3½-inch pieces of Fabric B to the top of three hearts. Press to Fabric B. See **Diagram 16**.

**STEP 2.** Sew three 4½ × 5½-inch pieces of Fabric B to the bottom of the heart sections, referring to **Diagram 16**. Press seams to Fabric B.

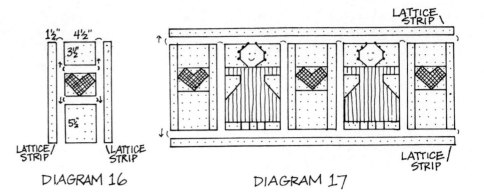

DIAGRAM 16

DIAGRAM 17

**STEP 3.** Cut two 1½ × 44-inch Fabric B lattice strips into thirds. Sew one of these strips to each side of the three heart sections as shown in **Diagram 16**. Trim the excess and press all seams to the lattice.

**STEP 4.** Sew the doll and heart sections together, alternating the sections as shown in **Diagram 17**. Press seams to the lattice.

**STEP 5.** Sew remaining lattice strips to the quilt top and bottom. Trim the excess and press.

### Half-Inch Border

**STEP 1.** Sew 1 × 44-inch strips of Fabric E to the quilt top and bottom. Trim the excess and press all seams to the border.

**STEP 2.** Sew border strips to the quilt sides. Trim and press.

### Miniature Checkerboard Border

**STEP 1.** Sew together six 1 × 44-inch strips each of Fabrics B and D, alternating the fabrics. This will make a 6½ × 44-inch strip set like the one in **Diagram 18**. Press all seams toward Fabric D as you go.

**STEP 2.** Cut this strip set into thirds, referring to the cutting lines in **Diagram 18**. Resew the thirds together side by side to make an 18½ × 14-inch strip set as shown in **Diagram 19**.

**STEP 3.** Cut the strip set in half, referring to the cutting line in **Diagram 19**. Resew the halves together to make a 36½ × 7-inch strip set as shown in **Diagram 20**.

**STEP 4.** Cut six 1 × 36½-inch strips from the strip set made in Step 3. Rematch two strips so they form a

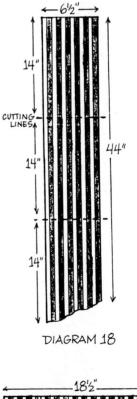

DIAGRAM 18

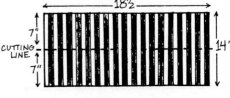

DIAGRAM 19

checkerboard and sew together. Make three 1½ × 36½-inch checkerboard sets like the one in **Diagram 21**.

**STEP 5.** See Hints on Fitting a Checkerboard Border on page 29. Fit and sew checkerboard borders to the quilt top and bottom.

**STEP 6.** The third strip of checkerboard is long enough for both quilt sides. Fit the strip to one side, measuring up to but not including the borders you just added to the top and bottom. Allow ¼ inch on each end of the strip, so it will fit correctly after the corner squares are added. Repeat for the other side.

**STEP 7.** For the corner squares, sew a 1½-inch square of Fabric A to each end of the side checkerboard strips. Press. Pin the strips in position, and sew to the quilt sides.

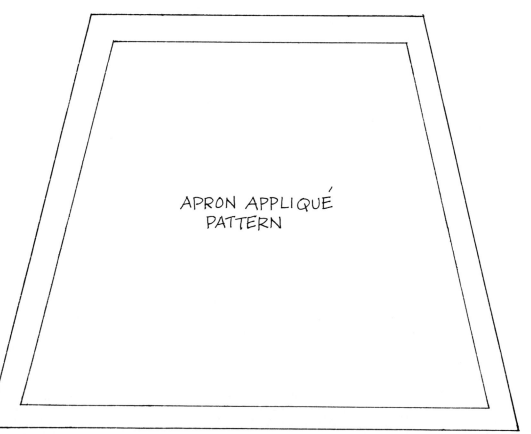

DIAGRAM 20

DIAGRAM 21

## Layering the Quilt

Arrange and baste the backing, batting, and top together following directions for Layering the Quilt on page 32. Trim the batting and backing to ¼ inch from the raw edge of the quilt top.

## Binding the Quilt

Using the strips cut from Fabric E, follow the directions on page 33 for Binding the Quilt.

## The Finishing Stitches

Outline your dolls and hearts by quilting in the ditch or ¼ inch from the seam line. Stitch a 1-inch diagonal grid in the background. A little blush from your own makeup drawer applied with a cotton swab to the dolls' cheeks can add a nice rosy glow that comes from country living!

APRON APPLIQUÉ
PATTERN

# Springtime Tulips

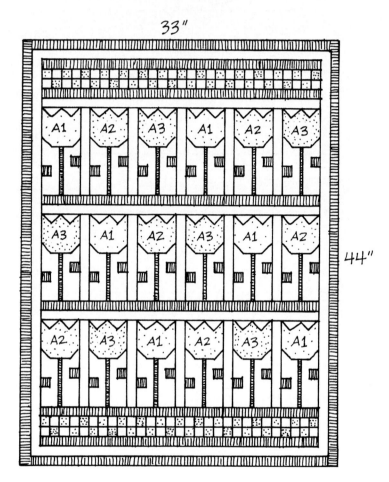

33"

44"

QUILT LAYOUT

Enjoy the freshness of spring year-round
with this cheerful tulip wallhanging.
Pastels, primaries, or your favorite country
colors all work great for this design,
and Speedy Triangles make it a breeze to
put together!

Finished Quilt: 33 × 44 inches
Finished Block: 4 × 9 inches

## Materials

Obvious directional prints are not
recommended.

**FABRIC A** *(tulips, checkerboard)*
Use three fabrics.
| | |
|---|---|
| Blocks | ¼ yard |
| Checkerboard | ⅛ yard |
| TOTAL | ⅜ yard |
| | *each* of *three* fabrics |

**FABRIC B** *(block background,
lattice, checkerboard)*
| | |
|---|---|
| Blocks | 1 yard |
| Lattice | ⅝ yard |
| Checkerboard | ¼ yard |
| TOTAL | 1⅞ yards |

**FABRIC C** *(leaves, stems, lattice,
binding)*
| | |
|---|---|
| Leaves | ⅛ yard |
| Stems | ⅛ yard |
| Green Lattice | ¼ yard |
| Binding | ⅞ yard |
| TOTAL | 1⅜ yards |

| | |
|---|---|
| **BACKING** | 1⅓ yards |
| **BATTING** | 1⅓ yards |

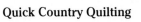

## Cutting Directions

Prewash and press all of your fabrics. Using a rotary cutter, see-through ruler, and cutting mat, prepare the strips as described in the first column in the chart below.

Then from those strips, cut the pieces listed in the second column. Some portions of the quilt need to be cut only once, so no additional cutting information will appear in the second column.

## Speedy Triangles

**STEP 1.** Refer to Speedy Triangle directions on page 11 for how to mark, sew, and cut.

**FABRIC KEY**

FABRIC A ⬚
FABRIC B ☐
FABRIC C ▨

| | FIRST CUT | | SECOND CUT | |
|---|---|---|---|---|
| | NO. OF STRIPS | DIMENSIONS | NO. OF PIECES | DIMENSIONS |
| **FABRIC A** | TULIP BLOCKS: from *each* of the *three* fabrics, cut the following | | | |
| | 1 | 2½ × 44-inch strip | 6 | 2½ × 4½-inch pieces |
| | | | 6 | 2½ × 1½-inch pieces |
| | 1 | 6 × 22-inch strip | | |
| | CHECKERBOARD ROWS: from *each* of the *three* fabrics, cut the following | | | |
| | 1 | 1½ × 44-inch strip | | |
| **FABRIC B** | TULIP BLOCKS | | | |
| | 1 | 4½ × 44-inch strip | 18 | 4½ × 1½-inch pieces |
| | 2 | 4½ × 44-inch strips | 18 | 4½ × 2½-inch pieces |
| | 2 | 6 × 44-inch strips | 3 | 6 × 22-inch pieces |
| | 2 | 3½ × 44-inch strips | | |
| | LATTICE | | | |
| | **Before You Cut:** From four of the 44-inch strips, cut the pieces as directed in the second column. The remaining eight strips require no further cutting. | | | |
| | 12 | 1½ × 44-inch strips | 15 | 1½ × 9½-inch pieces |
| | CHECKERBOARD ROWS | | | |
| | 3 | 1½ × 44-inch strips | | |
| **FABRIC C** | LEAVES/STEMS | | | |
| | 2 | 1½ × 44-inch strips | | |
| | 3 | 1 × 44-inch strips | | |
| | GREEN LATTICE | | | |
| | 6 | 1½ × 44-inch strips | | |
| | BINDING | | | |
| | 5 | 5½ × 44-inch strips | | |

**STEP 2.** Position the 6 × 22-inch pieces of Fabrics A and B with right sides together. You will have three sets. On each set, draw a 1⅞-inch grid of eighteen squares. See **Diagram 1.**

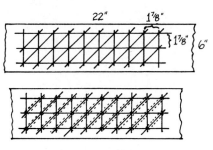

DIAGRAM 1

**STEP 3.** After sewing and cutting are complete, press seam allowances of twelve triangle sets from each Fabric A toward Fabric A and the other twenty-four triangle sets toward Fabric B. You will have made a total of 108 triangle sets, thirty-six of each tulip fabric.

## Assembling the Blocks

Throughout this section, refer to the Fabric Key at left to identify the fabric placements in the diagrams. Also, it's a good idea to review Assembly Line Piecing on page 13 before you get started. It's more efficient to do the same step for each block at the same time than to piece one entire block together at a time. Be sure to press as you go, and follow the arrows for pressing direction.

### SECTION ONE (Flower Top)

**STEP 1.** Sew thirty-six triangle sets (pressed toward Fabric B) to thirty-six triangle sets (pressed toward Fabric A), as shown in **Diagram 2.** Use twelve triangle sets of each Fabric A, and match up the same Fabric A's for each tulip. Position them right sides together and line up next to your sewing machine. Use the Continuous Seam tech-

nique on page 14 to join all thirty-six sets together. Pay close attention that the triangle sets are positioned the same way as shown in **Diagram 2.** Press seams toward the triangle set that has seams pressed to Fabric A, and cut joining threads. You will be making a total of thirty-six blocks, twelve of each Fabric A.

DIAGRAM 2

**STEP 2.** Sew the Step 1 triangle units together in pairs. Make sure the triangle sets are positioned as shown in **Diagram 3** and the Fabric A's match. Press. You will make a total of eighteen units, six of each Fabric A.

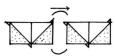

DIAGRAM 3

**STEP 3.** Sew the units from Step 2 to eighteen 4½ × 2½-inch pieces of Fabric A. See **Diagram 4.** Press toward Fabric A.

DIAGRAM 4

### SECTION TWO (Flower Base)

**STEP 1.** Sew eighteen 2½ × 1½-inch pieces of Fabric A (six of each Fabric A) to eighteen triangle sets (with seams pressed toward Fabric B). See **Diagram 5.** Press toward Fabric A.

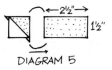

DIAGRAM 5

**STEP 2.** Sew eighteen triangle sets (with seams pressed toward Fabric B) to the right side of each of the units from Step 1. Make sure the triangle set being added is positioned as shown in **Diagram 6.** Press away from the new triangle set.

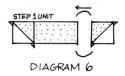

DIAGRAM 6

### FLOWER ASSEMBLY

**STEP 1.** Sew the units from Section One to the units from Section Two, as shown in **Diagram 7.** Press toward Section One. You should have a total of six tulips of each color for a grand total of eighteen tulip sections.

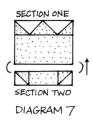

DIAGRAM 7

### SECTION THREE (Leaves)

**STEP 1.** Sew a 1½ × 44-inch strip of Fabric C to the right side of a 3½ × 44-inch strip of Fabric B. See **Diagram 8.** Press seam toward Fabric C.

**STEP 2.** Sew a 1½ × 44-inch strip of Fabric C to the left side of a 3½ × 44-inch strip of Fabric B. See **Diagram 9.** Press seam toward Fabric C.

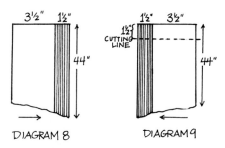

DIAGRAM 8          DIAGRAM 9

**STEP 3.** Stack the two strip sets (with Fabric C strips on opposite sides) and cut into 1½ × 4½-inch strips, referring to the cutting line in **Diagram 9**. Make eighteen cuts, for a total of eighteen strips from each strip set. Each set of eighteen strips will have Fabric C on opposite ends, as shown in **Diagram 10**.

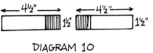

DIAGRAM 10

**STEP 4.** Sew eighteen 4½ × 1½-inch pieces of Fabric B to eighteen strips from Step 3. Make sure the strips from Step 3 are positioned as shown in **Diagram 11**. Press toward Fabric B.

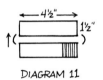

DIAGRAM 11

**STEP 5.** Sew eighteen 4½ × 2½-inch pieces of Fabric B to the remaining eighteen strips from Step 3, positioning the strips as shown in **Diagram 12**. Press toward Fabric B.

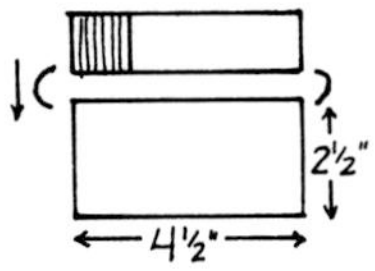

DIAGRAM 12

**STEP 6.** Sew the units from Step 4 to the units from Step 5 as shown in **Diagram 13**. Press toward the Step 4 units.

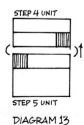

STEP 4 UNIT

STEP 5 UNIT

DIAGRAM 13

**SECTION FOUR (Stems)**

**STEP 1.** Take the eighteen units from Section Three (the leaves) and cut down the center of each unit as shown in **Diagram 14**. Use a see-through ruler to help locate the center of the units.

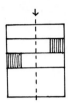

DIAGRAM 14

**STEP 2.** With right sides together, making sure the edges are even, sew the three 1 × 44-inch strips of Fabric C (stems) to the eighteen left-side leaf sections using the Continuous Seam method. You should be able to fit seven leaf sections on a 44-inch stem strip. Press toward the stem strips. Cut stem strips between leaf sections. See **Diagram 15**.

**STEP 3.** Using the Continuous Seam method, sew the eighteen right-side leaf sections to the stem strip/leaf units from Step 2. Press toward the stem strips. The finished block should look like **Diagram 16**.

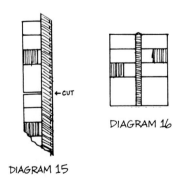

←CUT

DIAGRAM 16

DIAGRAM 15

**FLOWER AND STEM ASSEMBLY**

Sew the eighteen units from the flower section to the eighteen units from the stem/leaf section as shown in **Diagram 17**. Press toward the stem section.

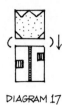

DIAGRAM 17

**The Lattice**

**STEP 1.** Lay out the tulip blocks according to the **Quilt Layout**, with three rows of six blocks each. Keep track of your layout while sewing on the lattice.

**STEP 2.** Sew the 1½ × 9½-inch Fabric B lattice strips to the right side of all the blocks *except* one block of each Fabric A. This will be the last block in each row. Press all seam allowances toward the lattice. See **Diagram 18**.

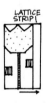

LATTICE STRIP

DIAGRAM 18

**STEP 3.** Sew one row of blocks together following the sequence of tulip fabrics in **Diagram 19**. The last block in the row will not have lattice on the right.

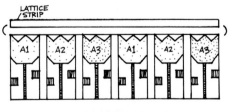

LATTICE STRIP

| A1 | A2 | A3 | A1 | A2 | A3 |

DIAGRAM 19

**STEP 4.** For rows two and three, follow the tulip fabric sequence illustrated in the **Quilt Layout**.

**STEP 5.** Sew a 1½ × 44-inch Fabric B lattice strip across the top of each row of tulips. See **Diagram 19**. Trim excess and press toward the lattice. Set aside five remaining lattice strips.

## The Checkerboard Rows

**STEP 1.** Sew together the six 1½ × 44-inch strips of Fabrics A and B, using one of each Fabric A and alternating the Fabric A and B strips. See **Diagram 20**. Press as you go, facing all seams toward Fabric A.

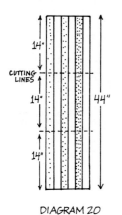

DIAGRAM 20

**STEP 2.** Cut the strip set into thirds referring to the cutting lines in **Diagram 20**. Each third will be approximately 14 inches. Resew those thirds together to make an 18½ × 14-inch strip set. See **Diagram 21**.

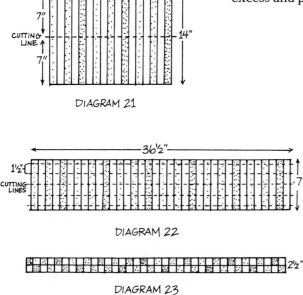

DIAGRAM 21

DIAGRAM 22

2½"

DIAGRAM 23

**STEP 3.** Cut the strip set from Step 2 in half as shown in **Diagram 21**. Resew the halves together to make a 36½ × 7-inch strip set. See **Diagram 22**.

**STEP 4.** From this 36½-inch strip, cut four 1½ × 36½-inch strips, referring to the cutting lines in **Diagram 22**. Rematch the strips so they form a checkerboard, and stitch them together. Make two 2½ × 36½-inch checkerboard sets that look like the one shown in **Diagram 23**.

## Putting It All Together

**STEP 1.** Sew a 1½ × 44-inch Fabric C lattice strip below each row of tulips and across the top edge of the top row of tulips. Trim the excess and press toward the lattice.

**STEP 2.** Stitch the three tulip rows together. Press toward the lattice.

**STEP 3.** Refer to Hints on Fitting a Checkerboard Border on page 29. Fit the checkerboard to the top and bottom of the quilt top and stitch. Press toward the lattice.

**STEP 4.** Sew 1½ × 44-inch lattice strips of Fabric C to the top and bottom of the quilt top. Trim excess and press.

**STEP 5.** Sew two of the five remaining 1½ × 44-inch strips of Fabric B lattice to the quilt top and bottom. Trim excess and press. Sew two of the strips to the quilt sides, using the fifth strip to add length to the side strips if necessary. Trim excess and press.

## Layering the Quilt

Arrange and baste the backing, batting, and top together following the directions for Layering the Quilt on page 32. Trim batting and backing to ¾ inch from the raw edge of the quilt top.

## Binding the Quilt

Using the strips cut from Fabric C, follow the directions on page 33 for Binding the Quilt.

## The Finishing Stitches

Outline your tulips by quilting ¼ inch away from the seam line, and stitch a tulip pattern inside each flower using the **Tulip Quilting Template**. Stitch a diagonal grid in the checkerboard rows.

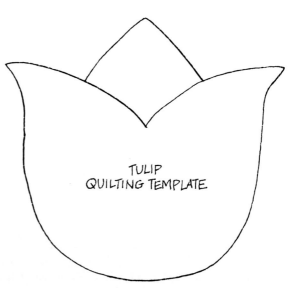

TULIP QUILTING TEMPLATE

# Autumn Leaves

48½"

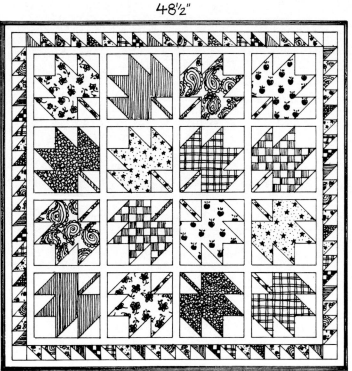

QUILT LAYOUT

48½"

## Large Quilt

Finished Quilt: 48½ × 48½ inches
Finished Block: 9 × 9 inches

**Materials**

Obvious directional prints are not recommended.

**FABRIC A** *(leaves, stems, sawtooth border)*
Use eight fabrics.
Blocks and Border        ⅓ yard
*each* of *eight* fabrics

**FABRIC B** *(block background, lattice, sawtooth border, one-inch border, corner squares)*
Blocks, Sawtooth
  Border, and Corner
  Squares               1½ yards
Lattice                      ½ yard
One-Inch Border        ¼ yard
  TOTAL             2¼ yards

**FABRIC C**
Binding                  ⅝ yard

**BACKING**            2 yards

**BATTING**            2 yards

Do you look forward to autumn each year, that wonderful season of crisp, clear days and juicy, red apples? Are you awed by the dazzling display of color in the trees around you? Well, here are some autumn leaves that won't disappear with the first snows of winter. Use the warm colors of autumn or your favorite decorator colors; Speedy Triangles and Assembly Line techniques make it quick and easy! Directions are given for both a large and a small version.

## Cutting Directions

Prewash and press all of your fabrics. Using a rotary cutter, see-through ruler, and cutting mat, prepare the strips as described in the first column in the chart below.

Then from those strips, cut the pieces listed in the second column. Some portions of the quilt need to be cut only once, so no additional cutting information will appear in the second column.

| | FIRST CUT | | SECOND CUT | |
|---|---|---|---|---|
| | NO. OF STRIPS | DIMENSIONS | NO. OF PIECES | DIMENSIONS |
| **FABRIC A** | LEAVES AND SAWTOOTH BORDER: from *each* of the *eight* fabrics, cut the following | | | |
| | 1 | 11 × 44-inch strip | 1 | 8 × 11-inch piece |
| | | | 1 | 10 × 10-inch piece |
| | | | 2 | 3½ × 6½-inch pieces |
| | | | 2 | 3½ × 3½-inch pieces |
| | STEMS: from *each* of the *eight* fabrics, cut the following | | | |
| | 2 | 1 × 6-inch strips | | |
| **FABRIC B** | BLOCKS | | | |
| | 2 | 10 × 44-inch strips | 8 | 10 × 10-inch pieces |
| | 3 | 3½ × 44-inch strips | 32 | 3½ × 3½-inch pieces |
| | LATTICE | | | |
| | **Before You Cut:** From three of the 44-inch strips, cut the strips as directed in the second column. The remaining seven strips require no further cutting. | | | |
| | 10 | 1½ × 44-inch strips | 12 | 1½ × 9½-inch pieces |
| | SAWTOOTH BORDER | | | |
| | 2 | 8 × 44-inch strips | 8 | 8 × approx. 11-inch pieces |
| | CORNER SQUARES | | | |
| | 4 | 2½ × 2½-inch squares | | |
| | ONE-INCH BORDER | | | |
| | 5 | 1½ × 44-inch strips | | |
| **FABRIC C** | BINDING | | | |
| | 5 | 3½ × 44-inch strips | | |

## Speedy Triangles

**STEP 1.** Refer to Speedy Triangle directions on page 11 for how to mark, sew, and cut.

**STEP 2.** For the blocks, position the 10 × 10-inch squares of Fabrics A and B with right sides together. You will have eight sets. On each set, mark a 3⅞-inch grid of four squares. See **Diagram 1**.

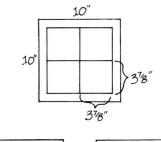

DIAGRAM 1

**STEP 3.** After sewing and cutting are complete, press seam allowances toward Fabric A. You will have made a total of sixty-four triangle sets, eight of each Fabric A.

**STEP 4.** For the sawtooth border, position the 8 × 11-inch pieces of Fabrics A and B with right sides together. On each of the eight sets, mark a 2⅞-inch grid of six squares, as shown in **Diagram 2**.

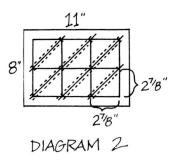

DIAGRAM 2

**STEP 5.** After sewing and cutting are complete, press seam allowances toward Fabric A. You will have a total of ninety-six triangle sets, twelve of each Fabric A. Set these triangle sets aside while you assemble the blocks.

## Assembling the Blocks

Throughout this section, refer to the Fabric Key to identify the fabric placements in the diagrams. Also, it's a good idea to review Assembly Line Piecing on page 13 before you get started. It's more efficient to do the same step for each block at the same time than to piece one entire block together at a time. Be sure to press as you go, and follow the arrows for pressing direction.

FABRIC KEY — FABRIC A (LEAVES); FABRIC B (BACKGROUND)

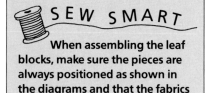

**SEW SMART** When assembling the leaf blocks, make sure the pieces are always positioned as shown in the diagrams and that the fabrics match.

### SECTION ONE

**STEP 1.** Sew sixteen of the 3½-inch triangle sets, two of each Fabric A, to sixteen 3½ × 3½-inch pieces of Fabric B. Position them right sides together and line them up next to your sewing machine. Use the Continuous Seam technique on page 14 to join all sixteen sets together. Pay close attention that the triangle sets are positioned as shown in **Diagram 3**. Press seams toward Fabric B and cut joining threads.

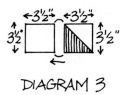

DIAGRAM 3

In each of the remaining steps, use the same Continuous Seam method. You will be making two blocks each of the eight different leaf fabrics, for a total of sixteen blocks. Match up the same Fabric A's for each leaf.

**STEP 2.** Sew sixteen of the 3½-inch triangle sets, two of each Fabric A, to the right side of the Step 1 units. Press toward the Step 1 unit. See **Diagram 4**.

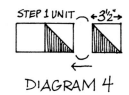

DIAGRAM 4

### SECTION TWO

Sew sixteen of the 3½-inch triangle sets to the 6½ × 3½-inch pieces of Fabric A, as shown in **Diagram 5**. Press toward Fabric A.

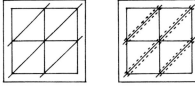

DIAGRAM 5

### SECTION THREE (Stems)

**STEP 1.** Lay out sixteen 3½-inch squares of Fabric B. Using your ruler and the rotary cutter, cut the 3½-inch squares on the diagonal. See **Diagram 6**.

DIAGRAM 6

**STEP 2.** With right sides together, line up and sew the 1 × 6-inch strips of Fabric A to the diagonal cut of the left triangle halves, as shown in **Diagram 7**. Let the strip overhang at least ½ inch on both ends. You are sewing on the bias, so be careful not to stretch the triangle.

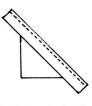

DIAGRAM 7

**STEP 3.** Press seam allowances toward the stem. See **Diagram 8**.

**STEP 4.** With right sides together, sew the other half of the 3½-inch square to the 1-inch strip, making sure the points line up. See **Diagram 9**. Press seam toward the stem.

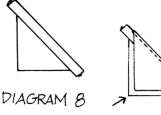

DIAGRAM 8

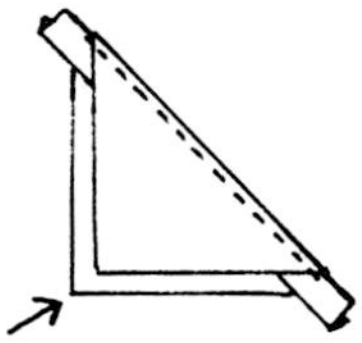

DIAGRAM 9

**STEP 5.** Using your see-through ruler and rotary cutter, trim the excess of the stem as shown in **Diagram 10**. The finished size of the square is 3½ × 3½ inches. See **Diagram 11**.

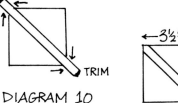

DIAGRAM 10

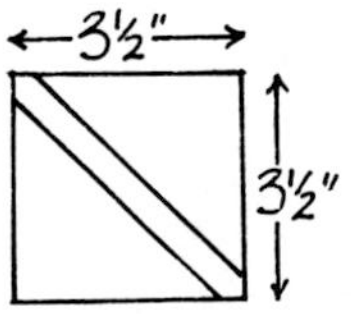

DIAGRAM 11

## SECTION FOUR

**STEP 1.** Sew the remaining sixteen 3½-inch triangle sets to the sixteen 3½ × 3½-inch pieces of Fabric A. Press toward the triangle sets. See **Diagram 12**.

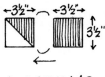

DIAGRAM 12

**STEP 2.** Sew the Step 1 units to the 3½-inch-square stem sections. Press toward the Step 1 units. See **Diagram 13**.

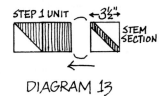

DIAGRAM 13

## Leaf Assembly

Sew the three sections together, making sure the units are positioned as shown in **Diagram 14**. Press all seams toward Section Two.

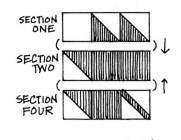

DIAGRAM 14

## The Lattice

**STEP 1.** Lay out the leaf blocks according to the **Quilt Layout**, with four rows of four blocks each. In each row, make sure that the two blocks on the left face one direction and the two blocks on the right face the opposite direction. Keep track of your layout while sewing on the lattice.

**STEP 2.** Sew the 1½ × 9½-inch Fabric B lattice strips to the right side of twelve blocks. The last block in each row will not have lattice on the right. See **Diagram 15**. Press all seam allowances toward the lattice.

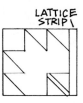

DIAGRAM 15

**STEP 3.** Sew four blocks together to make a row of four leaves. See **Diagram 16**. Press. Repeat for the remaining three rows.

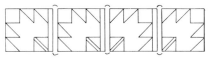

DIAGRAM 16

**STEP 4.** Sew 1½ × 44-inch lattice strips to the bottom of each row of blocks and to the top of the top row. Trim excess and press. Sew the four rows together. Make sure the leaves in the top two rows face up and the leaves in the bottom two rows face down. Press.

**STEP 5.** Sew lattice strips to the quilt sides. Trim and press.

## The Sawtooth Border

**STEP 1.** Arrange the 2½-inch triangle sets in a pleasing order, using one each of the eight different Fabric A's. Make sure the triangles are positioned as shown in **Diagram 17**.

DIAGRAM 17

DIAGRAM 18

DIAGRAM 19

**STEP 2.** Using the Continuous Seam technique, sew the triangles together in pairs, then sew the pairs together to make fours. See **Diagram 18.** Then sew the fours together to make sets of eight, as shown in **Diagram 19.** Make eight sets of eight.

**STEP 3.** Sew sets of eight together to make four sets of sixteen. Use the extra triangle sets to add five triangle sets to each strip of sixteen. Make sure the five added triangle sets are in the same sequence of fabrics. You should have a total of four strips of twenty-one triangle sets each.

**STEP 4.** Fit, pin, and sew the border to the quilt top and bottom. Press toward the lattice.

**STEP 5.** Compare the remaining two borders to the sides of the quilt. Measure up to but do not include the sawtooth borders you just added to the top and bottom. Add an extra ½ inch to each strip so they will fit correctly after corner squares are added. Make these adjustments by slightly taking in or letting out a few seam allowances so that you won't have uneven triangle sets on the ends.

**STEP 6.** Sew the 2½-inch Fabric B corner squares to each end of the side border strips. Pin in position and sew the border strips to the sides of the quilt.

## One-Inch Border

**STEP 1.** Sew the 1½ × 44-inch Fabric B border strips to the quilt top and bottom. Trim excess and press all seams toward Fabric B.

**STEP 2.** Sew two of the strips to the quilt sides, using the fifth strip to add length if necessary. Trim and press.

## Layering the Quilt

Arrange and baste the backing, batting, and top together following the directions for Layering the Quilt on page 32. Trim batting and backing to ½ inch from the raw edge of the quilt.

## Binding the Quilt

Using the 3½ × 44-inch strips cut from Fabric C, follow the directions on page 33 for Binding the Quilt. Cut the fifth strip in half. Add one half to each of the side binding strips to achieve the needed length.

## The Finishing Stitches

Outline the leaves and the sawtooth border by quilting ¼ inch away from the seam line as shown in **Diagrams 20 and 21.**

DIAGRAM 20

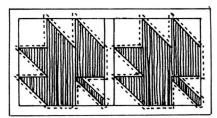

DIAGRAM 21

# Small Quilt

Finished Quilt: 28½ × 28½ inches
Finished Block: 4½ × 4½ inches

## Materials

Obvious directional prints are not recommended.

**FABRIC A** *(leaves, stems, sawtooth border)*
Use eight fabrics.
Blocks and Border                ¼ yard
*each* of *eight* fabrics

**FABRIC B** *(block background, lattice, sawtooth border, one-inch border, corner squares)*

| | |
|---|---|
| Blocks, Sawtooth Border, and Corner Squares | 1 yard |
| Lattice and One-Inch Border | ⅝ yard |
| TOTAL | 1⅝ yards |

**FABRIC C**
Binding                ½ yard

**BACKING**                1 yard

**BATTING**                1 yard

## Before You Begin

Many of the assembly techniques for the Small Quilt are the same as those given earlier for the Large Quilt. Throughout these directions, you will be referred back to the Large Quilt for steps that are identical. Specific assembly directions needed for the Small Quilt are given in detail here. Note that the layout is the same for both quilts.

## Cutting Directions

Prewash and press all of your fabrics. Using a rotary cutter, see-through ruler, and cutting mat, prepare the strips as described in the first column in the chart below. Then from those strips, cut the pieces listed in the second column. Some portions of the quilt need to be cut only once, so no additional cutting information will appear in the second column.

## Speedy Triangles

**STEP 1.** Refer to Speedy Triangle directions on page 11 for how to mark, sew, and cut.

**STEP 2.** For the blocks and saw-tooth border, position the 7 × 12-inch pieces of Fabrics A and B with right sides together. You will have eight sets. On each of the eight sets, mark a 2⅜-inch grid of eight squares. See **Diagram 22**.

**STEP 3.** After sewing and cutting are complete, press seam allowances toward Fabric A. You will have made a total of 128 triangle sets, sixteen of each Fabric A.

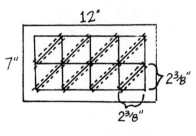

DIAGRAM 22

## Assembling the Blocks

Throughout this section, refer to the Fabric Key to identify the fabric placements in the diagrams. Also, it's a good idea to review Assembly Line Piecing on page 13 before you get started. It's

FABRIC KEY

FABRIC A (LEAVES)

FABRIC B (BACKGROUND)

| | FIRST CUT | | SECOND CUT | |
|---|---|---|---|---|
| | **NO. OF STRIPS** | **DIMENSIONS** | **NO. OF PIECES** | **DIMENSIONS** |
| **FABRIC A** | LEAVES, STEMS, AND SAWTOOTH BORDER: from *each* of the *eight* fabrics, cut the following | | | |
| | 1 | 7 × 44-inch strip | 1 | 7 × 12-inch piece |
| | | | 2 | 2 × 2-inch pieces |
| | | | 2 | 2 × 3½-inch pieces |
| | | | 2 | 1 × 4-inch pieces |
| **FABRIC B** | BLOCKS AND SAWTOOTH BORDER | | | |
| | 2 | 7 × 44-inch strips | 8 | 7 × 12-inch pieces |
| | 2 | 2 × 44-inch strips | 32 | 2 × 2-inch pieces |
| | LATTICE | | | |
| | 3 | 1⅝ × 44-inch strips | | |
| | **Before You Cut:** From two of the 44-inch strips, cut the pieces as directed in the second column. The remaining two strips require no further cutting. | | | |
| | 4 | 1¼ × 44-inch strips | 12 | 1¼ × 5-inch pieces |
| | CORNER SQUARES | | | |
| | 4 | 2 × 2-inch squares | | |
| | ONE-INCH BORDER | | | |
| | 4 | 1⅝ × 44-inch strips | | |
| **FABRIC C** | BINDING | | | |
| | 4 | 2¾ × 44-inch strips | | |

more efficient to do the same step for each block at the same time than to piece one entire block together at a time. Be sure to press as you go, and follow the arrows for pressing direction. You will be making two blocks of each Fabric A, for a total of sixteen blocks.

## SECTION ONE

**STEP 1.** Using the Continuous Seam technique, sew sixteen of the 2 × 2-inch triangle sets, two of each Fabric A, to sixteen 2 × 2-inch pieces of Fabric B. Position the triangles as shown in **Diagram 23**. Press toward Fabric B.

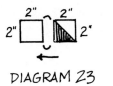

DIAGRAM 23

**STEP 2.** Sew sixteen triangle sets to the Step 1 units. Press toward the Step 1 units. See **Diagram 24**.

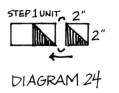

DIAGRAM 24

## SECTION TWO

Sew sixteen 2 × 3½-inch pieces of Fabric A to sixteen triangle sets as shown in **Diagram 25**. Press.

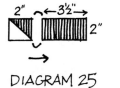

DIAGRAM 25

## SECTION THREE (Stems)

Use the sixteen 1 × 4-inch strips of Fabric A and the 2 × 2-inch squares of Fabric B to make the stem sections. Follow Steps 1 through 5 of Section Three of the Large Quilt, beginning on page 137.

## SECTION FOUR

**STEP 1.** Sew sixteen triangle sets to sixteen 2 × 2-inch pieces of Fabric A. Press toward the triangle sets. See **Diagram 26**.

DIAGRAM 26

**STEP 2.** Sew the 2-inch stem sections to the right side of the Step 1 units as shown in **Diagram 27**. Press toward the Step 1 units.

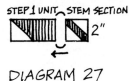

DIAGRAM 27

## Leaf Assembly

Sew the three sections together, making sure the units are positioned as shown in **Diagram 28**. Press all seams toward Section Two.

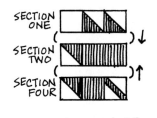

DIAGRAM 28

## The Lattice

**STEP 1.** Refer to the lattice directions for the Large Quilt beginning on page 138. Sew the 1¼ × 5-inch strips to the right side of twelve blocks. Press all seam allowances toward the lattice.

**STEP 2.** Sew the blocks together into rows. The last block in each row will not have lattice on the right. Sew the remaining 1¼-inch strips between the four rows of blocks. Use the two 44-inch pieces and the piece left after cutting the

5-inch strips. Trim excess and press toward the lattice.

**STEP 3.** Cut one 1⅝ × 44-inch Fabric B lattice strip in half. Sew one half to each side of the quilt. Trim and press. Sew the other two 1⅝-inch strips to the quilt top and bottom. Trim and press.

## The Sawtooth Border

Follow the directions for the sawtooth border under the Large Quilt beginning on page 138. Use the remaining 2-inch triangle sets for the border. You should use approximately fifteen triangle sets per side, with 2-inch corner squares.

## One-Inch Border

**STEP 1.** (For simplicity, I am calling this a one-inch border even though it technically measures 1⅛-inch on the finished quilt.) Sew the 1⅝ × 44-inch Fabric B border strips to the quilt top and bottom. Trim excess and press all seams toward Fabric B.

**STEP 2.** Sew the remaining two strips to the quilt sides. Trim and press.

## Layering the Quilt

Arrange and baste the backing, batting, and top together following the directions for Layering the Quilt on page 32. Trim batting and backing to ¼ inch from the raw edge of the quilt top.

## Binding the Quilt

Using the four 2¾ × 44-inch strips cut from Fabric C, follow the directions for Binding the Quilt on page 33.

## The Finishing Stitches

Outline the leaves and the sawtooth border by quilting ¼ inch away from the seam line.

# Frosty & Friends

27"

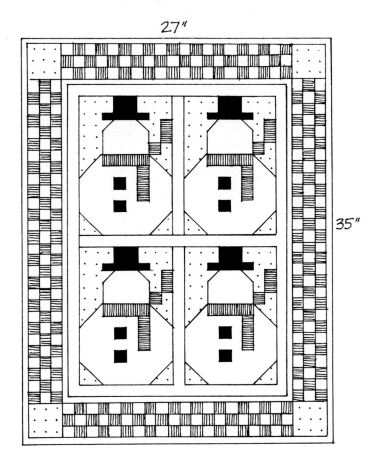

QUILT LAYOUT

35"

Finished Quilt: 27 × 35 inches
Finished Block: 8 × 12 inches

## Materials

Obvious directional prints are not recommended.

**FABRIC A** *(snowmen, checkerboard)*

| | |
|---|---|
| Blocks | ½ yard |
| Checkerboard | ⅓ yard |
| TOTAL | ⅞ yard |

**FABRIC B** *(block background, lattice)*

| | |
|---|---|
| Blocks | ½ yard |
| Lattice | ¼ yard |
| TOTAL | ¾ yard |

**FABRIC C** *(hats, buttons)*

| | |
|---|---|
| Hats and Buttons | ⅛ yard |

**FABRIC D** *(scarves, checkerboard)*

| | |
|---|---|
| Blocks | ⅛ yard |
| Checkerboard | ⅓ yard |
| TOTAL | ½ yard |

**FABRIC E** *(border, corner squares, binding)*

| | |
|---|---|
| Border One, Corner Squares, and Binding | ⅝ yard |

| | |
|---|---|
| **BATTING** | 1 yard |
| **BACKING** | 1 yard |

Pray for snow! And when the flurries start to fly, settle down in your cozy sewing room to whip up some snowmen who are guaranteed not to melt. Frosty and Friends makes a wonderful holiday gift, especially since it is so quick and easy to put together.

## Cutting Directions

Prewash and press all of your fabrics. Using a rotary cutter, see-through ruler, and cutting mat, prepare the strips as described in the first column in the chart below.

Then from those strips, cut the pieces listed in the second column. Some portions of the quilt need to be cut only once, so no additional cutting information will appear in the second column.

| | FIRST CUT | | SECOND CUT | |
| --- | --- | --- | --- | --- |
| | **NO. OF STRIPS** | **DIMENSIONS** | **NO. OF PIECES** | **DIMENSIONS** |
| **FABRIC A** | **SNOWMEN** | | | |
| | 1 | 5 × 44-inch strip | 2 | 5 × 14-inch pieces |
| | | | 1 | 4 × 10-inch piece |
| | 2 | 1½ × 44-inch strips | 4 | 1½ × 3½-inch pieces |
| | | | 16 | 1½ × 2½-inch pieces |
| | | | 8 | 1½ × 1½-inch pieces |
| | 2 | 2½ × 44-inch strips | 8 | 2½ × 3½-inch pieces |
| | | | 8 | 2½ × 4½-inch pieces |
| | **CHECKERBOARD BORDER** | | | |
| | 7 | 1½ × 40-inch strips | | |
| **FABRIC B** | **BACKGROUND** | | | |
| | 1 | 1½ × 44-inch strip | 4 | 1½ × 1½-inch pieces |
| | | | 4 | 1½ × 2½-inch pieces |
| | | | 8 | 1½ × 2-inch pieces |
| | 1 | 2½ × 44-inch strip | 4 | 2½ × 3½-inch pieces |
| | | | 8 | 2½ × 2½-inch pieces |
| | 1 | 5 × 44-inch strip | 2 | 5 × 14-inch pieces |
| | | | 1 | 4 × 10-inch piece |
| | **LATTICE** | | | |
| | **Before You Cut:** From one of the 44-inch strips, cut the pieces as directed in the second column. The remaining four 44-inch strips require no further cutting. | | | |
| | 5 | 1½ × 44-inch strips | 2 | 1½ × 12½-inch pieces |
| **FABRIC C** | **HATS** | | | |
| | 1 | 1½ × 44-inch strip | 8 | 1½ × 1-inch pieces |
| | | | 8 | 1½ × 1½-inch pieces |
| | 1 | 2½ × 44-inch strip | 4 | 2½ × 2½-inch pieces |

| FIRST CUT | | SECOND CUT | |
|---|---|---|---|
| NO. OF STRIPS | DIMENSIONS | NO. OF PIECES | DIMENSIONS |
| **FABRIC D** | **SCARVES** | | |
| 2 | 1½ × 44-inch strips | 4 | 1½ × 1½-inch pieces |
| | | 4 | 1½ × 2½-inch pieces |
| | | 4 | 1½ × 3½-inch pieces |
| | | 4 | 1½ × 4½-inch pieces |
| | **CHECKERBOARD BORDER** | | |
| 7 | 1½ × 40-inch strips | | |
| **FABRIC E** | **BORDER ONE** | | |
| 4 | 1 × 44-inch strips | | |
| | **CORNER SQUARES** | | |
| 4 | 3½ × 3½-inch squares | | |
| | **BINDING** | | |
| 4 | 2¾ × 44-inch strips | | |

## Speedy Triangles

**STEP 1.** Refer to Speedy Triangle directions on page 11 for how to mark, sew, and cut. You will be making two different size triangle sets to complete this project.

**STEP 2.** Position the 4 × 10-inch pieces of Fabrics A and B with right sides together. Draw a 1⅞-inch grid of four squares. See **Diagram 1.**

**STEP 3.** After sewing and cutting are complete, press seam allowances toward Fabric A. You will have made a total of eight 1½-inch triangle sets.

**STEP 4.** For the second group of triangle sets, you will use two pieces of Fabric A and two pieces of Fabric B. Match up two pairs of 5 × 14-inch pieces of Fabrics A and B. Mark a 2⅞-inch grid of four squares on each pair. See **Diagram 2.**

**STEP 5.** After sewing and cutting are complete, press seam allowances toward Fabric A. You will have made a total of sixteen 2½-inch triangle sets.

## Assembling the Blocks

Throughout this section, refer to the Fabric Key to identify the fabric placement in the diagrams. Also, it's a good idea to review Assembly Line Piecing on page 13 before you get started. It is more efficient to do the same step for each block at the same time than to piece one entire block together at a time. Be sure to press as you go, and follow the arrows for pressing direction.

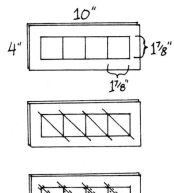

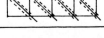
DIAGRAM 1

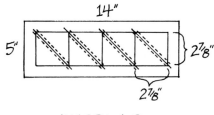
DIAGRAM 2

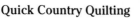

## SECTION ONE (Hat)

**STEP 1.** Sew eight 1½ × 1-inch pieces of Fabric C to eight 1½ × 2-inch pieces of Fabric B. Position them right sides together and line them up next to your sewing machine. Stitch the first set together, then butt the next set directly behind them and continue sewing each set without breaking your seam. Press seams toward Fabric C and cut joining threads. See **Diagram 3**.

DIAGRAM 3

In each of the remaining steps, use the same Continuous Seam method (for a refresher on this technique, see page 14). You will be making a total of four blocks.

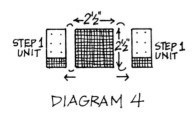

**Pay close attention to the diagrams as you assemble the pieces for the blocks. Be sure your triangle sets are facing the same way as shown in the diagrams.**

**STEP 2.** Sew the units from Step 1 to two sides of four 2½ × 2½-inch pieces of Fabric C. Press seams toward units from Step 1. See **Diagram 4**.

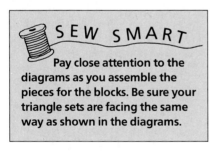

DIAGRAM 4

**STEP 3.** Sew four 2½ × 2½-inch pieces of Fabric B to each side of the four units from Step 2. Press seams to the Step 2 units. See **Diagram 5**.

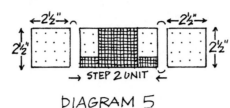

DIAGRAM 5

## SECTION TWO (Head)

**STEP 1.** Sew four 1½-inch triangle sets to each side of four 1½ × 2½-inch pieces of Fabric A. Press seams to Fabric A. See **Diagram 6**.

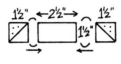

DIAGRAM 6

**STEP 2.** Sew the units from Step 1 to four 2½ × 4½-inch pieces of Fabric A. Press seams to Fabric A. See **Diagram 7**.

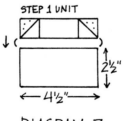

DIAGRAM 7

**STEP 3.** Sew four 1½ × 2½-inch pieces of Fabric B to four 1½ × 2½-inch pieces of Fabric D. Press seams to Fabric D. See **Diagram 8**.

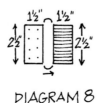

DIAGRAM 8

**STEP 4.** Sew four 1½ × 1½-inch pieces of Fabric D to four 1½ × 1½-inch pieces of Fabric B. Press seams to Fabric D. See **Diagram 9**.

DIAGRAM 9

**STEP 5.** Sew the units from Step 3 to the units from Step 4. Be sure you place the fabrics in the positions shown in **Diagram 10**. Press seams toward the Step 3 units.

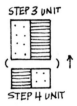

DIAGRAM 10

**STEP 6.** Sew the units from Step 5 to the units from Step 2. Press seams to the Step 5 unit. Sew those units to four 2½ × 3½-inch pieces of Fabric B. Press seams to Fabric B. See **Diagram 11**.

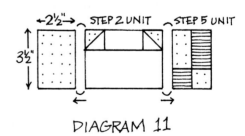

DIAGRAM 11

## SECTION THREE (Body)

**STEP 1.** Sew four 1½ × 1½-inch pieces of Fabric C to four 1½ × 1½-inch pieces of Fabric A. Press seams to Fabric C. See **Diagram 12**.

DIAGRAM 12

**STEP 2.** Sew the units from Step 1 to four 1½ × 2½-inch pieces of Fabric A. See **Diagram 13**.

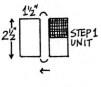

DIAGRAM 13

**STEP 3.** Sew four 1½ × 1½-inch pieces of Fabric A to four 1½ × 1½-inch pieces of Fabric C. Press seams to Fabric C. See **Diagram 14**.

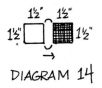

DIAGRAM 14

**STEP 4.** Sew the units from Step 2 to the units from Step 3. Press seams toward the Step 3 units. See **Diagram 15**.

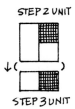

DIAGRAM 15

**STEP 5.** Sew the units from Step 4 to four 1½ × 2½-inch pieces of Fabric A. Press seams to Fabric A. See **Diagram 16**.

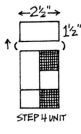

DIAGRAM 16

**STEP 6.** Sew four 1½ × 3½-inch pieces of Fabric A to four 1½ × 3½-inch pieces of Fabric D. Press seams to Fabric D. See **Diagram 17**.

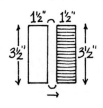

DIAGRAM 17

**STEP 7.** Sew the units from Step 6 to four 1½ × 2½-inch pieces of Fabric A. Press seams to the Step 6 units. See **Diagram 18**.

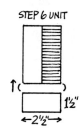

DIAGRAM 18

**STEP 8.** Sew the units from Step 5 to the units from Step 7. Press seams to the Step 7 units. See **Diagram 19**.

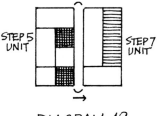

DIAGRAM 19

**STEP 9.** Sew four 1½ × 4½-inch pieces of Fabric D to the units from Step 8. Press seams to Fabric D. See **Diagram 20**.

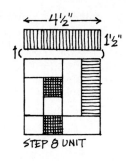

DIAGRAM 20

**STEP 10.** Sew the units from Step 9 to four 2½ × 4½-inch pieces of Fabric A. Press seams to Fabric A. See **Diagram 21**.

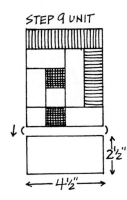

DIAGRAM 21

**STEP 11.** Sew eight 2½-inch triangle sets to eight 2½ × 3½-inch pieces of Fabric A. On four of these units, have the triangle sets facing as shown on the left of **Diagram 22**. On the other four units, have the triangle sets facing the opposite way, as shown on the right in the diagram. Press seams to Fabric A.

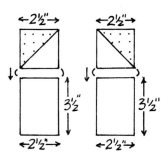

DIAGRAM 22

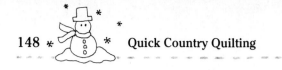

**STEP 12.** Sew eight 2½-inch triangle sets to the units from Step 11. Be sure to refer to **Diagram 23** as you position the triangle sets. Four of the units must have the sets positioned as shown on the left of the diagram, and four units should be positioned as shown on the right. Press seams toward Step 11 units.

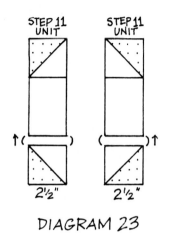

DIAGRAM 23

**STEP 13.** Sew units from Step 12 to each side of the units from Step 10. Refer to **Diagram 24** to be sure you position the Step 12 units properly. Press seams to the Step 10 units.

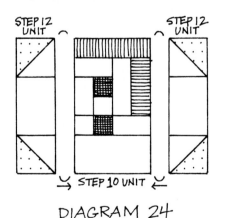

DIAGRAM 24

## SECTION ASSEMBLY

**STEP 1.** Sew the units from Section One to the units from Section Two. Press seams toward Section One. See **Diagram 25.**

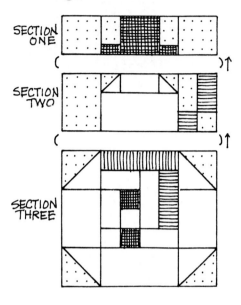

DIAGRAM 25

**STEP 2.** Sew the units from Section Three to the units from Step 1. Press seams to the Step 1 units. Your Frosty blocks are now complete!

## The Lattice

**STEP 1.** Sew the 1½ × 12½-inch strips to the right side of two blocks. Press all seams toward the lattice. Sew a block to the right side of each of those lattice strips to make two rows of two snowmen. See **Diagram 26.**

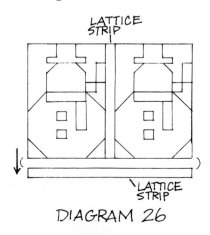

DIAGRAM 26

**STEP 2.** Cut one 1½ × 44-inch lattice strip in half. Sew one half to the bottom of each row. Trim the excess and press all seams toward the lattice. Sew the two rows together. Press.

**STEP 3.** Sew a lattice strip to the quilt top. Trim the excess and press. Sew lattice strips to the quilt sides. Trim and press.

## Border One

**STEP 1.** Sew 1 × 44-inch Fabric E border strips to the quilt top and bottom. Trim the excess and press all seams toward the border.

**STEP 2.** Sew border strips to the quilt sides. Trim and press.

## Triple Checkerboard Border

**STEP 1.** Sew together seven 1½ × 40-inch strips of Fabrics A and D, alternating the fabrics. See **Diagram 27.** Press all seams toward Fabric D as you go.

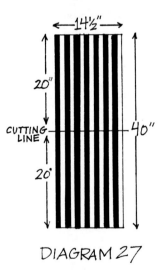

DIAGRAM 27

**STEP 2.** Cut the strip set in half across the width, referring to the cutting line in **Diagram 27**. Resew the halves together so the strip set is now 28½ × 20 inches. See **Diagram 28**.

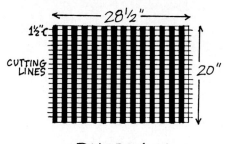

DIAGRAM 28

**STEP 3.** From the strip set made in Step 2, cut twelve 1½ × 28½-inch strips. Refer to the cutting lines shown in **Diagram 28**.

**STEP 4.** Refer to Hints on Fitting a Checkerboard Border on page 29. Fit one strip cut in Step 3 to the top edge of the quilt. Match a second and third strip to the first strip. Make sure you flip the position of the middle strip (so the right end becomes the left end) to create the checkerboard effect. See **Diagram 29**. Sew the three strips together and then sew to the quilt top. Repeat to create the checkerboard border for the bottom of the quilt.

DIAGRAM 29

**STEP 5.** Repeat the same fitting process described in Step 4 for the sides. Compare the strips to the quilt sides and measure up to but do not include the checkerboard borders you just added to the top and bottom. Then allow ¼ inch on both ends of each strip so they will fit correctly after the corner squares are added. After you have fit the strips and assembled the checkerboard borders, sew 3½-inch corner squares to each end of the borders. See **Diagram 30**. Pin the borders in position and sew to the quilt sides.

DIAGRAM 30

## Layering the Quilt

Arrange and baste the backing, batting, and top together following the directions for Layering the Quilt on page 32. Trim batting and backing to ¼ inch from the raw edge of the quilt top.

## Binding the Quilt

Using the 2¾ × 44-inch strips cut from Fabric E, follow the directions on page 33 for Binding the Quilt. Bind the sides first, then the top and bottom.

## The Finishing Stitches

Quilt in the ditch around the snowmen bodies as well as around their accessories (hats, scarves, and buttons). In the background, randomly stitch some snowflakes using the **Snowflake Templates** below. To make the templates, draw paper or cardboard circles of the desired size. (I have provided circles the same size as those on my quilt, but you can make yours larger or smaller if you wish.) Trace around the circles onto the background fabric. Then use a ruler to draw the four lines that cross in the middle. Stitch only on the lines. Do not stitch on the circles. A couple strands of white embroidery floss will stand out even better than quilting thread.

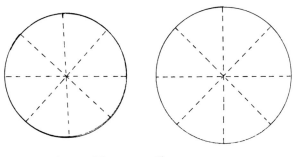

SNOWFLAKE TEMPLATES

# Trio of Trees

33"

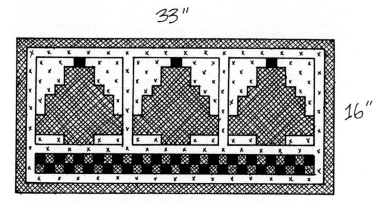

16"

QUILT LAYOUT

$A$dd to the festive spirit in your home with this trio of holiday decorations. The Christmas Tree Wallhanging is the perfect size to fit over a mantle or nestle above a jelly cupboard in the kitchen. The extra blocks you don't use for the wallhanging can be transformed into a Christmas card holder and a pair of plump seasonal pillows. Since these projects all go together quickly with the Speedy Strip technique, they make great last-minute gift ideas.

## Christmas Tree Wallhanging

(shown on wall in the photograph)

Finished Quilt: 33 × 16 inches
Finished Block: 9 × 9 inches

### Materials

The yardages given here are enough to complete six blocks. Three blocks are used for the wallhanging, one for the cardholder, and two for the pillow tops. Directional print may be used for Fabric A only; it is not recommended for Fabrics B or C.

**FABRIC A** *(trees, checkerboard, binding)*

| | |
|---|---|
| Blocks | ½ yard |
| | (⅔ yard if directional print is used) |
| Checkerboard | ⅛ yard |
| Binding | ½ yard |
| TOTAL | 1⅛ yards |
| | (1½ yards if using directional print) |

**FABRIC B** *(block background, lattice)*

| | |
|---|---|
| Blocks | ⅜ yard |
| Lattice | ¼ yard |
| TOTAL | ⅝ yard |

**FABRIC C** *(stars, checkerboard)*

| | |
|---|---|
| Block | ⅛ yard |
| Checkerboard | ⅛ yard |
| TOTAL | ¼ yard |

**BACKING** ⅝ yard

**BATTING** ⅝ yard

## Cutting Directions

Prewash and press all of your fabrics. Using a rotary cutter, see-through ruler, and cutting mat, prepare the strips as described in the two charts below. The first chart tells you how to cut the strips for the tree blocks. The second chart explains how to cut pieces for the rest of the quilt.

### CUTTING THE STRIPS

Refer to the fabric requirements for the *blocks only.* Cut the block yardage in half lengthwise (on the fold) so you will have two approx-imately 22-inch-wide pieces. From these pieces, cut the strips for Fabrics A, B, and C. Refer to the **Fabrics A and B Cutting Diagrams** as you work.

**SEW SMART**

For a directional fabric, cut strips so the direction of the print is parallel to the length of the strip.

| CUTTING THE STRIPS | FIRST CUT | | SECOND CUT | |
|---|---|---|---|---|
| | NO. OF STRIPS | DIMENSIONS | NO. OF PIECES | DIMENSIONS |
| **FABRIC A** | TREES | | | |
| | 1 | 3½ × 22-inch strip | | |
| | 1 | 9½ × 22-inch strip | | |
| | 1 | 3½ × 11-inch strip | | |
| | 1 | 5½ × 11-inch strip | | |
| | 1 | 7½ × 22-inch strip | | |
| **FABRIC B** | BACKGROUND | | | |
| | 2 | 1½ × 22-inch strips | | |
| | 2 | 3½ × 22-inch strips | | |
| | 2 | 2½ × 11-inch strips | | |
| | 2 | 3½ × 11-inch strips | | |
| | 2 | 4½ × 11-inch strips | | |
| **FABRIC C** | STAR | | | |
| | 1 | 1½ × 11-inch strip | | |

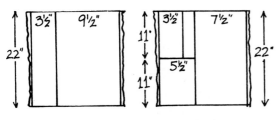

FABRIC A CUTTING DIAGRAMS                FABRIC B CUTTING DIAGRAMS

## CUTTING THE OTHER QUILT PIECES

| | FIRST CUT | | SECOND CUT | |
|---|---|---|---|---|
| | NO. OF STRIPS | DIMENSIONS | NO. OF PIECES | DIMENSIONS |
| **FABRIC A** | CHECKERBOARD | | | |
| | 2 | 1½ × 44-inch strips | | |
| | BINDING | | | |
| | 3 | 5½ × 44-inch strips | | |
| **FABRIC B** | LATTICE | | | |
| | **Before You Cut:** From two 44-inch strips cut the shorter strips as directed in the second column. It is important that you cut one 9½-inch strip from *each* of the two 44-inch strips. The approximately 34½-inch strips that remain will be used in the lattice. | | | |
| | 4 | 1½ × 44-inch strips | 2 | 1½ × 9½-inch pieces |
| **FABRIC C** | CHECKERBOARD | | | |
| | 2 | 1½ × 44-inch strips | | |

### Sewing the Strip Sets

Sew the strips together following **Diagrams 1 through 6.** Use accurate ¼-inch seam allowances. Be sure to press seams toward Fabrics A and C as you go. Refer to the Fabric Key for fabric identification. All finished strip sets will be 9½ inches wide.

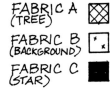

FABRIC KEY
FABRIC A (TREE)
FABRIC B (BACKGROUND)
FABRIC C (STAR)

**STRIP SET 1.** Use one 1½ × 11-inch strip of Fabric C and two 4½ × 11-inch strips of Fabric B. See **Diagram 1.**

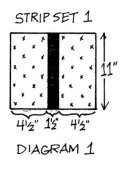

STRIP SET 1

4½"  1½"  4½"

DIAGRAM 1

**STRIP SET 2.** Use one 3½ × 22-inch strip of Fabric A and two 3½ × 22-inch strips of Fabric B. See **Diagram 2.**

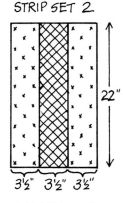

STRIP SET 2

22"

3½"  3½"  3½"

DIAGRAM 2

**STRIP SET 3.** Use one 5½ × 11-inch strip of Fabric A and two 2½ × 11-inch strips of Fabric B. See **Diagram 3.**

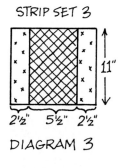

STRIP SET 3

11"

2½"  5½"  2½"

DIAGRAM 3

**STRIP SET 4.** Use one 7½ × 22-inch strip of Fabric A and two 1½ × 22-inch strips of Fabric B. See **Diagram 4.**

**STRIP SET 5.** Use one 9½ × 22-inch strip of Fabric A. No sewing here! See **Diagram 5.**

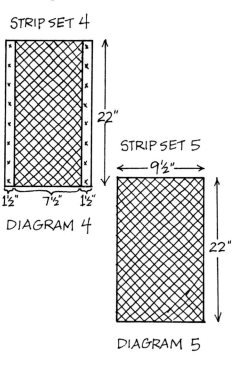

STRIP SET 4

22"

1½"  7½"  1½"

DIAGRAM 4

STRIP SET 5

9½"

22"

DIAGRAM 5

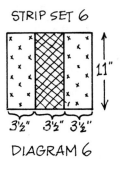

**STRIP SET 6.** Use one 3½ × 11-inch strip of Fabric A and two 3½ × 11-inch strips of Fabric B. See **Diagram 6.**

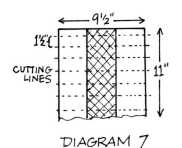

STRIP SET 6

11"

3½"   3½"   3½"

DIAGRAM 6

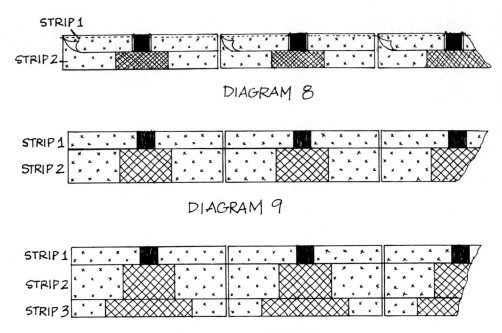

STRIP 1
STRIP 2

DIAGRAM 8

STRIP 1
STRIP 2

DIAGRAM 9

STRIP 1
STRIP 2
STRIP 3

DIAGRAM 10

### Stacking and Cutting the Strip Sets

**STEP 1.** Make two stacks of the strip sets, one with the three 11-inch-long sets, and the other with the three 22-inch-long sets.

**STEP 2.** From the 11-inch-long sets, cut six 1½ × 9½-inch strips of each, as shown in **Diagram 7.** Cut through all three layers at once. In the same way, from the 22-inch-long sets, cut six 2½ × 9½-inch strips of each. (You *may* be able to cut seven strips from each set for an extra block.)

9½"

1½"

CUTTING LINES

11"

DIAGRAM 7

**STEP 3.** Reorganize your strips and stack them in order, making six piles. Each pile will need one strip from each strip set, stacked in sequence, starting with Strip 6 on the bottom and ending with Strip 1 on the top.

### Making the Blocks

**STEP 1.** Lay out the six piles of strips next to your sewing machine.

**STEP 2.** From the first pile, sew one Strip 1 to one Strip 2 (right sides together). Repeat until you have sewn together all Strips 1 and 2 from all six piles. Butt all strips behind one another, and sew together in a Continuous Seam. Do not backstitch and do not cut threads. See **Diagram 8.** Press seams to Strip 2. You will end up with six joined pieces that look like those in **Diagram 9.** Resist the temptation to cut them apart!

**STEP 3.** Sew all Strip 3 pieces from all six piles to the units made from Strips 1 and 2. Again, do not cut threads. Press seams to Strip 3. See **Diagram 10.**

**STEP 4.** Sew all Strip 4 pieces to the units made from Strips 1, 2, and 3. Do not cut threads. Press seams to Strip 4.

**STEP 5.** Sew all the remaining strips together using the same method. Be sure to add your strips in sequence, and do not cut threads. Press all seams in the direction of the piece you have just added.

Once all the strips have been sewn together, you can cut the threads that join your blocks.

### The Lattice

**STEP 1.** Sew the 1½ × 9½-inch strips of Fabric B to each side of one tree block. Press all seams to the lattice.

**STEP 2.** Sew a block to each side of those lattice strips to make a row of three trees. Press.

**STEP 3.** Sew the 1½ × 34½-inch lattice strips to the top and bottom of the tree row. Trim off the excess so the end of the lattice is even with the edge of the blocks. See **Diagram 11.** Press. Set aside the two remaining 1½ × 44-inch lattice strips.

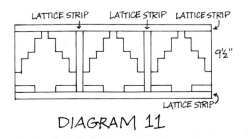

LATTICE STRIP   LATTICE STRIP   LATTICE STRIP

9½"

LATTICE STRIP

DIAGRAM 11

## Checkerboard Row

**STEP 1.** Sew together the four 1½ × 44-inch-long strips of Fabrics A and C, alternating the colors. See **Diagram 12**. Press the seam toward Fabric A after adding each strip.

S E W  S M A R T

In sewing together the strips as described in Step 1, it doesn't matter which color you put first.

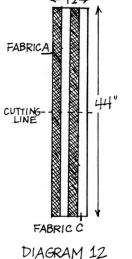

FABRIC A

CUTTING LINE

44"

4½"

FABRIC C

DIAGRAM 12

**STEP 2.** Cut the strip set shown in **Diagram 12** in half across the width. Each half will be approximately 22 inches long. Resew those halves together to make an 8½ × 22-inch strip set that is eight strips wide. See **Diagram 13**.

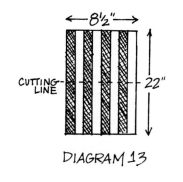

8½"

CUTTING LINE

22"

DIAGRAM 13

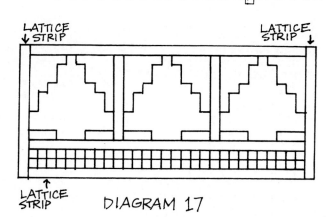

LATTICE STRIP

LATTICE STRIP

LATTICE STRIP

DIAGRAM 17

**STEP 3.** Cut the strip set shown in **Diagram 13** in half across the width. Resew those halves together to make a 16½ × 11-inch strip set that is sixteen strips wide. See **Diagram 14**.

**STEP 4.** Cut the strip set shown in **Diagram 14** in half. Resew those halves together end to end to make a 32½ × 5½-inch strip set that is thirty-two strips wide. See **Diagram 15**.

**STEP 5.** From this final strip set, cut three 1½ × 32½-inch strips, referring to the cutting lines in **Diagram 15**. Rematch two strips and sew them together to create the checkerboard. See **Diagram 16**. The third strip is an extra to use for the Christmas Card Holder.

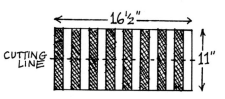

16½"

CUTTING LINE

11"

DIAGRAM 14

**STEP 6.** See Hints on Fitting a Checkerboard Border on page 29. Fit and sew the checkerboard to the lattice strip at the bottom of the tree row.

## Finishing the Lattice

**STEP 1.** Sew one of the two remaining lattice strips below the checkerboard. Trim so the end of the lattice is even with the edge of the checkerboard. Press toward the lattice.

**STEP 2.** Use the last strip for both quilt sides. Cut the strip in half, then sew those strips to the sides, trimming the excess. Press. See **Diagram 17**.

## Layering the Quilt

Arrange and baste the backing, batting, and top together following directions for Layering the Quilt on page 32. Trim the batting and backing to ¾ inch from the raw edge of the quilt top.

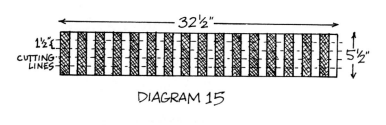

32½"

1½"
CUTTING LINES

5½"

DIAGRAM 15

2½"

DIAGRAM 16

## Binding the Quilt

**STEP 1.** Review Binding the Quilt on page 33.

**STEP 2.** Use one 5½ × 44-inch strip of Fabric A to bind the top of the quilt and another strip to bind the bottom.

**STEP 3.** Cut the remaining 5½ × 44-inch strip in half, and use these pieces to bind the sides.

## The Finishing Stitches

Quilt around each tree in the seam line. The **Holly Leaves and Berries Quilting Template** on page 161 fits nicely into the corner of each block. Stitch a diamond pattern in the checkerboard as shown in **Diagram 18.**

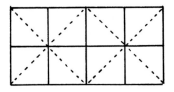

DIAGRAM 18

# Christmas Card Holder

(shown hanging from the knob on the cupboard in the photo on page 150)

Finished Size: 13 × 18 inches

## Materials

Directional print can be used for Fabric A, but it is not recommended for Fabric B.

One 9½ × 9½-inch tree block (left over from the wallhanging)
One checkerboard strip (left over from the wallhanging)

**FABRIC A** *(block backing, decorative top, card holder panel)*

⅞ yard

**FABRIC B** *(block border, decorative top)*

⅛ yard

**BATTING**                 ½ yard

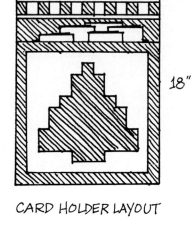

CARD HOLDER LAYOUT

13"

18"

## Cutting Directions

Prewash and press all of your fabrics. Using a rotary cutter, see-through ruler, and cutting mat, prepare the strips as described in the chart below.

| | FIRST CUT | | SECOND CUT | |
|---|---|---|---|---|
| | **NO. OF STRIPS** | **DIMENSIONS** | **NO. OF PIECES** | **DIMENSIONS** |
| **FABRIC A** | **BLOCK BACKING AND POCKET** | | | |
| | 1 | 6½ × 11½-inch piece | | |
| | 1 | 11½ × 11½-inch piece | | |
| | **DECORATIVE TOP** | | | |
| | 1 | 1½ × 13½-inch piece | | |
| | **CARD HOLDER PANEL AND BACKING** | | | |
| | 1 | 13½ × 15½-inch piece | | |
| | 1 | 13½ × 18½-inch piece | | |

**Note:** If you are using a directional print for Fabric A, the direction of the print should be parallel to the length of the piece or strip. The only exceptions are the 1½ × 13½-inch decorative top and the 6½ × 11½-inch block pocket. On those pieces the print direction should be parallel to the width of the piece.

| | FIRST CUT | | SECOND CUT | |
|---|---|---|---|---|
| | NO. OF STRIPS | DIMENSIONS | NO. OF PIECES | DIMENSIONS |
| **FABRIC B** | **BLOCK BORDER** | | | |
| | 2 | 1½ × 9½-inch strips | | |
| | 2 | 1½ × 11½-inch strips | | |
| | **DECORATIVE TOP** | | | |
| | 2 | 1 × 13½-inch strips | | |
| **BATTING** | 1 | 11½ × 11½-inch piece | | |
| | 1 | 13½ × 18½-inch piece | | |

## Sewing Directions

**STEP 1.** Sew the 1½ × 9½-inch border strips of Fabric B to the sides of the tree block. Press toward border. Sew the 1½ × 11½-inch strips of Fabric B to the block top and bottom. Press. Set aside the tree block for now.

**STEP 2.** Stitch a ¼-inch hem on the long sides of the 6½ × 11½-inch piece of Fabric A. Topstitch this piece to the *right side* of the 11½ × 11½-inch piece of Fabric A. Position this smaller piece 1½ inches from the top edge of the larger piece as shown in **Diagram 19**. Topstitch ⅛ inch from the edges of three sides as shown in the diagram. This will be the block backing with a pocket for Christmas cards.

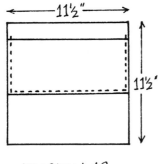

DIAGRAM 19

**STEP 3.** With right sides together, place the tree block on top of the

backing from Step 2. Then place these two layers on top of an 11½ × 11½-inch piece of batting. This three-layer "sandwich" should have the tree block on the top, backing in the middle and batting on the bottom. Sew all three layers together, leaving an opening at the bottom for turning. Trim the corners, turn right side out, and handstitch the opening shut. Pin or baste the layers together and hand or machine quilt around the tree in the seam line. Set aside the completed tree block.

**STEP 4.** Next make the card holder panel onto which the tree block will be mounted. For the decorative top section, piece together strips in the following order, referring to **Diagram 20**. Press the seams as you attach each strip:

1. 1½ × 13½-inch strip of Fabric A
2. 1 × 13½-inch strip of Fabric B
3. 13½-inch strip of checkerboard (left over from wallhanging)
4. 1 × 13½-inch strip of Fabric B

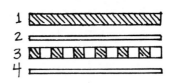

DIAGRAM 20

Sew this section of strips to the 13½ × 15½-inch piece of Fabric A. Press toward Fabric B.

**STEP 5.** With right sides together, place the card holder panel from Step 4 on top of a 13½ × 18½-inch piece of Fabric A. Then place these two layers on top of a 13½ × 18½-inch piece of batting. This "sandwich" should have the card holder panel on the top, rectangle of Fabric A in the middle, and batting on the bottom. Sew all three layers together, leaving an opening at the bottom for turning. Trim the corners, turn right side out, and stitch the opening shut. You may choose to quilt a diamond pattern on the checkerboard.

**STEP 6.** Center the tree block on the card holder panel. To guide your placement, the panel should extend an inch around the sides and the bottom of the block. Pin in position and topstitch the block in place around three sides, leaving the top open.

**STEP 7.** Tack some plastic rings to the back for hanging, and just wait for those cards and letters to start rolling in!

# Christmas Pillow with Checkerboard

(shown on the bench in the photo on page 150)

Finished Pillow (without ruffle): 13 × 13 inches

## Materials

One 9½ × 9½-inch tree block (left over from the wallhanging)

**FABRIC A** *(backing, checkerboard)*

| | |
|---|---|
| Backing | ½ yard |
| Checkerboard | ⅛ yard |
| TOTAL | ⅝ yard |

**FABRIC B** *(plain border)*

| | |
|---|---|
| Plain Border | ⅛ yard |

**FABRIC C** *(ruffle, checkerboard)*

| | |
|---|---|
| Ruffle | ⅝ yard |
| Checkerboard | ⅛ yard |
| TOTAL | ¾ yard |

**BATTING** *(for pillow form)*

½ yard

**STUFFING** *(for pillow form)*

One 1-lb. bag of smooth stuffing like FiberFil; shredded foam is not recommended.

## Cutting Directions

Prewash and press all of your fabrics. Using a rotary cutter, see-through ruler, and cutting mat, prepare the strips as described in the chart below.

| | | FIRST CUT | | SECOND CUT | |
|---|---|---|---|---|---|
| | | **NO. OF STRIPS** | **DIMENSIONS** | **NO. OF PIECES** | **DIMENSIONS** |
| **FABRIC A** | **BACKING** | | | | |
| | | 1 | 15 × 15-inch piece | | |
| | **CHECKERBOARD** | | | | |
| | | 2 | 1½ × 32-inch strips | | |
| **FABRIC B** | **PLAIN BORDER** | | | | |
| | | 2 | 1½ × 9½-inch strips | | |
| | | 2 | 1½ × 11½-inch strips | | |
| **FABRIC C** | **RUFFLE** | | | | |
| | | 3 | 6 × 44-inch strips | | |
| | **CHECKERBOARD** | | | | |
| | | 2 | 1½ × 32-inch strips | | |
| **BATTING** | **PILLOW FORM** | | | | |
| | | 2 | 15 × 15-inch pieces | | |

## Plain Border

Sew the 1½ × 9½-inch strips of Fabric B to the top and bottom of the tree block. Press toward the borders. Sew the 1½ × 11½-inch strips to the sides. Press.

## Checkerboard Border

**STEP 1.** Review Hints on Fitting a Checkerboard Border on page 29.

**STEP 2.** Sew together the four 32-inch-long strips of Fabrics A and C, alternating the colors. See **Diagram 21**. Press the seam toward Fabric A after adding each strip.

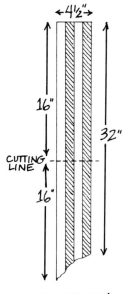

DIAGRAM 21

**STEP 3.** Cut the strip set shown in **Diagram 21** in half across the width. Each half will be approximately 16 inches long. Resew those halves together to make an 8½ × 16-inch strip set that is eight strips wide. See **Diagram 22**.

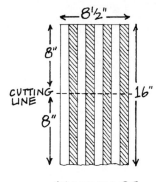

DIAGRAM 22

**STEP 4.** Cut the strip set shown in **Diagram 22** in half across the width. Resew those halves together to make a 16½ × 8-inch strip set that is sixteen strips wide. See **Diagram 23**.

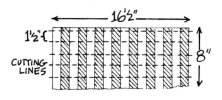

DIAGRAM 23

**STEP 5.** From this final strip set, cut four 1½ × 16½-inch strips, referring to the cutting lines in **Diagram 23**.

**STEP 6.** Using a seam ripper, remove excess checkerboard squares to make two 1½ × 11½-inch and two 1½ × 13½-inch strips of checkerboard.

**STEP 7.** Sew the 1½ × 11½-inch strips to the block top and bottom. Press all seams toward the plain border. Sew the 1½ × 13½-inch strips to the sides. Press.

## The Ruffle

**STEP 1.** Sew the three 6 × 44-inch strips of Fabric C together end to end to make a 6 × 132-inch strip. Press seam allowances open.

**STEP 2.** Press ruffle strip in half with wrong sides together. Sew two rows of machine basting ¼ inch and ⅜ inch from the raw edge along the length of the ruffle. Leave a few inches of thread extending from both rows of stitching at both ends of the ruffle. Securely knot the stitching at one end.

**STEP 3.** Pull the free ends of the basting thread to gather the ruffle. Evenly distribute the gathering as you fit the ruffle to the pillow top. Pin the ruffle securely in position and sew ½ inch from the raw edges of the pillow top and ruffle.

## Finishing

**STEP 1.** Use the pillow top (without counting the ruffle) as a pattern to trim the 15 × 15-inch backing piece to fit. With right sides together and the ruffle safely tucked out of the way toward the center of the tree block, sew the pillow front to back, using a ½-inch seam allowance. Leave a large opening at the bottom for turning and for inserting the pillow form.

**STEP 2.** Make a custom-fit pillow form from the batting and stuffing, referring to the directions on page 37.

**STEP 3.** Insert pillow form and handstitch opening.

# Christmas Pillow with Double Border

(not shown in the photograph)

Finished Pillow (without ruffle):
12 × 12 inches

PILLOW LAYOUT

## Materials

One 9½ × 9½-inch tree block
  (left over from the wallhanging)

**FABRIC A** *(border two)*
⅛ yard

**FABRIC B** *(border one)*
⅛ yard

**FABRIC C** *(corner squares)*
Scraps

**FABRIC D** *(ruffle, backing)*
Ruffle        ⅓ yard
Backing       ⅜ yard
  TOTAL        ¾ yard

**BATTING** *(for pillow form)*
⅜ yard

**STUFFING** *(for pillow form)*

One 1-lb. bag of smooth stuffing
  like FiberFil; shredded foam
  is not recommended.

## Cutting Directions

Prewash and press all of your
fabrics. Using a rotary cutter, see-
through ruler, and cutting mat,
prepare the strips as described in
the chart below.

| | FIRST CUT | | SECOND CUT | |
| --- | --- | --- | --- | --- |
| | **NO. OF STRIPS** | **DIMENSIONS** | **NO. OF PIECES** | **DIMENSIONS** |
| **FABRIC A** | BORDER TWO | | | |
| | 4 | 2 × 10½-inch strips | | |
| **FABRIC B** | BORDER ONE | | | |
| | 2 | 1 × 9½-inch strips | | |
| | 2 | 1 × 10½-inch strips | | |
| **FABRIC C** | CORNER SQUARES | | | |
| | 4 | 2 × 2-inch squares | | |
| **FABRIC D** | RUFFLE | | | |
| | 2 | 5 × 44-inch strips | | |
| | BACKING | | | |
| | 1 | 13½ × 13½-inch piece | | |
| **BATTING** | PILLOW FORM | | | |
| | 2 | 13½ × 13½-inch pieces | | |

## Border One

Sew the 1 × 9½-inch strips of Fabric B to the block top and bottom. Press all seams to the border. Sew the 1 × 10½-inch strips to the sides. Press.

## Border Two

**STEP 1.** Sew two of the 2 × 10½-inch strips of Fabric A to the top and bottom. Press all seams to Border Two.

**STEP 2.** Sew the 2-inch corner squares to the ends of the other two 2 × 10½-inch border strips. Press.

**STEP 3.** Pin in position and sew border strips to the sides. Press.

## The Ruffle

**STEP 1.** Sew the two 5 × 44-inch strips together end to end to make a 5 × 88-inch strip. Press seam allowance open.

**STEP 2.** Press ruffle strip in half with wrong sides together. Sew two rows of machine basting ¼ inch and ⅜ inch from the raw edge along the length of the ruffle. Leave a few inches of thread extending from both rows of stitching at both ends of the ruffle. Securely knot the stitching at one end.

**STEP 3.** Pull the free ends of the basting threads to gather the ruffle. Evenly distribute the gathering as you fit the ruffle to the pillow top. Pin the ruffle securely in position and sew ½ inch from the raw edges of the pillow top and ruffle.

## Finishing

**STEP 1.** Use the pillow top (without counting the ruffle) as a pattern to trim the 13½-inch backing piece to fit. With right sides together and the ruffle safely tucked out of the way toward the center of the tree block, sew the pillow front to back, using a ½-inch seam allowance. Leave a large opening at the bottom for turning and for inserting the pillow form.

**STEP 2.** Make a custom-fit pillow form from the batting and stuffing, referring to the directions on page 37.

**STEP 3.** Insert pillow form and handstitch opening.

HOLLY LEAVES AND BERRIES
QUILTING TEMPLATE

# Made in Heaven

## Four-Angel Quilt

Finished Quilt: 29 × 39 inches
Finished Block: 9 × 14 inches

### Materials

Obvious directional prints are not recommended.

**FABRIC A** *(dresses, scrap border, binding)*

| | |
|---|---|
| Blocks and Scrap Border | ½ yard |
| Binding | ⅜ yard |
| TOTAL | ⅞ yard |

**FABRIC B** *(block background, borders, lattice)*

| | |
|---|---|
| Blocks and Scrap Border | ½ yard |
| Lattice | ¾ yard |
| One-Inch Border | ¼ yard |
| TOTAL | 1½ yards |

**FABRIC C** *(wings, scrap border)*

| | |
|---|---|
| Blocks and Scrap Border | ½ yard |

**FABRIC D** *(heads, feet)*

| | |
|---|---|
| Blocks | ⅓ yard |

**SCRAP BORDER**

Four 1½ × 44-inch strips of coordinated fabrics from your scrap bag of fabrics

| | |
|---|---|
| **BACKING** | 1 yard |
| **BATTING** | 1 yard |

**Tear-away paper** *(for machine appliqué only)*

Some angels are made in heaven, but others can be made right in your own sewing room (the next best place!). Depending on the colors you choose, you can create a decidedly holiday feel or a more timeless one. Angels in an array of pastels could make a particularly angelic gift for a newly arrived cherub.

You have your choice of two sizes—a Four-Angel or a Three-Angel Quilt. If you make the smaller quilt, there's a block left over to transform into a heavenly pillow.

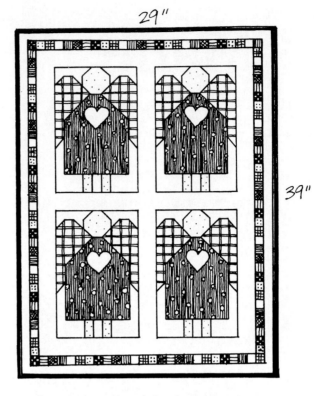

29"

39"

FOUR-ANGEL QUILT LAYOUT

## Cutting Directions

Prewash and press all of your fabrics. Using a rotary cutter, see-through ruler, and cutting mat, prepare the strips as described in the first column in the chart below. Then from those strips, cut the pieces listed in the second column. Some portions of the quilt need to be cut only once, so no additional cutting information will appear in the second column.

| | FIRST CUT | | SECOND CUT | |
|---|---|---|---|---|
| | NO. OF STRIPS | DIMENSIONS | NO. OF PIECES | DIMENSIONS |
| **FABRIC A** | **DRESSES** | | | |
| | 1 | 6 × 18-inch strip | | |
| | **Before You Cut:** Set aside one 44-inch strip for the scrap border. Cut the four pieces in the second column from the other 44-inch strip. | | | |
| | 2 | 1½ × 44-inch strips | 4 | 1½ × 3½-inch pieces |
| | 1 | 6½ × 44-inch strip | 4 | 6½ × 7½-inch pieces |
| | **BINDING** | | | |
| | 4 | 2¾ × 44-inch strips | | |
| **FABRIC B** | **BACKGROUND** | | | |
| | 1 | 6 × 44-inch strip | 1 | 6 × 14-inch piece |
| | | | 1 | 6 × 6-inch piece |
| | 1 | 3½ × 44-inch strip | 16 | 3½ × 1½-inch pieces |
| | 1 | 2½ × 44-inch strip | 8 | 2½ × 3½-inch pieces |
| | **Before You Cut:** Set aside one 1½ × 44-inch strip for the scrap border. Cut the four pieces in the second column from the other 44-inch strip. | | | |
| | 2 | 1½ × 44-inch strips | 4 | 1½ × 2½-inch pieces |

*(continued on next page)*

| | FIRST CUT | | SECOND CUT | |
|---|---|---|---|---|
| | **NO. OF STRIPS** | **DIMENSIONS** | **NO. OF PIECES** | **DIMENSIONS** |
| **FABRIC B,** *continued* | **LATTICE** | | | |
| | **Before You Cut:** From one of the 44-inch strips, cut the strips as directed in the second column. The remaining four strips require no further cutting. | | | |
| | 5 | 2½ × 44-inch strips | 2 | 2½ × 14½-inch pieces |
| | **ONE-INCH BORDER** | | | |
| | 4 | 1½ × 44-inch strips | | |
| **FABRIC C** | **WINGS** | | | |
| | 1 | 6 × 44-inch strip | 1 | 6 × 14-inch piece |
| | | | 1 | 6 × 18-inch piece |
| | | | 1 | 6 × 6-inch piece |
| | **Before You Cut:** Set aside one 44-inch strip for the scrap border. Cut the pieces listed in the second column from the remaining three 44-inch strips. | | | |
| | 4 | 1½ × 44-inch strips | 8 | 1½ × 1½-inch pieces |
| | | | 8 | 1½ × 3½-inch pieces |
| | | | 8 | 1½ × 5½-inch pieces |
| **FABRIC D** | **HEADS AND FEET** | | | |
| | 1 | 6 × 44-inch strip | 2 | 6 × 6-inch pieces |
| | 2 | 1½ × 44-inch strips | 8 | 1½ × 2½-inch pieces |
| | | | 8 | 1½ × 1½-inch pieces |
| | | | 4 | 1½ × 3½-inch pieces |

## Speedy Triangles

**STEP 1.** Refer to the Speedy Triangle directions on page 11 for how to mark, sew, and cut. You will be making four different sizes of triangle sets to complete this project.

**STEP 2.** Position the 6 × 14-inch pieces of Fabrics B and C with right sides together. Draw a 1⅞-inch grid of twelve squares. See **Diagram 1**.

**STEP 3.** After sewing and cutting are complete, press seam allowances toward Fabric C. You will have made a total of twenty-four 1½-inch Fabric B/C triangle sets.

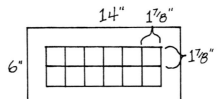
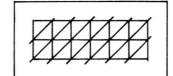
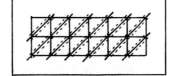

DIAGRAM 1

**STEP 4.** For the second set of triangles, use a 6 × 6-inch piece each of Fabrics B and D. Mark a 1⅞-inch grid of four squares. See **Diagram 2**. Press seam allowances toward Fabric D. You will have made eight 1½-inch Fabric B/D triangle sets.

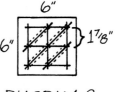

DIAGRAM 2

**STEP 5.** For the third set of triangles, use a 6 × 6-inch piece each of Fabrics C and D. Mark a 1⅞-inch grid of four squares. See **Diagram 2**. Press seam allowances toward

Fabric D. You will have made eight 1½-inch Fabric C/D triangle sets.

**STEP 6.** For the fourth set of triangles, use a 6 × 18-inch piece each of Fabrics A and C. Mark a 3⅞-inch grid of four squares. See **Diagram 3.** Press seam allowances toward Fabric A. You will have made eight 3½-inch Fabric A/C triangle sets.

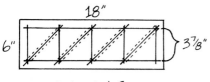

DIAGRAM 3

## Assembling the Blocks

Throughout this section, refer to the Fabric Key to identify the fabric placements in the diagrams. Also, it's a good idea to review Assembly Line Piecing on page 13 before you get started. It's more efficient to do the same step for each block at the same time than to piece one entire block together at a time. Be sure to press as you go, and follow the arrows for pressing direction.

FABRIC KEY    FABRIC A (DRESS)
              FABRIC B (BACKGROUND)
              FABRIC C (WINGS)
              FABRIC D (HEADS, FEET)

### SECTION ONE (Head and Wing Tops)

**STEP 1.** (Note: Steps 1 through 6 make the angels' heads.) Sew four 1½-inch Fabric B/D triangle sets to four 1½ × 1½-inch pieces of Fabric D. Place them right sides together with the triangle sets in the position shown in **Diagram 4.** Line them up next to your sewing machine. Stitch the first set together, then butt the next set directly behind them and continue sewing each set without breaking the seam. Press seams toward Fabric D and cut the joining threads.

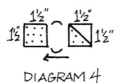

DIAGRAM 4

In each of the remaining steps, use the same Continuous Seam method. You will be making a total of four blocks.

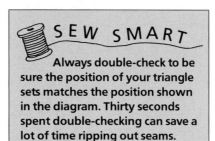

**SEW SMART**
Always double-check to be sure the position of your triangle sets matches the position shown in the diagram. Thirty seconds spent double-checking can save a lot of time ripping out seams.

**STEP 2.** Sew the units from Step 1 to four 1½-inch Fabric B/D triangle sets. Press toward Step 1 units. See **Diagram 5.**

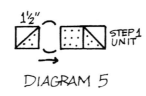

DIAGRAM 5

**STEP 3.** Sew four 1½-inch Fabric C/D triangle sets to four 1½ × 1½-inch pieces of Fabric D. Press toward Fabric D. See **Diagram 6.**

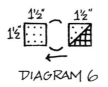

DIAGRAM 6

**STEP 4.** Sew units from Step 3 to four 1½-inch Fabric C/D triangle sets. Press toward Step 3 units. See **Diagram 7.**

DIAGRAM 7

**STEP 5.** Sew units from Step 2 to four 3½ × 1½-inch pieces of Fabric D. Press toward Fabric D. See **Diagram 8.**

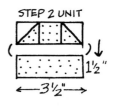

DIAGRAM 8

**STEP 6.** Sew units from Step 4 to units from Step 5. Press toward Step 5 units. See **Diagram 9.**

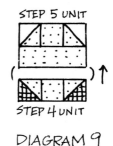

DIAGRAM 9

**STEP 7.** (Note: Steps 7 through 11 make the angels' wing tops.) Sew four 1½ × 1½-inch pieces of Fabric C to four 1½-inch Fabric B/C triangle sets. Press toward Fabric C. See **Diagram 10.**

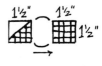

DIAGRAM 10

**STEP 8.** Sew four 1½-inch Fabric B/C triangle sets to units from Step 7. Press toward Step 7 units. See **Diagram 11**.

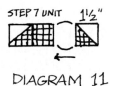

STEP 7 UNIT    1½"

DIAGRAM 11

**STEP 9.** Sew units from Step 8 to four 3½ × 1½-inch pieces of Fabric C. Press toward Fabric C. See **Diagram 12**.

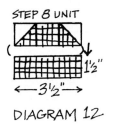

STEP 8 UNIT

1½"

←—3½"—→

DIAGRAM 12

**STEP 10.** Sew four 3½ × 1½-inch pieces of Fabric B to units from Step 9. Press toward Fabric B. See **Diagram 13**.

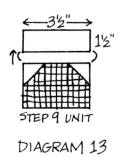

←—3½"—→

1½"

STEP 9 UNIT

DIAGRAM 13

**STEP 11.** To make the angels' other wing tops, repeat Steps 7 through 10 as described above.

**STEP 12.** To join the head and wings, sew one wing unit to the left of the head unit from Step 6. Press toward the head unit. See **Diagram 14**.

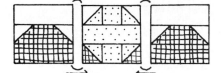

DIAGRAM 14

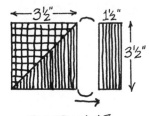

←—3½"—→    1½"

3½"

DIAGRAM 15

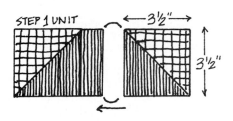

STEP 1 UNIT     ←—3½"—→

3½"

DIAGRAM 16

STEP 2 UNIT

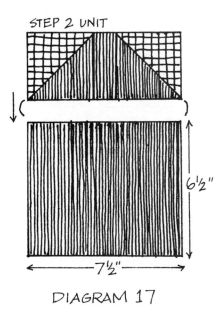

6½"

←————7½"————→

DIAGRAM 17

**STEP 13.** Sew the other wing unit to the units from Step 12. Press toward the Step 12 units. Refer to **Diagram 14**.

**SECTION TWO (Dresses and Lower Wings)**

**STEP 1.** Sew four 1½ × 3½-inch pieces of Fabric A to four 3½-inch Fabric A/C triangle sets. Press toward Fabric A. See **Diagram 15**.

**STEP 2.** Sew four 3½-inch Fabric A/C triangle sets to the units from Step 1. Press toward the Step 1 units. See **Diagram 16**.

**STEP 3.** Sew the units from Step 2 to four 7½ × 6½-inch pieces of Fabric A. Press toward Fabric A. See **Diagram 17**.

**STEP 4.** Sew four 1½ × 5½-inch pieces of Fabric C to four 1½-inch Fabric B/C triangle sets. Press toward Fabric C. See **Diagram 18**.

**STEP 5.** Sew the units from Step 4 to four 1½ × 3½-inch pieces of Fabric B. Press toward Fabric B. See **Diagram 19**.

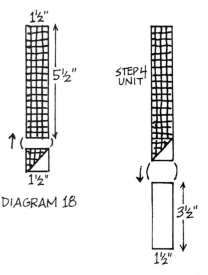

1½"

5½"

1½"

DIAGRAM 18

STEP 4 UNIT

3½"

1½"

DIAGRAM 19

**STEP 6.** Sew four 1½ × 5½-inch pieces of Fabric C to four 1½-inch Fabric B/C triangle sets. Press toward Fabric C. See **Diagram 20**.

**STEP 7.** Sew the units from Step 6 to four 1½ × 3½-inch pieces of Fabric B. Press toward Fabric B. See **Diagram 21**.

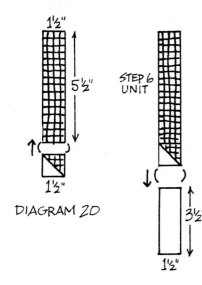

DIAGRAM 20

DIAGRAM 21

**STEP 8.** Sew the units from Step 5 to the units from Step 3, referring to **Diagram 22**. Press toward the Step 3 units.

**STEP 9.** Sew the units from Step 7 to the opposite side of the Step 3 units, referring to **Diagram 22**. Press toward the Step 3 units.

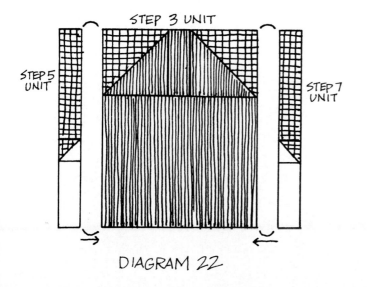

DIAGRAM 22

## SECTION THREE (Feet)

**STEP 1.** Sew four 1½ × 2½-inch pieces of Fabric D to four 2½ × 3½-inch pieces of Fabric B. Press toward Fabric D. See **Diagram 23**.

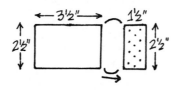

DIAGRAM 23

**STEP 2.** Sew four 1½ × 2½-inch pieces of Fabric D to four 1½ × 2½-inch pieces of Fabric B. Press toward Fabric D. See **Diagram 24**.

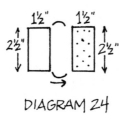

DIAGRAM 24

**STEP 3.** Sew the units from Step 2 to the units from Step 1. Press toward the Step 1 units. See **Diagram 25**.

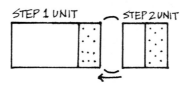

DIAGRAM 25

**STEP 4.** Sew four 3½ × 2½-inch pieces of Fabric B to the units from Step 3. Press toward the Step 3 units. See **Diagram 26**.

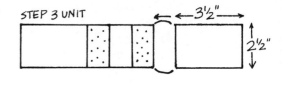

DIAGRAM 26

## SECTION ASSEMBLY

**STEP 1.** Sew the units from Section One (head and wing tops) to the units from Section Two (dresses and lower wings). Press toward Section Two. Refer to **Diagram 27**.

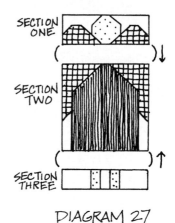

DIAGRAM 27

**STEP 2.** Sew the units from Section Three (feet) to the units from Step 1. Press toward the Step 1 units.

## The Hearts

Hand or machine appliqué a heart on each angel. See Timesaving Techniques for Appliqué on page 16 to decide which appliqué technique you will use (machine or hand). Use the **Heart Appliqué Pattern** provided on page 170. Refer to the photographs and **Quilt Layout** for placement.

## The Lattice

**STEP 1.** Sew the 2½ × 14½-inch strips of Fabric B to the right side of two blocks. Press all seams toward the lattice. Sew a block to the right side of each of those lattice strips to make two rows of two angels. See **Diagram 28**.

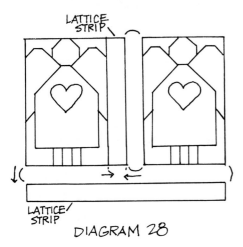

LATTICE STRIP

LATTICE STRIP

DIAGRAM 28

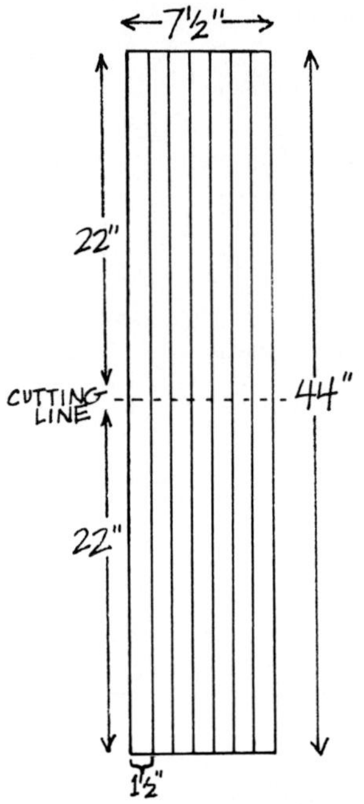

←—7½"—→

22"

CUTTING LINE ─ ─ ─ ─ ─ 44"

22"

1½"

DIAGRAM 29

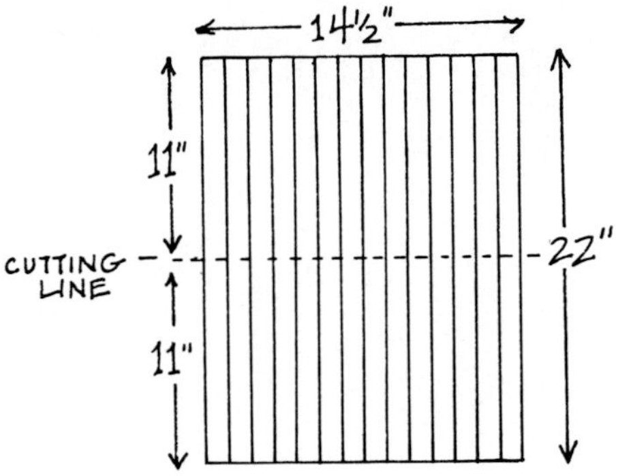

←——— 14½" ———→

11"

CUTTING LINE ─ ─ ─ ─ ─ 22"

11"

DIAGRAM 30

←——————— 28½" ———————→

1½"

CUTTING LINES

11"

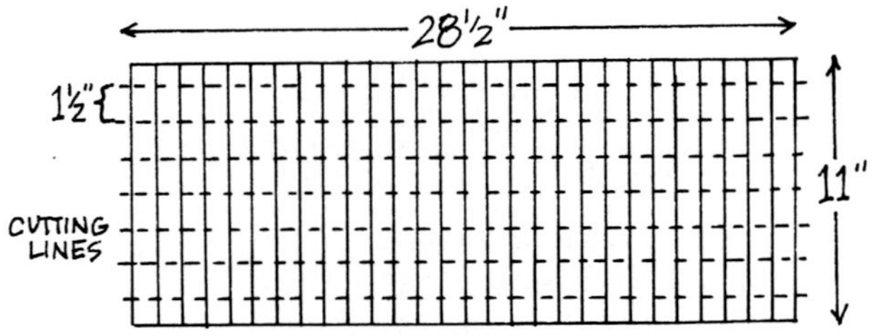

DIAGRAM 31

**STEP 2.** Cut one 2½ × 44-inch lattice strip in half. Sew one half to the bottom of each row. Trim the excess and press all seams toward the lattice. Sew the two rows together. Press.

**STEP 3.** Sew a lattice strip to the quilt top. Trim and press. Sew lattice strips to the quilt sides. Trim and press.

## The Scrap Border

**STEP 1.** Use one 1½ × 44-inch strip each of Fabrics A, B, and C, plus the four 1½ × 44-inch strips from your scrap bag. Arrange in a pleasing order and stitch together the seven strips to make a 7½ × approximately 44-inch strip set. See **Diagram 29**. Press all the seams in one direction as you go.

**STEP 2.** Cut this strip set in half widthwise, referring to the cutting lines in **Diagram 29**. Resew the halves together to make a 14½ × 22-inch Strip Set. See **Diagram 30**.

**STEP 3.** Cut the 14½ × 22-inch strip set in half, referring to **Diagram 30**. Resew the halves together to make a 28½ × 11-inch strip set. See **Diagram 31**.

**STEP 4.** Cut six 1½ × 28½-inch strips from the strip set made in Step 3, referring to the cutting lines in **Diagram 31**.

**STEP 5.** See Hints on Fitting a Scrap Border on page 28 for details on how to fit a scrap border to the quilt. Fit and sew border strips to the quilt top and bottom. You will need to sew two 28½-inch strips together end to end to create a border strip long enough to fit each side of the quilt. Fit and sew these lengthened strips to the quilt sides.

## One-Inch Border

**STEP 1.** Sew 1½ × 44-inch long strips of Fabric B to quilt sides. Trim excess and press seams toward the border.

**STEP 2.** Sew remaining Fabric B borders to the top and bottom of the quilt. Trim and press.

## Layering the Quilt

Arrange and baste the backing, batting, and top together following directions for Layering the Quilt on page 32. Trim batting and backing to ¼ inch from the raw edge of the quilt top.

## Binding the Quilt

Using the 2¾ × 44-inch strips cut from Fabric A, follow directions for Binding the Quilt on page 33.

## The Finishing Stitches

Outline your angels and hearts by quilting in the ditch or ¼ inch away from the seam line. To create some stars in the heavens, use the **Star Templates** on page 170 and randomly quilt stars in the background. Use a contrasting color of quilting thread for the stars.

# Three-Angel Quilt

Finished Quilt: 40 × 23 inches
Finished Block: 9 × 14 inches

## Before You Begin

Refer to the Materials list and Cutting Directions for the Four-Angel Quilt beginning on page 163. You will need the same amount of fabric cut into the same pieces to make the Three-Angel Quilt. The fourth, or extra block not used for the Three-Angel Quilt can be made into a pillow. Follow the directions for the Four-Angel Quilt, starting on page 165 with Speedy Triangles and working all the way through the step for appliquéing the hearts. Then refer to the specific directions given below for the Three-Angel Quilt.

## The Lattice

**STEP 1.** From two of the 2½ × 44-inch strips of Fabric B given under Cutting Directions, cut four 2½ × 14½-inch strips.

**STEP 2.** Sew the 14½-inch strips to the right side of all three blocks. On just one block, also sew a strip to the left side; this will be the block that appears on the left of the quilt. Press all seams toward the lattice.

**STEP 3.** Sew the three blocks together, making sure the block with two lattice strips is placed on the left. Press.

**STEP 4.** Sew 2½ × 44-inch lattice strips to the quilt top and bottom. Trim the excess and press.

## The Scrap Border

**STEP 1.** Follow Steps 1 through 5 on page 169 for the Four-Angel Quilt, using the lengthened strips of the scrap border for the quilt top and bottom and the shorter strips for the sides. Save any excess scrap border strips to use for the pillow border.

## One-Inch Border

**STEP 1.** Sew 1½ × 44-inch strips of Fabric B to the quilt top and bottom. Trim the excess and press all seams toward the border.

**STEP 2.** Sew border strips to quilt sides. Trim excess and press.

## Completing the Quilt

Refer to Layering the Quilt through The Finishing Stitches under the Four-Angel Quilt on page 169.

STAR TEMPLATES

HEART APPLIQUÉ PATTERN

# Heavenly Pillow

(in the rocking chair in the photo on page 162)

Finished Pillow: 14 × 17 inches

## Materials

**ONE ANGEL BLOCK** *(left over from the Three-Angel Quilt)*

**SCRAP BORDER STRIPS** *(left over from the Three-Angel Quilt)*

**FABRIC A** *(binding)*
⅛ yard or scraps left over from the Three-Angel Quilt

**FABRIC B** *(lattice strips)*
Scraps left over from the Three-Angel Quilt

**BACKING**                    ½ yard

**BATTING** *(for pillow form)*
                                 ½ yard

**STUFFING** *(for pillow form)*
One 1-lb. bag of smooth stuffing like FiberFil; shredded foam is not recommended.

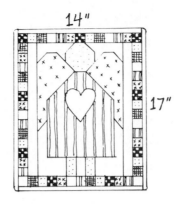

14"

17"

PILLOW LAYOUT

## Cutting Directions

Prewash and press all of your fabrics. Using a rotary cutter, see-through ruler, and cutting mat, prepare the strips as described in the chart below.

## Lattice and Borders

**STEP 1.** Sew 1½ × 14½-inch lattice strips from Fabric B to both sides of the block. Press toward the strips.

**STEP 2.** Fit and sew leftover scrap border strips to the pillow sides. Press toward the Fabric B strips. Fit and sew to the pillow top and bottom. Press.

**STEP 3.** Sew the 1 × 13½-inch binding strips cut from Fabric A to the pillow top and bottom. Press all seams toward the binding. Sew the 1 × 17½-inch strips to the pillow sides. Press.

**STEP 4.** Using the pillow front as a pattern, trim the backing piece to fit. With right sides together, sew the pillow front to the back. Leave a large opening at the bottom for turning and for inserting the pillow form.

**STEP 5.** Make a custom-fit pillow form from the batting and stuffing, referring to the directions on page 37.

**STEP 6.** After turning the pillow right side out, insert the pillow form and handstitch the opening.

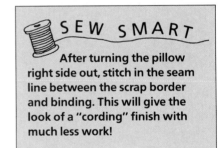

**SEW SMART**

After turning the pillow right side out, stitch in the seam line between the scrap border and binding. This will give the look of a "cording" finish with much less work!

|  | FIRST CUT | | SECOND CUT | |
|---|---|---|---|---|
|  | **NO. OF STRIPS** | **DIMENSIONS** | **NO. OF PIECES** | **DIMENSIONS** |
| **FABRIC A** | **BINDING** | | | |
|  | 2 | 1 × 13½-inch strips | | |
|  | 2 | 1 × 17½-inch strips | | |
| **FABRIC B** | **LATTICE STRIPS** | | | |
|  | 2 | 1½ × 14½-inch strips | | |
| **BACKING** | 1 | 15 × 18-inch piece | | |
| **BATTING** | 2 | 14½ × 17½-inch pieces | | |

# Appliqué Country Quilting Projects

You'll find a lot of fun projects in this section that go together
quickly. Before you begin any of them, review this checklist.
These pointers will help make sure you haven't overlooked any
materials or techniques you'll need to turn out a great finished
appliqué project.

☐ Read Tools and Accessories You Will Need on page 6 and the materials list for your specific project to make sure you have everything on hand.

☐ Prewash and press your fabrics only if you anticipate that you may want to launder your appliqué project.

☐ Read the step-by-step directions from start to finish, and look at all the diagrams before you cut and sew any fabric.

☐ Throughout the directions, there will be references to information found in Speedy Quilting Techniques and Quiltmaking Essentials. Take the time to flip back and review the material to make sure you understand everything you need to know about a specific technique.

☐ You will have your choice of appliqué technique for many of the projects. To help make your decision, be sure to review the directions for machine, buttonhole embroidery, Penstitch, and hand appliqué that start on page 18.

☐ All of the appliqué patterns are provided full size so there is no need for enlarging. However, if you plan to use an appliqué technique that requires a seam allowance, such as hand appliqué, be sure to add that seam allowance by cutting out the pattern ¼ inch outside the traced line.

☐ When assembling the background piece and borders, always use a ¼-inch seam allowance.

☐ Some appliqué projects still require strips and pieces to be cut. Don't forget to use your rotary cutter and see-through ruler for these.

# Alley Cats

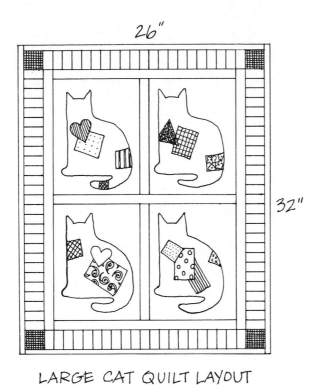

26"

32"

LARGE CAT QUILT LAYOUT

**T**hese hobo kitties from the alley want to settle down and are looking for a home to call their own. Maybe you have just the spot for them! These cats come in a variety of sizes, ranging from large, medium, and small wall quilts to a plump and cozy pillow. There's also a pattern for huggable, soft sculpture cats, which make ideal low-maintenance pets! Any of these projects are "purrfectly" suited for a cat-loving quilter with a big bag of fabric scraps.

## Large Cat Wallhanging

*(shown draped over the quilt rack in the photo)*

Finished Size: 26 × 32 inches

**Materials**

**FABRIC A** *(cats, scrap border)*
Use four different fabrics.

¼ yard
*each* of *four* fabrics

**FABRIC B** *(background, scrap border)*
Background and Scrap Border ½ yard

**FABRIC C** *(lattice, corner squares)*
Lattice and Corner Squares ⅓ yard

**COORDINATED SCRAPS**
Three 1½ × 44-inch strips of different fabrics for scrap border
Scrap pieces for patches and hearts

**BINDING** ⅓ yard

**BACKING** 1 yard

**BATTING** 1 yard

**Appliqué film**

**Tear-away paper** *(for machine appliqué only)*

**Black, extra-fine point, permanent felt-tip pen** *(for Penstitch only)*

## Cutting Directions

Prewash and press all of your fabrics if you anticipate that you may want to launder your appliqué project. Using a rotary cutter, see-through ruler, and cutting mat, prepare the strips as described in the first column in the chart below. Then from those strips, cut the pieces listed in the second column. Some portions of the quilt need to be cut only once, so no additional cutting information will appear in the second column.

| | FIRST CUT | | SECOND CUT | |
| --- | --- | --- | --- | --- |
| | NO. OF STRIPS | DIMENSIONS | NO. OF PIECES | DIMENSIONS |
| **FABRIC A** | SCRAP BORDER: from *each* of the *four* fabrics, cut the following | | | |
| | 1 | 1½ × 44-inch strip | | |
| **FABRIC B** | BACKGROUND PIECES | | | |
| | 4 | 9½ × 12½-inch pieces | | |
| | SCRAP BORDER | | | |
| | 1 | 1½ × 44-inch strip | | |
| **FABRIC C** | LATTICE | | | |
| | 5 | 1½ × 44-inch strips | 2 | 1½ × 12½-inch pieces |
| | | | 3 | 1½ × 19½-inch pieces |
| | | | 2 | 1½ × 27½-inch strips |
| | CORNER SQUARES | | | |
| | 4 | 2½ × 2½-inch squares | | |
| **FABRIC D** | BINDING | | | |
| | 4 | 2¾ × 44-inch strips | | |
| **SCRAPS** | SCRAP BORDER | | | |
| | 3 | 1½ × 44-inch strips | | |

## Appliqué

**STEP 1.** Refer to Timesaving Techniques for Appliqué on page 16 to decide which technique you will use (Penstitch, machine, buttonhole embroidery, or hand appliqué). Trace and cut appliqué designs for four large cats from the four Fabric A's you have chosen, using the **Large Cat Appliqué Pattern** on pages 184 and 185.

SEW SMART
The Large Cat Quilt shown in the photograph on page 174 was done in machine appliqué.

**STEP 2.** Decorate the cats with an assortment of patches and hearts cut from scraps. Refer to General Directions for Using Appliqué Film on page 17. Fuse selected scraps to the appliqué film and cut a variety of patch sizes and hearts. Use the **Heart Appliqué Patterns** on page 185. The patches you can cut freehand. Arrange them randomly around the cats' bodies, as shown in the quilt in the photograph and in the layout.

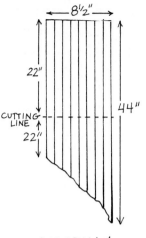

DIAGRAM 1

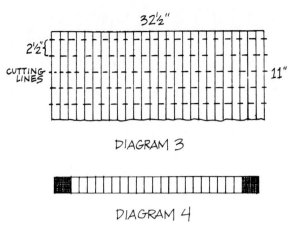

DIAGRAM 3

DIAGRAM 4

If you've chosen to fuse the cats to the background pieces, be sure to iron patches and hearts to the main cat pieces *before* removing the paper backing of the appliqué film from the cats. Otherwise, the appliqué film on the back of the cat will be activated while you're fusing the patches, and the cat will stick to your ironing board.

**STEP 3.** Center and appliqué each cat to the background pieces.

## The Lattice

**STEP 1.** Sew a 1½ × 12½-inch lattice strip from Fabric C between two sets of cat blocks to make two rows of two blocks each. Press all seams to the lattice.

**STEP 2.** Sew one 1½ × 19½-inch lattice strip between the two rows of cats. Sew the other two 1½ × 19½-inch strips to the top and bottom of the wallhanging. Press.

**STEP 3.** Sew a 1½ × 27½-inch strip to each side. Press.

## Scrap Border

**STEP 1.** Arrange the eight 1½ × 44-inch strips cut from Fabrics A and B and scraps in a pleasing order. Sew the strips together to make an 8½ × 44-inch strip set as shown in **Diagram 1**. Press all seams in one direction as you go.

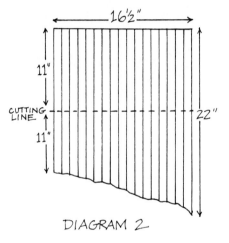

DIAGRAM 2

**STEP 2.** Cut this strip set in half and resew together to make a 16½ × 22-inch strip set. See **Diagram 2**.

**STEP 3.** Cut the strip set from Step 2 in half and resew together to make a 32½ × 11-inch strip set. See **Diagram 3**.

**STEP 4.** From this strip set, cut four 2½ × 32½-inch strips, referring to the cutting lines in **Diagram 3**.

**STEP 5.** Fit and sew the scrap border to the quilt sides. See Hints on Fitting a Scrap Border on page 28. Fit the scrap border strips to the top and bottom edges, up to but not including the side borders.

Allow ¼ inch on each end for seam allowance. Do not sew these strips to the quilt yet.

**STEP 6.** Sew a 2½ × 2½-inch corner square cut from Fabric C to each end of the top and bottom border strips. See **Diagram 4**. Press toward the border.

**STEP 7.** Pin the top and bottom borders in position and sew. Press.

## Layering the Quilt

Arrange and baste the backing, batting, and top together following the directions for Layering the Quilt on page 32. Trim the batting and backing to ¼ inch from the raw edge of the quilt top.

## Binding the Quilt

Using the 2¾ × 44-inch strips cut from Fabric D, attach the binding following the directions given under Binding the Quilt on page 33.

## The Finishing Stitches

Machine or hand quilt around the cats and the background pieces. Quilt in the ditch or ¼ inch from the seam lines. A 1-inch grid of quilting fills in the background just beautifully.

# Medium Cat Wallhanging

(shown at the left in the photo on the opposite page)

Finished Size: 20 × 22½ inches

MEDIUM CAT QUILT LAYOUT

## Materials

**FABRIC A** *(cats, hearts, patches)*

Use nine different fabrics or a coordinated assortment from your scrap bag.

⅛ yard
*each* of *nine* fabrics

**FABRIC B** *(background, backing, border)*

Background, Backing,
Heart Border     ⅝ yard

**FABRIC C** *(border, corner squares, binding)*

Half-Inch Border, Corner
Squares, and Binding     ⅓ yard

**BATTING**     ⅔ yard
cut into 22 × 26-inch piece

**Appliqué film**

**Tear-away paper** *(for machine appliqué only)*

**Black, extra-fine point, permanent felt-tip pen** *(for Penstitch only)*

## Cutting Directions

Prewash and press all of your fabrics if you anticipate that you may want to launder your appliqué project. Using a rotary cutter, see-through ruler, and cutting mat, prepare the strips as described in the first column in the chart below. Then from those strips, cut the pieces listed in the second column. Some portions of the quilt need to be cut only once, so no additional cutting information will appear in the second column.

| | | FIRST CUT | | SECOND CUT | |
|---|---|---|---|---|---|
| | | **NO. OF STRIPS** | **DIMENSIONS** | **NO. OF PIECES** | **DIMENSIONS** |
| **FABRIC B** | **BACKGROUND** | | | | |
| | | 1 | 15 × 17½-inch piece | | |
| | **HEART BORDER** | | | | |
| | | 2 | 2¼ × 44-inch strips | 2 | 2¼ × 19-inch pieces |
| | | | | 2 | 2¼ × 16-inch pieces |
| **FABRIC C** | **HALF-INCH BORDER** | | | | |
| | | 2 | 1 × 44-inch strips | 2 | 1 × 15-inch pieces |
| | | | | 2 | 1 × 19-inch pieces |
| | **CORNER SQUARES** | | | | |
| | | 4 | 2¼ × 2¼-inch squares | | |
| | **BINDING** | | | | |
| | | 3 | 2¾ × 44-inch strips | | |

## Appliqué

**STEP 1.** Refer to Timesaving Techniques for Appliqué on page 16 to decide which appliqué technique you will use (Penstitch, machine, buttonhole embroidery, or hand appliqué). Cut the appliqué designs from Fabric A using the **Medium Cat** and **Medium Cat Border Heart Appliqué Patterns** on pages 184 and 185. Cut nine cats and thirty-six hearts. (Set aside the hearts for use in the border at a later stage.)

**SEW SMART**

The Medium Cat Wallhanging shown in the photograph was done using Penstitch appliqué.

**STEP 2.** Cut a variety of patches and hearts to decorate your cats. Cut an assortment of square and triangular patches freehand. Use the **Heart Appliqué Patterns** on page 185 to cut different sizes of hearts. If you will be fusing the cats to the background fabric, be sure to fuse patches and hearts to the main cat pieces *before* removing the paper backing from the cats. Otherwise, the appliqué film on the back of the cat will be activated while you're fusing the patches, and the cat will stick to your ironing board.

**STEP 3.** Arrange and center the nine cats on the background fabric. The cats on the perimeter should be 1⅛ inch from the raw edge of the fabric. Start with the corner cats, then position the rest of the perimeter cats, and position the center cat last. Use your see-through ruler to help you with the positioning. Fuse and appliqué in position. (Of course, if you're using hand appliqué, you won't need to fuse.)

## Half-Inch Border

**STEP 1.** Sew the 1 × 15-inch strips of Fabric C to the top and bottom of the quilt. Press all seams to the border.

**STEP 2.** Sew the 1 × 19-inch strips of Fabric C to the quilt sides. Press.

## Heart Border

**STEP 1.** Sew the 2¼ × 19-inch strips of Fabric B to the quilt sides. Press seams toward the border.

**STEP 2.** Sew a corner square of Fabric C to each end of the 2¼ × 16-inch border strips. Press. Pin in position and sew to the top and bottom of the quilt.

**STEP 3.** Arrange and center nine hearts on the border sides, seven on the border top and bottom, and one in each corner square. Remember to allow for ¼-inch seam allowance on the outside fabric edge of the borders. Position the center and end hearts first, and then fill in the rest. Use your see-through ruler to make sure all the hearts are spaced an equal distance apart. Fuse all the hearts in position.

## Layering the Quilt

Arrange and baste the backing, batting, and top together following the directions for Layering the Quilt on page 32. Trim the batting and backing to ¼ inch from the raw edge of the quilt top.

## Binding the Quilt

**STEP 1.** Refer to Binding the Quilt on page 33 for directions. Cut one of the 2¾ × 44-inch strips of Fabric C in half and sew to the top and bottom of the quilt.

**STEP 2.** Use the remaining two strips of Fabric C to bind the sides.

## The Finishing Stitches

Quilt in the ditch on both sides of the half-inch border. Quilt around the cats in the background if you like.

# Four-Cat Wallhanging

(shown on the right in the photo on page 179)

Finished Size: 13½ × 15½ inches

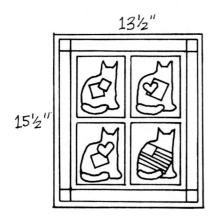

**13½"**

**15½"**

FOUR-CAT QUILT LAYOUT

## Materials

### FABRIC A (cats)

Use a coordinated assortment of four fabrics from your scrap bag or

⅛ yard *each* of *four* different fabrics

### FABRIC B (background, backing, border)

Background, Backing, Border                                ½ yard

### FABRIC C (lattice, binding)

Lattice and Binding              ¼ yard

### BATTING                          ½ yard
cut into 15 × 17-inch piece

**Appliqué film**

**Tear-away paper** (for machine appliqué only)

**Black, extra-fine point, permanent felt-tip pen** (for Penstitch only)

## Cutting Directions

Prewash and press all of your fabrics if you anticipate that you may want to launder your appliqué project. Using a rotary cutter, see-through ruler, and cutting mat, prepare the strips as described in the first column in the chart below. Then from those strips, cut the pieces listed in the second column. Some portions of the quilt need to be cut only once, so no additional cutting information will appear in the second column.

| | FIRST CUT | | SECOND CUT | |
|---|---|---|---|---|
| | **NO. OF STRIPS** | **DIMENSIONS** | **NO. OF PIECES** | **DIMENSIONS** |
| **FABRIC B** | **BACKGROUND** | | | |
| | 4 | 5 × 6-inch pieces | | |
| | **BORDER** | | | |
| | 2 | 1½ × 44-inch strips | 2 | 1½ × 13-inch pieces |
| | | | 2 | 1½ × 11-inch pieces |
| **FABRIC C** | **LATTICE** | | | |
| | 2 | 1 × 44-inch strips | 2 | 1 × 6-inch pieces |
| | | | 3 | 1 × 10-inch pieces |
| | | | 2 | 1 × 12½-inch pieces |
| | **BINDING** | | | |
| | 2 | 2¾ × 44-inch strips | 2 | 2¾ × 13-inch pieces |
| | | | 2 | 2¾ × 16-inch pieces |
| | **CORNER SQUARES** | | | |
| | 4 | 1½ × 1½-inch squares | | |
| | **Note:** You may use scraps from cat or patches fabric. | | | |

## Appliqué

**STEP 1.** Refer to Timesaving Techniques for Appliqué on page 16 to decide which technique you will use (Penstitch, machine, buttonhole embroidery, or hand appliqué). Cut one cat appliqué design from each Fabric A using the **Medium Cat Appliqué Pattern** on page 185. Cut four cats.

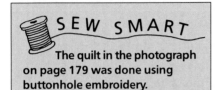

S E W   S M A R T

**The quilt in the photograph on page 179 was done using buttonhole embroidery.**

**STEP 2.** Fuse selected scraps to appliqué film and cut a variety of patches and hearts to decorate the cats. Cut an assortment of square patches freehand. Use the **Heart Appliqué Patterns** on page 185 to cut different sizes of hearts. If you will be fusing the main cat shapes to the background, be sure to fuse patches and hearts to the main cat pieces *before* removing the paper backing from the cats. Otherwise, the appliqué film on the back of the cat will be activated while you're fusing the patches, and the cat will stick to your ironing board.

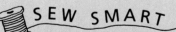

S E W   S M A R T

**Since I made my quilt out of a patriotic trio of colors, a flag patch seemed very appropriate! I cut this patch from a larger piece of fabric printed with flags. You can also find miniature flag patches for sale in fabric stores or craft catalogs.**

**STEP 3.** Center and appliqué the cats to background pieces cut from Fabric B.

## Lattice

**STEP 1.** Sew the two 1 × 6-inch strips of Fabric C between two sets of cat blocks to make two rows. Press all seams to the lattice.

**STEP 2.** Sew a 1 × 10-inch strip between the two rows to join them together. Press. Sew the two remaining 10-inch strips to the top and bottom. Press.

**STEP 3.** Sew 1 × 12½-inch lattice strips to the sides. Press.

## The Border

**STEP 1.** Sew 1½ × 13-inch strips of Fabric B to the sides. Press seams to the border.

**STEP 2.** Sew a 1½ × 1½-inch corner square to each end of the 1½ × 11-inch borders. Press. Sew these border strips to the top and bottom of the quilt. Press.

## Layering the Quilt

Arrange and baste the backing, batting, and top together following the directions for Layering the Quilt on page 32. Trim the batting and backing to ¼-inch from the raw edge of the quilt top.

## Binding the Quilt

See Binding the Quilt directions on page 33. Sew 2¾ × 13-inch strips to the top and bottom. Press. Sew 16-inch strips to the quilt sides.

## The Finishing Stitches

Quilt in the ditch around the blocks. Then "sprinkle" some stars in the border by using the **Star Quilting Templates** shown here.

STAR QUILTING TEMPLATES

# Miniature Cat Pillow

(shown in the photograph on page 174)

Finished Pillow (without ruffle): 13 × 13¾ inches

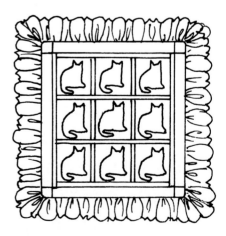

PILLOW LAYOUT

## Materials and Cutting

Prewash and press all of your fabrics. Using a rotary cutter, see-through ruler, and cutting mat, prepare the pieces as directed in the chart below.

## Appliqué

**STEP 1.** Refer to Time-Saving Techniques for Appliqué on page 16 to decide which technique you will use (machine appliqué or buttonhole embroidery). Cut nine cat designs from the Fabric A's using the **Miniature Cat Appliqué Pattern** on page 185.

**STEP 2.** Center one cat on each background square and appliqué in place to complete nine blocks.

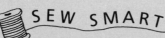

**S E W   S M A R T**

The pillow in the photograph was done in buttonhole embroidery appliqué. Penstitch appliqué is not recommended for this design because a pillow is likely to be handled and may need to be laundered. The Penstitch method wouldn't hold up well with this kind of use.

## Lattice

**STEP 1.** Arrange the blocks in a pleasing order of three rows of three blocks each. Refer to the **Pillow Layout.**

**STEP 2.** Sew a 1 × 3¾-inch Fabric C lattice strip to each side of the three center blocks. Press all seams to the lattice.

**STEP 3.** Sew a cat block to each side of the three center blocks with lattice to make three rows of cats. Press.

**STEP 4.** Sew 1 × 10½-inch lattice strips between each row of cats and to the top and bottom of the pillow front. Press.

**STEP 5.** Sew 1 × 12¼-inch lattice strips to the sides. Press.

## The Border

**STEP 1.** Sew the 1¾ × 11½-inch border strips to the top and bottom of the pillow front. Press all seams to the border.

**STEP 2.** Sew the 1¾-inch corner squares to each end of the 1¾ × 12¼-inch border strips. Press.

| | YARDAGE | CUTTING | |
|---|---|---|---|
| | | **NO. OF PIECES** | **DIMENSIONS** |
| **Fabric A** Cats | Coordinated scraps from your scrap bag for nine cats | | |
| **Fabric B** Background | ⅛ yard | 9 | 3½ × 3¾-inch pieces |
| **Fabric C** Lattice | ⅛ yard | 6 | 1 × 3¾-inch strips |
| | | 4 | 1 × 10½-inch strips |
| | | 2 | 1 × 12¼-inch strips |
| Corner Squares | | 4 | 1¾ × 1¾-inch squares |
| **Ruffle** | ½ yard | 3 | 5 × 44-inch strips |
| **Border (choose one Fabric A)** | ⅛ yard | 2 | 1¾ × 12¼-inch strips |
| | | 2 | 1¾ × 11½-inch strips |
| **Backing** | ½ yard | 1 | 14 × 14¾-inch piece |
| **Batting (for pillow form)** | ½ yard | 2 | 14 × 14¾-inch pieces |

Stuffing (for pillow form): One 1-lb. bag of smooth stuffing like FiberFil; shredded foam is not recommended.
Appliqué film
Tear-away paper (for machine appliqué only)

**STEP 3.** Pin in position and sew the border strips to the pillow sides. Press.

## The Ruffle

**STEP 1.** Sew the three 5 × 44-inch strips together to make a 130-inch-long strip. Press in half with wrong sides together.

**STEP 2.** Sew two rows of machine basting along the long raw edge of the ruffle (approximately ¼ inch and ⅜ inch from the raw edge). Pull basting stitches to gather the ruffle.

**STEP 3.** Fit the raw edge of the ruffle to the raw edge of the pillow top all the way around the pillow. Pin in position and sew ½ inch from the edge.

**STEP 4.** Use the pillow top (without counting the ruffle) as a pattern to trim the backing piece to fit. Sew the pillow top and backing together with right sides facing, using a ½-inch seam allowance. Leave a large opening (approximately 10 inches) in the bottom for turning and inserting the pillow form.

**STEP 5.** Make a custom-fit pillow form from the batting and stuffing, referring to the directions on page 37.

# Soft Sculpture Kitties

(shown in the photographs on pages 174 and 179)

Finished Size: approximately 8 × 10 inches

## Materials

### CAT

¼ yard or two 9 × 12-inch pieces for each cat

### PATCHES AND HEARTS

Coordinated scraps

### NEEDLEPUNCH

¼ yard or one 9 × 12-inch piece and one 3½ × 7-inch piece for each cat

### NONFUSIBLE INTERFACING

¼ yard

### STUFFING

Use a smooth stuffing like FiberFil; shredded foam is not recommended.

### Appliqué film

### Tear-away paper *(for machine appliqué only)*

### Black, extra-fine point, permanent felt-tip pen *(for Penstitch only)*

## Assembly

**STEP 1.** Use the **Soft Sculpture Cat** and **Tail Patterns** on pages 184 and 185. Trace the pattern lines onto the nonfusible interfacing and cut out one cat and one tail to make a pattern.

**STEP 2.** Position cat fabric pieces right sides together. Trace around the cat and tail patterns onto the wrong side of fabric. This will be the sewing line. Cut the shapes out of the fabric approximately ¼ inch from the traced sewing line.

**STEP 3.** Cut one tail and one cat out of needlepunch.

**STEP 4.** Refer to Timesaving Techniques for Appliqué on page 16 to decide which technique you will use to appliqué the hearts and patches to the cats. Fuse selected scraps to appliqué film and cut a variety of patches and hearts from these coordinated fabric scraps. Cut the square and triangular patches freehand. Use the **Heart Appliqué Patterns** on page 185 to cut out hearts of assorted sizes. Position and appliqué the hearts and patches to cat fronts.

**STEP 5.** Position the tail pieces right sides together and lay both pieces on the needlepunch tail. Sew the three layers together following the sewing lines you marked in Step 2. Leave the end open for turning. Turn and press.

**STEP 6.** Pin the open end of the tail to the cat front where indicated on the pattern. The tail piece should extend across the front of the cat's body and be clear of the seam allowance along the bottom edge.

**STEP 7.** Position the cat front and back with right sides together. Lay both pieces on the needlepunch cat piece. Sew the three layers together following the sewing lines you marked in Step 2. Leave an approximately 5-inch opening at the bottom for turning.

**STEP 8.** Clip curves and trim ear seam allowances to ⅛ inch. Turn, stuff, and handstitch the opening.

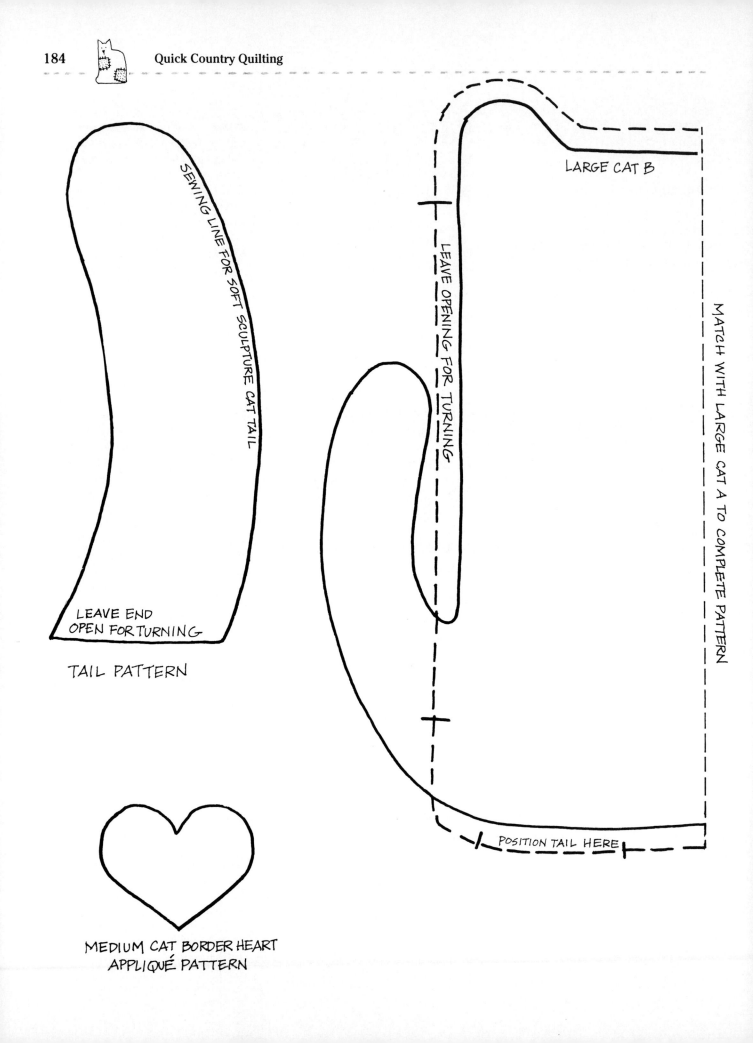

SEWING LINE FOR SOFT SCULPTURE CAT TAIL

LEAVE END OPEN FOR TURNING

TAIL PATTERN

LEAVE OPENING FOR TURNING

LARGE CAT B

MATCH WITH LARGE CAT A TO COMPLETE PATTERN

POSITION TAIL HERE

MEDIUM CAT BORDER HEART APPLIQUÉ PATTERN

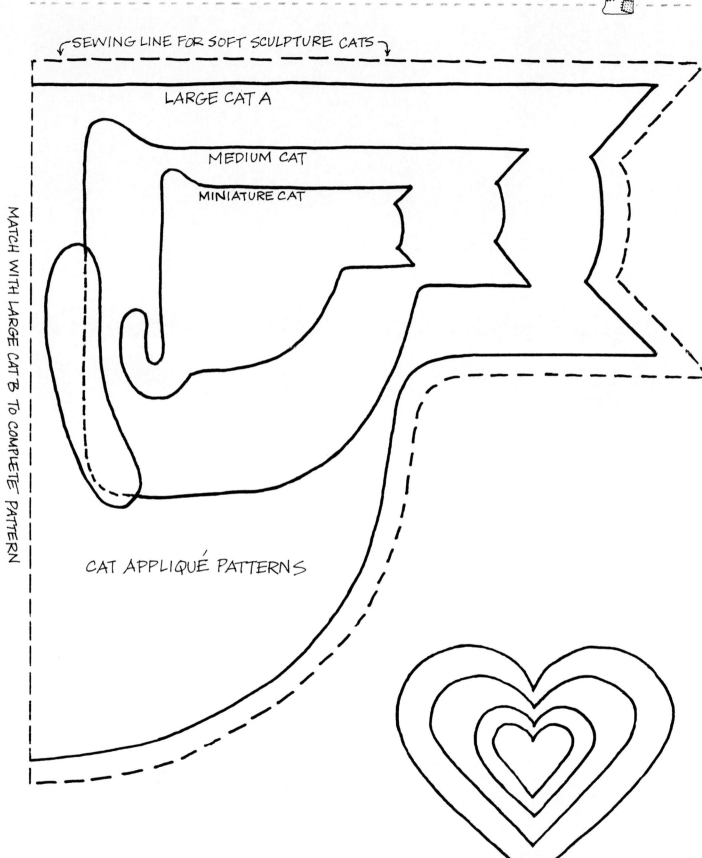

SEWING LINE FOR SOFT SCULPTURE CATS

LARGE CAT A

MEDIUM CAT

MINIATURE CAT

MATCH WITH LARGE CAT B TO COMPLETE PATTERN

CAT APPLIQUÉ PATTERNS

HEART APPLIQUÉ PATTERNS

# Baby Love

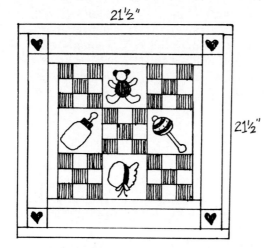

21½″

21½″

TINY TREASURES QUILT LAYOUT

## Tiny Treasures

Finished Size:
21½ × 21½ inches

### Materials and Cutting

Prewash and press all of your fabrics if you anticipate that you may want to launder your appliqué project. Using a rotary cutter, see-through ruler, and cutting mat, prepare the pieces as directed in the chart below.

| | YARDAGE | NO. OF PIECES | DIMENSIONS |
|---|---|---|---|
| | | **CUTTING** | |
| **Background Squares** | ⅙ yard (6 inches) | 4 | 5 × 5-inch squares |
| **Appliquéd Pieces** | ⅛ yard pieces or several coordinated scraps | | |
| **Border One** | ¼ yard | 2 | 1½ × 14-inch strips |
| | | 2 | 1½ × 16-inch strips |
| **Binding** | | 2 | 1½ × 20-inch strips |
| | | 2 | 1½ × 22-inch strips |
| **Border Two** | ¼ yard | 4 | 2½ × 16-inch strips |
| **Corner Squares** | ⅛ yard | 4 | 2½ × 2½-inch squares |
| **Ninepatch Squares** | | | |
| Fabric #1 | ⅛ yard | 2 | 2 × 22-inch strips |
| | | 1 | 2 × 11-inch strip |
| Fabric #2 | ⅛ yard | 1 | 2 × 22-inch strip |
| | | 2 | 2 × 11-inch strips |
| **Backing** | ⅔ yard or one 24-inch square | | |
| **Batting** | ⅔ yard or one 24-inch square | | |

**Appliqué film**
**Tear-away paper (for machine appliqué only)**
**Black, extra-fine point, permanent felt-tip pen (for Penstitch only)**

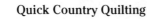

## Appliqué

**STEP 1.** Refer to Timesaving Techniques for Appliqué on page 16 and decide which technique you will use (Penstitch, machine, buttonhole embroidery, or hand appliqué). Cut appliqué designs from assorted scraps of fabric using the full-size **Tiny Treasures Appliqué Patterns** on page 194.

**STEP 2.** Appliqué the designs onto the four 5-inch background squares. Use the **Appliqué Patterns,** the **Appliqué Pattern Key,** and the **Quilt Layout** as reference for placement. Place the bottle and rattle on an angle to fit within the square. As an optional added touch, attach a ribbon bow to the base of the bonnet.

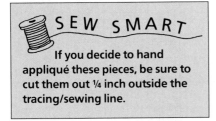

**SEW SMART**

If you decide to hand appliqué these pieces, be sure to cut them out ¼ inch outside the tracing/sewing line.

## Assembling the Ninepatch Squares

**STEP 1.** Sew together the three 2 × 11-inch strips, one of Fabric #1 and two of Fabric #2, alternating the colors as shown in **Diagram 1** to create Strip Set A. Sew together the three 2 × 22-inch strips, two of Fabric #1 and one of Fabric #2, alternating colors as shown in **Diagram 2** to create Strip Set B. Press all seams toward the darkest color.

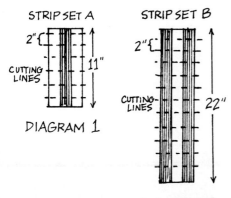

DIAGRAM 1

DIAGRAM 2

**STEP 2.** Cut five 2-inch strips from Strip Set A (refer to **Diagram 1**). Cut ten 2-inch strips from Strip Set B (refer to **Diagram 2**). Sew three 2-inch strips together to create a ninepatch block, sandwiching a strip from Set A between two strips from Set B. See **Diagram 3** for reference on how to place the strips. Repeat to make a total of five ninepatch blocks. Press toward Set A.

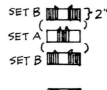

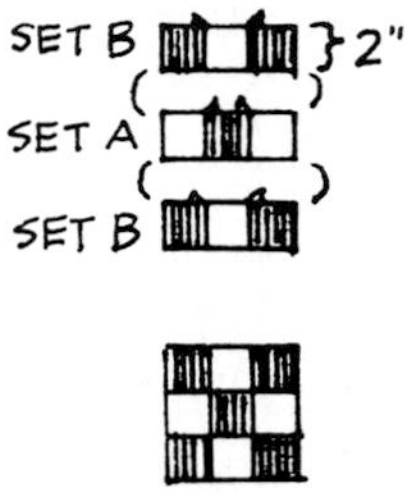

DIAGRAM 3

## Assembling the Top

Sew together the four 5-inch appliqué squares with the five ninepatch squares. Refer to the **Quilt Layout** as a guide for placement.

## The Borders

### BORDER ONE

**STEP 1.** Sew one 1½ × 14-inch border strip to each side of the wallhanging. Press all seams toward the border.

**STEP 2.** Sew one 1½ × 16-inch border strip to the top and another to the bottom. Press.

### BORDER TWO

**STEP 1.** Sew one 2½ × 16-inch strip to each side of the wall-hanging. Press all seams to the border.

**STEP 2.** Cut four heart appliqué shapes from scraps of fabric, using the full-size **Corner Square Heart** pattern on page 194. Following

the instructions for the appliqué method you've chosen, attach one heart to the center of each corner square.

**STEP 3.** Sew the four 2½-inch corner squares to the ends of the two remaining 2½ × 16-inch border strips. Press toward the border. Pin the strips in position and sew to the top and bottom edges of the wallhanging. Press.

## Binding

**STEP 1.** Sew one 1½ × 20-inch binding strip to each side of the wallhanging. Press all seams to the binding.

**STEP 2.** Sew 1½ × 22-inch strips to the top and bottom edges of the wallhanging. Press.

## Finishing

**STEP 1.** Position the top and backing right sides together. Lay both pieces on top of the batting and pin all three layers together. Trim the batting and backing to the same size as the top. Sew together, leaving a 3- to 4-inch opening for turning.

**STEP 2.** Turn right side out and handstitch the opening. Press.

**STEP 3.** Machine or hand quilt in the ditch around the ninepatch blocks and the borders.

# Ready to Roll

Finished Size: 16 × 14½ inches

## Materials and Cutting

Prewash and press all of your fabrics if you anticipate that you may want to launder your appliqué project. Using a rotary cutter, see-through ruler, and cutting mat, prepare the pieces as directed in the chart below.

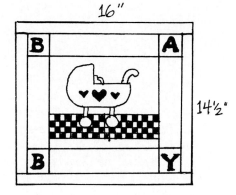

READY TO ROLL QUILT LAYOUT

| | YARDAGE | NO. OF PIECES | DIMENSIONS |
|---|---|---|---|
| | | | **CUTTING** |
| **Background** | ¼ yard | 1 | 6 × 10½-inch piece |
| | | 1 | 1½ × 10½-inch strip |
| **Corner Squares** | | 4 | 2½ × 2½-inch squares |
| **Appliquéd Pieces** | Several coordinated scraps including 6-inch-wide pieces for the buggy | | |
| **Sidewalk Checkerboard*** | | | |
| Fabric #1 | ⅛ yard | 2 | 1 × 44-inch strips |
| Fabric #2 | ⅛ yard | 2 | 1 × 44-inch strips |
| **Border** | ⅛ yard | 2 | 2½ × 10½-inch strips |
| | | 2 | 2½ × 9-inch strips |
| **Binding** | ⅛ yard | 2 | 1½ × 13½-inch strips |
| | | 2 | 1½ × 16½-inch strips |
| **Backing** | ½ yard or 16 × 18-inch piece | | |
| **Batting** | ½ yard or 16 × 18-inch piece | | |
| Appliqué film<br>Tear-away paper (for machine appliqué only)<br>Black, extra-fine point, permanent felt-tip pen (for Penstitch only) | | | |

*If you prefer a solid sidewalk, cut one 2½ × 10½-inch piece from one of these fabrics.

## Alternate Sidewalk

Instead of using the checkerboard described below, you can substitute a solid piece of fabric. Sew this solid piece to the background pieces as described in Step 4.

## Sidewalk Checkerboard

**STEP 1.** Cut two 1 × 44-inch strips of Fabrics #1 and #2 in half to make four 1 × 22-inch strips of each fabric. Sew together the strips, alternating fabrics as shown in **Diagram 4**. Press all seams to the darkest fabric.

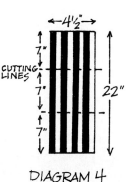

DIAGRAM 4

**STEP 2.** Cut the strip set into three 7-inch sections as shown in **Diagram 4.** Sew these sections together to make a 12½ × 7-inch strip set. From this unit, cut four 1 × 12½-inch strips. See **Diagram 5.**

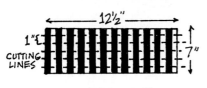

DIAGRAM 5

**STEP 3.** Fit each checkerboard strip to the 10½-inch-wide background pieces and trim as necessary. See Hints on Fitting a Checkerboard Border on page 29. Sew the four strips together to form the checkerboard as shown in **Diagram 6.**

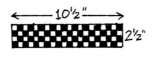

DIAGRAM 6

**STEP 4.** With right sides together, sew one background piece to each side of the checkerboard. See **Diagram 7.**

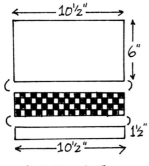

DIAGRAM 7

## Appliqué

**STEP 1.** Refer to Timesaving Techniques for Appliqué on page 16 to decide which technique you will use (Penstitch, machine, buttonhole embroidery, or hand appliqué). Cut appliqué designs from coordinated scraps of fabric using the full-size **Ready to Roll Appliqué Patterns** on page 195.

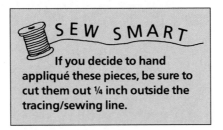

If you decide to hand appliqué these pieces, be sure to cut them out ¼ inch outside the tracing/sewing line.

**STEP 2.** Appliqué the buggy pieces to the background/checkerboard unit. Start by positioning the wheels; these should be about ⅛ inch above the bottom edge of the checkerboard and set a little to the left of the center to allow enough room for the handle. See the **Appliqué Patterns** and the **Appliqué Pattern Key** on page 195 for additional placement guidance and the order in which the pieces should be fused.

## The Border

**STEP 1.** Sew the 2½ × 10½-inch border strips to the wallhanging top and bottom. Press all seams toward the border.

**STEP 2.** Cut the appliqué shapes to spell *B A B Y* from fabric scraps, using the full-size patterns on page 195. Following the instructions for the appliqué method you've chosen, appliqué one letter to the center of each of the four corner squares.

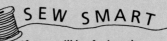

If you will be fusing these letters onto the border, remember that you must start by tracing them in *reverse* onto the paper side of the appliqué film. See page 17 for pointers.

**STEP 3.** Sew 2½-inch corner squares to both ends of each of the remaining 2½ × 9-inch border strips. Pay attention to the order of the letters. The strip for the left side should have a *B* in the top and bottom corners. The strip for the right side should have an *A* in the top corner and a *Y* in the bottom. Press seams toward the borders. Pin the strips in position and sew to the sides of the wallhanging. Press.

## Binding

**STEP 1.** Sew one 1½ × 13½-inch binding strip to each side of the wallhanging. Press seams toward the binding.

**STEP 2.** Sew the remaining 1½ × 16½-inch binding strips to the top and bottom of the wallhanging. Press.

## Finishing

Refer to Finishing under Tiny Treasures on page 188. Machine or hand quilt in the ditch around all borders and corner squares.

# Goodnight

Finished Size: 17½ × 23 inches

17½"

23"

GOODNIGHT QUILT LAYOUT

## Materials and Cutting

Prewash and press all of your fabrics if you anticipate that you may want to launder your appliqué project. Using a rotary cutter, see-through ruler, and cutting mat, prepare the pieces as directed in the chart below.

| | YARDAGE | NO. OF PIECES | DIMENSIONS |
|---|---|---|---|
| | | CUTTING | |
| **Background** | ⅜ yard | 1 | 9 × 11-inch piece |
| | | 1 | 3½ × 12-inch piece |
| **Appliqué Pieces** | | | |
|    **Goodnight lettering** | ⅛ yard or coordinated scraps | | |
|    **Bed cover** | ¼ yard or coordinated scraps | | |
|    **Clown, bear, and bunny** | ⅛ yard pieces or several coordinated scraps | | |
| **Border One** | ⅛ yard | 2 | 2 × 11-inch strips |
| | | 2 | 2 × 12-inch strips |
| **Corner Squares** | | 4 | 2½ × 2½-inch squares |
| **Border Two** | ⅛ yard | 3 | 1 × 12-inch strips |
| | | 2 | 1 × 18½-inch strips |
| **Binding** | | 2 | 1 × 22½-inch strips |
| | | 2 | 1 × 18½-inch strips |
| **Border Three** | ¼ yard | 2 | 2½ × 18½-inch strips |
| | | 2 | 2½ × 13-inch strips |
| **Backing** | ⅝ yard or 19 × 25-inch piece | | |
| **Batting** | ⅝ yard or 19 × 25-inch piece | | |
| **Appliqué film** <br> **Tear-away paper (for machine appliqué only)** <br> **Black, extra-fine point, permanent felt-tip pen (for Penstitch only)** | | | |

## Appliqué

**STEP 1.** Refer to Timesaving Techniques for Appliqué on page 16 to decide which technique you will use (Penstitch, machine, or buttonhole embroidery appliqué). Cut appliqué designs from assorted scraps of fabric using the full-size **Goodnight Appliqué Patterns** at right.

**STEP 2.** Appliqué all pieces of the design onto the center of the 9 × 11-inch background piece. Use the **Appliqué Patterns** and the **Appliqué Pattern Key** as reference for placement. The appliqué designs should be placed about ¾ inch in from the edges of the background piece.

**STEP 3.** Appliqué the letters for *Goodnight* to the 3½ × 12-inch background piece. Letters should be placed about ⅞ inch in from the sides and bottom of the background piece.

## The Borders

### BORDER ONE

Sew 2 × 11-inch strips to each side of the 9 × 11-inch background piece. Press toward the border. Sew 2 × 12-inch strips to the top and bottom and press.

### BORDER TWO

**STEP 1.** Sew a 1 × 12-inch border strip to the top of the animal appliqué piece. Sew 1 × 12-inch strips to the top and bottom of the Goodnight appliqué piece. Press toward the borders.

**STEP 2.** Sew the Goodnight appliqué piece to the animal appliqué piece. Press. Sew 1 × 18½-inch border strips to the sides. Press.

### BORDER THREE

**STEP 1.** Sew 2½ × 18½-inch border strips to the sides. Press all seams toward the border.

**STEP 2.** Sew 2½-inch corner squares to the ends of two 2½ × 13-inch border strips. Press. Pin the borders in position and sew to the top and bottom of the wallhanging. Press.

## Binding

Sew a 1 × 22½-inch binding strip to each side. Press all seams toward the binding. Sew 1 × 18-inch strips to the top and bottom of the wallhanging. Press.

## Finishing

Refer to Finishing under Tiny Treasures on page 188. Machine or hand quilt in the ditch around the background pieces, all borders, and corner squares.

USE FINE POINT, PERMANENT
FELT-TIP PEN TO IMARK EYES
AND MOUTHS.

APPLIQUÉ PATTERN KEY

———————— TRACING LINE

— — — — — TRACING LINE
(BUT WILL BE
HIDDEN BEHIND
OTHER FABRIC)

GOODNIGHT APPLIQUÉ PATTERNS

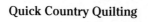 

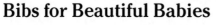

## Bibs for Beautiful Babies

### Materials

Plain, undecorated baby bibs
Scraps of fabric for appliqué
Appliqué film
Tear-away paper (for machine appliqué)

### Teddy Bib

Use the teddy bear and heart appliqué designs from Tiny Treasures. Cut out a bear and two hearts from fabric scraps. Center on the bib and machine appliqué in position. See Machine Appliqué directions on page 19.

### Toy Bib

Use the rattle and heart appliqué designs from Tiny Treasures. Cut out the rattle and three hearts from fabric scraps. Center on the bib and machine appliqué in position. See Machine Appliqué directions on page 19.

BONNET - ADD ½" RIBBON BOW (OPTIONAL)

← BOW

CORNER SQUARE HEART

TINY TREASURES APPLIQUÉ PATTERNS

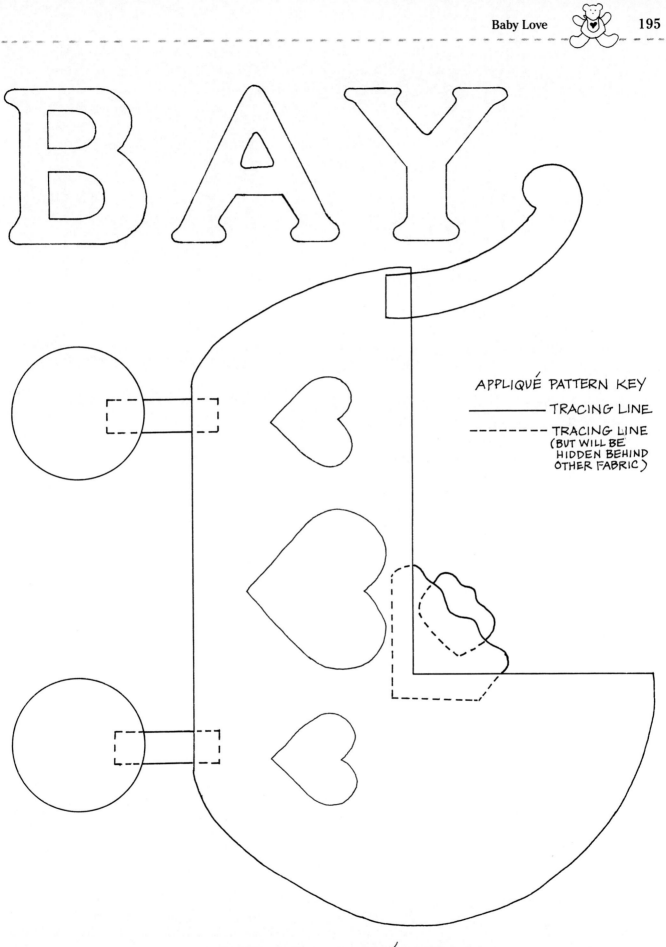

APPLIQUÉ PATTERN KEY

——————— TRACING LINE

- - - - - - - TRACING LINE
(BUT WILL BE
HIDDEN BEHIND
OTHER FABRIC)

READY TO ROLL APPLIQUÉ PATTERNS

Star Light, Star Bright
First star I see tonight,
I wish I may, I wish I might
Have the wish I wish tonight.

Hey Diddle Diddle
The cat and the fiddle,
The cow jumped over the moon,
The little dog laughed to see such sport
And the dish ran away
with the spoon.

# Nursery Rhyme Time

18"

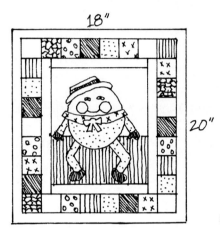

20"

HUMPTY DUMPTY LAYOUT

14"

19½"

STAR LIGHT, STAR BRIGHT LAYOUT

14"

19½"

HEY DIDDLE DIDDLE LAYOUT

**J**ust in time for baby's arrival! Here's a trio of terrific wallhangings to brighten the nursery. Toddlers will love them, too, because they feature two all-time favorite nursery rhymes, "Hey Diddle Diddle" and "Star Light, Star Bright" (shown on the wall and hanging from the child's dresser). Inexpensive screen-printed panels featuring the rhymes are available from the address provided on page 251. Everyone's favorite egg, Humpty Dumpty, sits astride a fabric "wall" in the third wallhanging.

# Hey Diddle Diddle

Finished Size: 14 × 19½ inches

## Materials and Cutting

Prewash and press all of your fabrics if you anticipate that you may want to launder your appliqué project. Using a rotary cutter, see-through ruler, and cutting mat, prepare the pieces as directed in the chart below.

| | YARDAGE | CUTTING | |
|---|---|---|---|
| | | NO. OF PIECES | DIMENSIONS |
| Appliqué Background | ¼ yard | 1 | 8½ × 10½-inch piece |
| Half-Inch Border | ⅛ yard | 3 | 1 × 8½-inch strips |
| | | 2 | 1 × 11½-inch strips |
| Binding | | 2 | 1 × 13½-inch strips |
| | | 2 | 1 × 20-inch strips |
| Checkerboard Border | | | |
| Fabric #1 | ¼ yard | 3 | 1½ × 44-inch strips |
| Fabric #2 | ¼ yard | 3 | 1½ × 44-inch strips |
| Corner Squares | ⅛ yard | 4 | 2½ × 2½-inch squares |
| Appliqué Pieces | | | |
| Cow and stars | ⅛ yard or scraps of several coordinated fabrics | | |
| Moon | ⅛ yard | | |
| Backing | ½ yard | 1 | 16 × 21-inch piece |
| Batting | ½ yard | 1 | 16 × 21-inch piece |
| Appliqué film<br>Black, extra-fine point, permanent felt-tip pen<br>Screen-printed "Hey Diddle Diddle" panel (ordering information on page 251) | | | |

## Appliqué

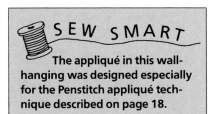

SEW SMART

The appliqué in this wall-hanging was designed especially for the Penstitch appliqué technique described on page 18.

**STEP 1.** Cut appliqué designs from assorted scraps of fabric using the **Hey Diddle Diddle Appliqué Patterns** on page 201.

**STEP 2.** Fuse and Penstitch appliqué the cow and moon pieces onto the 8½ × 10½-inch background fabric. Use the **Appliqué Patterns** and the **Appliqué Pattern Key** as guides for placing the pieces. With the felt-tip pen, draw the cow's eyes and nostrils.

**STEP 3.** Center, fuse, and Penstitch appliqué a star to each of the four 2½-inch corner squares.

## The Border

**STEP 1.** Cut out the screened nursery rhyme panel on the dotted lines.

**STEP 2.** Sew 1 × 8½-inch border strips to the top and bottom of the appliquéd background piece and to the bottom of the nursery rhyme panel. Press all seams toward the border.

**STEP 3.** Sew the appliquéd section to the nursery rhyme section. Press.

**STEP 4.** Sew 1 × 11½-inch border strips to the wallhanging sides. Press.

## Checkerboard Border

**STEP 1.** Sew together the six 1½ × 44-inch strips of checkerboard fabric, alternating colors as shown in **Diagram 1**. As you sew, press all seams toward the darkest fabric.

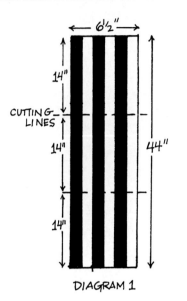

DIAGRAM 1

**STEP 2.** Cut the strip set into thirds. Each third measures approximately 14 inches. Resew those thirds together to make an 18½ × 14-inch strip set like the one shown in **Diagram 2**.

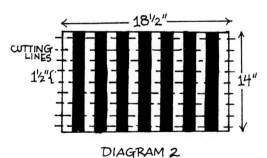

DIAGRAM 2

**STEP 3.** From this strip set, cut eight 1½ × 18½-inch strips, referring to the cutting lines in **Diagram 2**. Sew two of these strips

together to form a checkerboard like the one in **Diagram 3**. Make a total of four checkerboard border strips.

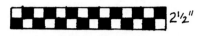

DIAGRAM 3

**STEP 4.** Fit two checkerboard borders to the wallhanging sides. See Hints on Fitting a Checkerboard Border on page 29. Sew and press.

**STEP 5.** Fit two checkerboard strips to the top and bottom, up to but not including the side checkerboard borders. Allow ¼ inch on the ends of each strip so they will fit correctly after corner squares are added. Sew a corner square to both ends of each border. Press. Pin in position and sew to the top and bottom. Press.

## Binding

**STEP 1.** Sew 1 × 13½-inch binding strips to the top and bottom of the wallhanging. Press all seams to the binding.

**STEP 2.** Sew 1 × 20-inch strips to the sides. Press.

## Finishing

**STEP 1.** Position the top and backing with right sides together. Lay both pieces on top of the batting and pin all three layers together. Trim the batting and backing to the same size as the top. Sew together, leaving a 3- to 4-inch opening for turning.

**STEP 2.** Turn right side out, press, and handstitch opening. Press.

**STEP 3.** Machine or hand quilt in the ditch on both sides of the border and the binding.

# Star Light, Star Bright

Finished Size: 14 × 19½ inches

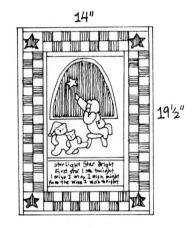

STAR LIGHT, STAR BRIGHT LAYOUT

This project uses the same basic materials, cutting information, and step-by-step directions as appear above for Hey Diddle Diddle. The only difference is that you will need ¼ yard of fabric for the sky appliqué piece and ¼ yard of fabric for the window appliqué piece. For the other appliqué shapes, ⅛ yard or several coordinated scraps will be adequate. Use the **Star Light, Star Bright Appliqué Patterns** on page 202. With the felt-tip pen, add noses and eyes to the bears. For the corner squares, use the star pattern on page 201.

# Humpty Dumpty

Finished Size: 18 × 20 inches

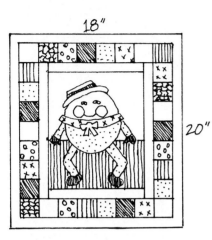

HUMPTY DUMPTY LAYOUT

## Materials and Cutting

Prewash and press all of your fabrics if you anticipate that you may want to launder your appliqué project. Using a rotary cutter, see-through ruler, and cutting mat, prepare the pieces as directed in the chart below.

## Appliqué

The appliqué in this wallhanging was designed especially to use the buttonhole embroidery technique described on page 19. However, you may use Penstitch if you prefer.

**STEP 1.** Sew the 7¼ × 10½-inch sky piece to the 5¾ × 10½-inch piece of wall fabric to make the background. Press seam toward the wall fabric.

**STEP 2.** Cut the appliqué designs from assorted fabrics using the **Humpty Dumpty Appliqué Pattern** on page 203. You will need to trace one arm as shown, plus one reversed. Line up points A and B to position the arms correctly.

**STEP 3.** Refer to the **Appliqué Pattern** and **Appliqué Pattern Key** as you position and fuse the design to the background. Humpty Dumpty should be seated with his hands resting on the wall. Center him between left and right edges.

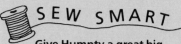

**S E W   S M A R T**

Give Humpty a great big smile by embroidering one from cheek to cheek using the chain stitch and two strands of embroidery floss. With one strand of floss, stitch the details for his eyes.

## Border One

**STEP 1.** Sew 1½ × 10½-inch border strips to the top and bottom of the appliquéd piece. Press all seams to the border.

**STEP 2.** Sew 1½ × 14½-inch border strips to the sides. Press.

## Scrap Border

**STEP 1.** Using the scraps left over from the appliqué and background fabrics, cut thirty 2½ × 2½-inch squares.

**STEP 2.** Sew together two strips of seven squares each and two strips of eight squares each. Press all seams in one direction.

| | YARDAGE | CUTTING | |
|---|---|---|---|
| | | NO. OF PIECES | DIMENSIONS |
| **Background** | | | |
| Sky | ¼ yard | 1 | 7¼ × 10½-inch piece |
| Wall | ¼ yard | 1 | 5¾ × 10½-inch piece |
| **Appliqué Pieces and Scrap Border** | ⅛ yard or scraps of several coordinated fabrics | | |
| **Border One** | ⅓ yard | 2 | 1½ × 10½-inch strips |
| | | 2 | 1½ × 14½-inch strips |
| **Binding** | | 2 | 1½ × 17½-inch strips |
| | | 2 | 1½ × 20½-inch strips |
| **Backing** | ⅝ yard | 1 | 20 × 22-inch piece |
| **Batting** | ⅝ yard | 1 | 20 × 22-inch piece |
| **Appliqué film** Buttonhole embroidery: Coordinating embroidery floss to match appliqué fabrics Black, extra-fine point, permanent felt-tip pen (for Penstitch only) | | | |

**STEP 3.** Sew the seven-square strips to the top and bottom of the wallhanging. Press all seams to Border One.

**STEP 4.** Sew the eight-square strips to the wallhanging sides. Press.

## Binding

**STEP 1.** Sew the 1½ × 17½-inch binding strips to the top and bottom. Press all seams to the binding.

**STEP 2.** Sew the 1½ × 20½-inch binding strips to the sides. Press.

## Finishing

**STEP 1.** Position the top and backing with right sides together. Lay both pieces on top of the batting and pin all three layers together. Trim the batting and backing to the same size as the top. Sew together, leaving a 3- to 4-inch opening for turning.

**STEP 2.** Turn right side out and handstitch the opening.

**STEP 3.** Machine or hand quilt in the ditch around both the borders.

HEY DIDDLE DIDDLE
APPLIQUÉ PATTERNS

APPLIQUÉ PATTERN KEY

——————— TRACING LINE

- - - - - - - TRACING LINE
(BUT WILL BE HIDDEN
BEHIND OTHER FABRIC)

APPLIQUÉ PATTERN KEY
——————— TRACING LINE
- - - - - - - TRACING LINE
(BUT WILL BE HIDDEN
BEHIND OTHER FABRIC)

SOLID LINES ARE WINDOW FRAME

SKY TRACING LINE ↓

SKY TRACING LINE ↓

STAR LIGHT, STAR BRIGHT
APPLIQUÉ PATTERNS

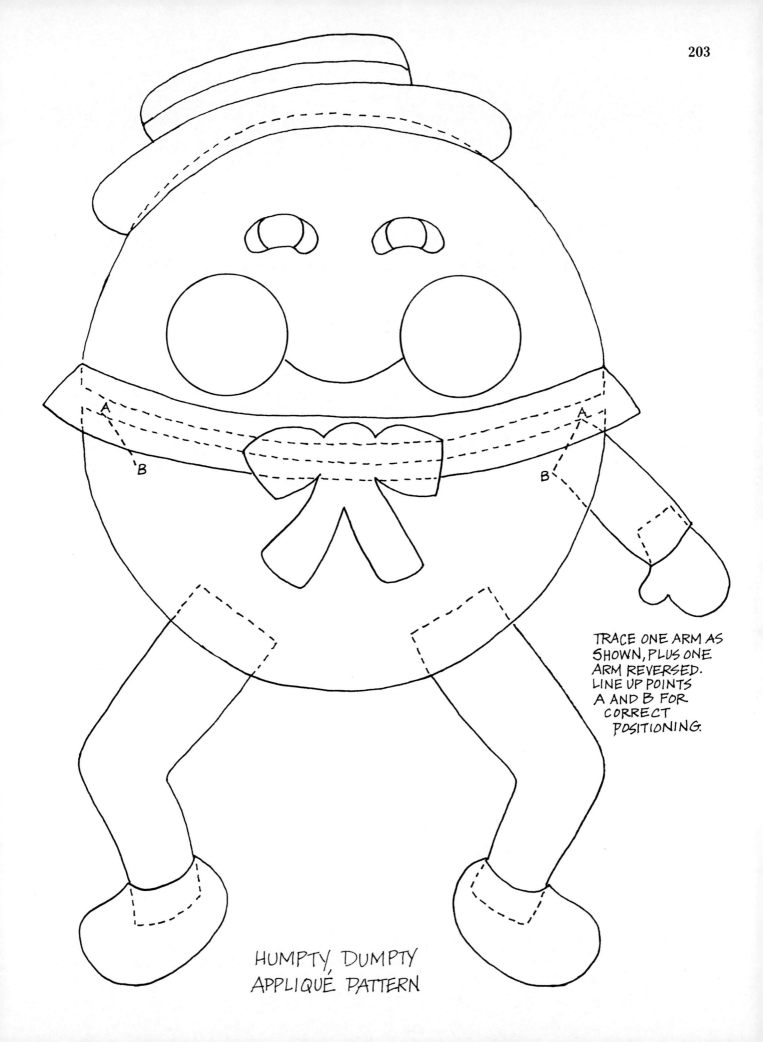

TRACE ONE ARM AS
SHOWN, PLUS ONE
ARM REVERSED.
LINE UP POINTS
A AND B FOR
CORRECT
POSITIONING.

A

B

A

B

HUMPTY DUMPTY
APPLIQUÉ PATTERN

# So Simple Sweatshirts

TEDDY BEAR APPLIQUÉ PATTERN

**O**nce you realize how easy it is to add appliqué to sweatshirts, you'll never wear a plain one again! The secret behind the ease of these no-sew sweatshirts is an appliqué film that stays put. That means you don't have to sew down the edges on all the appliqué pieces. Just cut out the appliqué shapes, fuse them in place with your iron, and your sweatshirt is ready to wear! You can't beat that for a last-minute gift idea!

## Teddy Bears

(shown in the front right of the photograph)

**Materials**

**SWEATSHIRT** *(adult or child-size)*

**APPLIQUÉ PIECES**

⅛ yard pieces or several coordinated scraps

**APPLIQUÉ FILM**

Choose an appliqué film product that doesn't need the edges sewn to remain intact and is laundry safe. I used Heat 'N Bond for the sweatshirts in the photograph.

**Black, extra-fine point, permanent felt-tip pen**

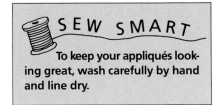

S E W   S M A R T
To keep your appliqués looking great, wash carefully by hand and line dry.

**STEP 1.** Before you begin, refer to Timesaving Techniques for Appliqué on page 16 for basic guidelines.

**STEP 2.** Trace the appliqué designs (six bears, six bows, and three 3-inch squares) onto appliqué film using the **Teddy Bear Appliqué Pattern** above. (You can trace the square on page 207.) Fuse to assorted scraps of fabric, then cut the appliqué shapes out of the fabric.

**STEP 3.** Center the designs on the sweatshirt front, alternating three bears with three squares (refer to the photograph). Position the designs approximately 2 inches down from the neckline, and space the bears and squares about 1 inch apart. For smaller sweatshirts, everything may need to be spaced a little closer. Press in position and Penstitch appliqué.

**STEP 4.** Press and Penstitch appliqué the remaining bears to the three squares. Fuse the bows to the fronts of the teddies.

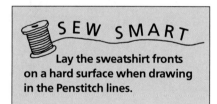

**SEW SMART**
Lay the sweatshirt fronts on a hard surface when drawing in the Penstitch lines.

# Hearts and Bunnies

(shown in the front left of the photograph on page 204)

**STEP 1.** Before you begin, refer to Timesaving Techniques for Appliqué on page 16 for basic guidelines.

**STEP 2.** Trace the appliqué designs (three hearts, three bunnies, and six 3-inch squares) onto appliqué film using the **Bunny Appliqué Pattern** and the **Large Heart Appliqué Pattern** on the opposite page. Fuse onto assorted scraps and then cut the shapes from the fabric.

**STEP 3.** Position the six squares on the sweatshirt front approximately 2 inches down from the neckline. Space squares about 1 inch apart. For smaller sweatshirts, everything may need to be spaced a little closer. Press in position and Penstitch appliqué.

**STEP 4.** Fuse and Penstitch appliqué bunnies (and their clothing) and hearts to the squares, alternating hearts and bunnies.

# Country Critters

(see the pink sweatshirt in the photograph on page 204)

**STEP 1.** Before you begin, refer to Timesaving Techniques for Appliqué on page 16 for basic guidelines.

**STEP 2.** Trace the appliqué designs (one bear, one bunny, one sheep, ten hearts, two ⅜ × 9½-inch strips, and one 4 × 9½-inch background piece) onto appliqué film. Use the **Small Heart Appliqué Pattern** and animal patterns on the opposite page. Fuse onto assorted scraps of fabric, then cut the shapes from the fabric.

**SEW SMART**
Instead of cutting the squares and rectangles with scissors, I usually cut an oversized piece of appliqué film and fuse it to an oversized piece of selected fabric. After the piece has cooled, remove the paper backing. Now, using a rotary cutter and see-through ruler, cut these pieces to size.

**STEP 3.** Center the design on the sweatshirt front. Position the background piece approximately 3 inches down from the neckline and press. Center, fuse, and Penstitch appliqué the animal designs on the background pieces. Position and fuse the ⅜-inch strips along the top and bottom edges of the background piece. Center, fuse, and Penstitch appliqué five hearts above and five hearts below the main design. Use the photograph for a visual guide.

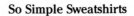

BUNNY APPLIQUÉ
PATTERN

DRAW IN
HEART LINE
WITH PEN

COUNTRY CRITTERS
BEAR APPLIQUÉ
PATTERN

SHEEP APPLIQUÉ PATTERN

SMALL HEART
APPLIQUÉ PATTERN

LARGE HEART APPLIQUÉ PATTERN

APPLIQUÉ PATTERN KEY

——————— TRACING LINE

- - - - - - - - - - TRACING LINE
(WILL BE HIDDEN
BEHIND OTHER
FABRIC)

209

# Easter Ensemble

Thereʼs a breath of springtime in the air, so why not get in the mood and add a fresh touch to the rooms in your home? This project features a bakerʼs dozen of cheery Easter and springtime designs that you can use in a number of different ways.

Stitch together some square or oval ornaments to hang on an "Easter Tree" or a pretty pastel wreath (as shown in the photograph on page 211). You can also perk up your kitchen table by stitching together an Easter Table Runner with your choice of appliqué designs. And maybe thereʼs a cozy little corner somewhere in the house thatʼs just the perfect place for a charming little Spring Is Here wall quilt.

## Easter Ornaments

(shown on wall, in teddyʼs lap and against base of lamp in the photo opposite)

**Materials**

**ORNAMENT BACKGROUND**

Square
  Two 3½ × 3½-inch squares per ornament
  (⅛ yard makes six ornaments)
Small Egg
  Two 3¾ × 4½-inch pieces per ornament
  (⅛ yard makes six ornaments)
Large Egg
  Two 4½ × 5¼-inch pieces per ornament
  (⅛ yard makes five ornaments)

**APPLIQUÉ DESIGNS**

Coordinated scraps or ⅛ yard each of several coordinated fabrics

**TRIM, BRAID, PIPING, OR LACE**

½ yard per ornament

**RIBBON HANGER**

½ yard per ornament (⅛ to ½ inch wide)

**BATTING** *(optional, for egg ornaments only)*

¼ yard lightweight batting makes sixteen eggs

**Black, extra-fine point, permanent felt-tip pen**

**Appliqué film**

**Stuffing** *(Use a smooth stuffing like FiberFil, not shredded foam.)*

## Appliqué

These ornaments were designed especially for the Penstitch appliqué technique described on page 18.

**STEP 1.** Cut two 3½ × 3½-inch pieces for each square ornament or two ovals for each egg-shaped ornament you wish to make. Use the **Egg Ornament Pattern** on page 215. (Note that there are patterns for two different size eggs; choose whichever one you like.) Cut with fabrics placed right sides together.

**STEP 2.** Cut out the appliqué designs of your choice from the thirteen **Appliqué Patterns** on pages 216 and 217. Note that the heart and tulip designs are suited for the small egg ornament only. The Easter bonnet design will not fit onto the small-size egg. All of the other designs can be used on whatever size or shape ornament you desire. Fuse and Penstitch the appliqué designs onto the ornament background pieces. Refer to the **Appliqué Patterns** and the **Appliqué Pattern Key** for help in placing the pieces.

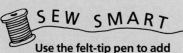

**SEW SMART**

Use the felt-tip pen to add eyes and noses to your appliqué designs. Tack a ribbon bow (½ to ⅝ inch wide) to the bottom of the tulip design. Also add a ribbon bow to the bottom of the Easter bonnet design.

## Assembling the Ornaments

**STEP 1.** Cut two 8- to 9-inch pieces of ribbon for a hanger for each ornament. Pin and sew to the right side of the front ornament piece as shown in **Diagram 1.** (Do this for both square and egg ornaments.)

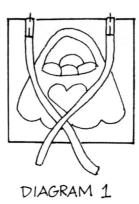

DIAGRAM 1

If you wish to use lace or trim on your ornaments, choose between the methods described in Steps 2 and 3. If you are not adding any trimming to your ornaments, proceed to Steps 4 and 5.

**STEP 2.** Pin lace or trim to the ornament front and stitch ¼-inch from the raw edge. See **Diagram 2.** Position ornament back and ornament front with right sides facing and sew together.

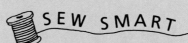

**SEW SMART**

You can line the front of the egg-shaped ornaments with a piece of lightweight batting to make stuffing easier. After you appliqué, position egg ornament pieces with right sides together. Lay both pieces on top of the batting (the egg front should be next to the batting). Add ribbon hanger and any lace trim at this time. Sew together, leaving an opening for turning.

Leave an opening at the bottom for turning. Fill with stuffing and handstitch the opening closed.

DIAGRAM 2

**STEP 3.** Here's a no-sew option for attaching trim. Sew the front to the back leaving an opening for turning. Stuff and handstitch the opening closed. Using a hot glue gun, glue braided trim around the edge of the ornament.

**STEP 4.** For ornaments you wish to leave plain, with no trim, simply sew the front to back with right sides together, leaving an opening for turning.

**STEP 5.** Here's another finishing option. For a pinking-sheared edge, sew the ornament front to back with the *wrong* sides together. Leave an opening at the top as shown in **Diagram 3.** Use pinking shears to trim the edge all the way around the ornament. Fill with stuffing. Pin two 8- to 9-inch ribbon pieces in position at the top of the back piece for hangers. Now finish stitching across the top.

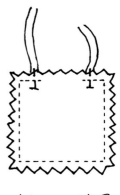

DIAGRAM 3

# Springtime Wreath

### Materials

18- to 22-inch white grapevine
   wreath
Country Blue Spray Paint (or any
   color of your choice)
6 or 7 Easter Ornaments (see
   directions above)
Bow made from 4 yards of 2½- to
   3-inch-wide florist ribbon or
   twisted-paper ribbon
Three satin ribbons in coordinating
   colors, ⅜ to 1½ inches wide,
   4 yards each
Hot glue gun and glue sticks

**STEP 1.** Spraypaint a white grapevine wreath (white is easier to cover evenly than a natural wreath) with Country Blue or the color of your choice. Let it dry thoroughly. If you're not pleased with the way the paint has gone on, a second coat may be necessary.

**STEP 2.** Leaving an approximately 6-inch tail, tie the three satin ribbons together in a knot. Tie a knot about every 6 inches or so, leaving a 6- to 8-inch tail on the other end of the ribbons. Using a hot glue gun, attach the ribbons to the wreath with a spot of glue under each knot.

**STEP 3.** Make a large bow with the florist or twisted-paper ribbon, and attach it with a hot glue gun at the top of the wreath.

**STEP 4.** Position the ornaments evenly around the wreath and glue in place.

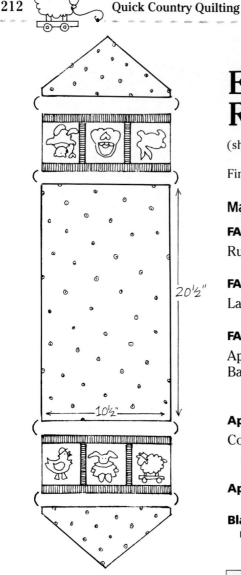

TABLE RUNNER LAYOUT

# Easter Table Runner

(shown in the photo on page 208)

Finished Size: 11 × 37 inches

## Materials

### FABRIC A

Runner and Backing        ¾ yard

### FABRIC B

Lattice and Binding        ¼ yard

### FABRIC C

Appliqué Design
Background Squares        ⅛ yard
    or six 3½ × 3½-inch squares

### Appliqué Designs

Coordinated scraps or ⅛ yard of
    several coordinated fabrics

### Appliqué film

### Black, extra-fine point, permanent felt-tip pen

## Cutting Directions

Prewash and press your fabrics. Using a rotary cutter, see-through ruler, and cutting mat, prepare the strips as described in the first column in the chart below. Then from those strips, cut the pieces listed in the second column. Some portions of the table runner need to be cut only once, so no additional cutting information will appear in the second column.

| | FIRST CUT | | SECOND CUT | |
|---|---|---|---|---|
| | **NO. OF STRIPS** | **DIMENSIONS** | **NO. OF PIECES** | **DIMENSIONS** |
| **FABRIC A** | RUNNER | | | |
| | 1 | 10½ × 20½-inch strip | | |
| | 2 | triangles, using the **Triangle Template** on page 243 | | |
| **FABRIC B** | LATTICE | | | |
| | **Before You Cut:** From one of the 44-inch strips, cut the pieces as directed in the second column. The remaining strip will require no further cutting. | | | |
| | 2 | 1 × 44-inch strips | 4 | 1 × 3½-inch pieces |
| | BINDING | | | |
| | 3 | 1 × 44-inch strips | | |
| **FABRIC C** | APPLIQUÉ DESIGN BACKGROUND SQUARES | | | |
| | 6 | 3½ × 3½-inch squares | | |

20½"

10½"

## Appliqué

Choose six appliqué designs from among the **Appliqué Patterns** on pages 216 and 217. Cut those patterns from the fabrics you have selected. Fuse and Penstitch the design onto each of the six background squares. Be sure to center the designs and use the **Appliqué Patterns** and **Appliqué Pattern Key** as guides for placing the pieces.

### The Lattice

**STEP 1.** Sew a 1 × 3½-inch lattice strip to each side of the two center appliqué squares. See **Diagram 4.** Press all seams toward the lattice.

DIAGRAM 4

**STEP 2.** Sew an appliqué square to each side of the center squares as shown in **Diagram 5.**

DIAGRAM 5

**STEP 3.** Use the remaining 1 × 44-inch lattice strip to sew to the top and bottom of both rows of appliqué designs. Sew the strip to the top of one row, press, and trim

the excess. Use that excess to sew to the bottom of the rows. Press and trim the excess. Repeat to add lattice to the other row of appliqué.

### Assembling the Runner

Referring to the **Table Runner Layout,** sew the appliquéd rows to each end of the 10½ × 20½-inch piece of runner fabric. Sew the triangles to each end. Press all seams to the lattice.

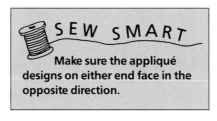

### The Binding

**STEP 1.** Sew one 1 × 44-inch strip to the left side of one of the triangle ends as shown in **Diagram 6.** A little bit of excess binding should extend beyond the left edge and the longer end of the strip should extend beyond the right edge. Press seams toward the binding. Align your ruler with the edge of the runner and trim the binding strips with a rotary cutter. Use the trimmed excess to bind the left side of the other triangle end.

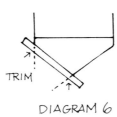

TRIM

DIAGRAM 6

**STEP 2.** Following Step 1 and using the remainder of the 44-inch strip from Step 1, sew binding to the right sides of the triangle ends. Refer to **Diagram 7** for guidance on how to trim the binding strips even with the edges of the runner.

Press and trim. Your triangle ends should look like the one in **Diagram 8.**

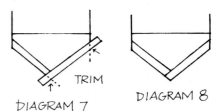

TRIM

DIAGRAM 7    DIAGRAM 8

**STEP 3.** Sew the two remaining 1 × 44-inch binding strips to the long sides of the runner. Press and trim the ends of the strips at the same angle as done for the triangle binding. See **Diagram 9.**

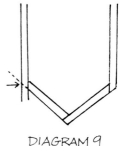

DIAGRAM 9

### Finishing

**STEP 1.** Use the completed runner top as a pattern to cut out the backing piece.

**STEP 2.** With right sides together, sew the top to the backing piece. Leave a 3- to 4-inch opening on the side for turning. Clip corners. Turn right side out, press, and stitch the opening.

**STEP 3.** You may choose to do a little machine or hand quilting around the lattice and binding strips.

# Spring Is Here! Wall Quilt

(shown on wall in the photograph on page 208)

Finished Size: 13 × 13 inches

## Materials and Cutting

Prewash and press all of your fabrics if you anticipate that you may want to launder your appliqué project. Using a rotary cutter, see-through ruler, and cutting mat, prepare the pieces as directed in the chart below.

## Appliqué

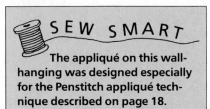

**SEW SMART**

The appliqué on this wall-hanging was designed especially for the Penstitch appliqué technique described on page 18.

Choose nine designs from the **Appliqué Patterns** on pages 216 and 217. Cut the designs from the fabrics you have chosen. Fuse and Penstitch appliqué one of these designs to the center of each of the nine background squares of Fabrics A and B. Use the **Appliqué Patterns** and **Appliqué Pattern Key** as guides for placing the pieces.

## The Lattice

**STEP 1.** Sew 1 × 3½-inch lattice strips to each side of the three appliquéd background squares that will be placed in the center of each row. Press all seams to the lattice.

**STEP 2.** Sew an appliquéd background square to each side of the three center squares to make three rows of three squares each. Remember to alternate Fabric A and B background squares as shown in **Diagram 10.** Press.

**STEP 3.** Sew a 1 × 10½-inch lattice strip to the bottom of each row. On one of these rows, also sew a lattice strip to the top edge. This

| | YARDAGE | CUTTING | |
|---|---|---|---|
| | | **NO. OF PIECES** | **DIMENSIONS** |
| **Fabric A**<br>Background Squares | ⅛ yard | 4 | 3½ × 3½-inch squares |
| **Fabric B**<br>Background Squares | ⅛ yard | 5 | 3½ × 3½-inch squares |
| **Fabric C**<br>Lattice | ⅙ yard (6 inches) | 6<br>4<br>2 | 1 × 3½-inch strips<br>1 × 10½-inch strips<br>1 × 11½-inch strips |
| Corner Squares | | 4 | 1½ × 1½-inch squares |
| **Fabric D**<br>Border | ⅛ yard | 4 | 1½ × 11½-inch strips |
| **Optional Binding*** | ⅛ yard | 4 | 1 × 15-inch strips |
| **Appliqué Designs** | ⅛ yard or scraps of several coordinated fabrics | | |
| **Backing** | ½ yard | 1 | 15 × 15-inch piece |
| **Batting** | ½ yard | 1 | 15 × 15-inch piece |
| **Appliqué film**<br>**Black, extra-fine point, permanent felt-tip pen** | | | |

*The binding is not shown on the quilt in the photograph.

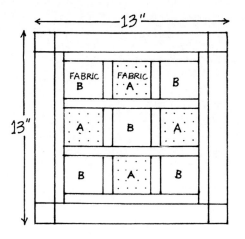

DIAGRAM 10

row with two lattice strips will become the top row of the wallhanging. Stitch the three rows together, referring to **Diagram 10** for placement. Press.

**STEP 4.** Sew 1 × 11½-inch lattice strips to each side. Press.

## The Border

**STEP 1.** Sew one 1½ × 11½-inch border strip to the wallhanging top and bottom. Press all seams to the border.

**STEP 2.** Sew the 1½-inch corner squares to the remaining two 1½ × 11½-inch border strips. Pin in position and sew to the sides. Press.

## Optional Binding

**STEP 1.** Sew 1 × 15-inch binding strips to the wallhanging top and bottom. Trim the excess and press all seams to the binding.

**STEP 2.** Sew 1 × 15-inch strips to the sides. Trim and press.

## Finishing

**STEP 1.** Use the finished top as a pattern to trim the backing piece and batting to fit.

**STEP 2.** Position the top and backing with right sides together. Lay both pieces on top of the batting and pin all three layers together. Sew together, leaving a 3- to 4-inch opening for turning.

**STEP 3.** Turn right side out, press, and handstitch the opening.

**STEP 4.** Machine or hand quilt in the ditch around the blocks and the borders.

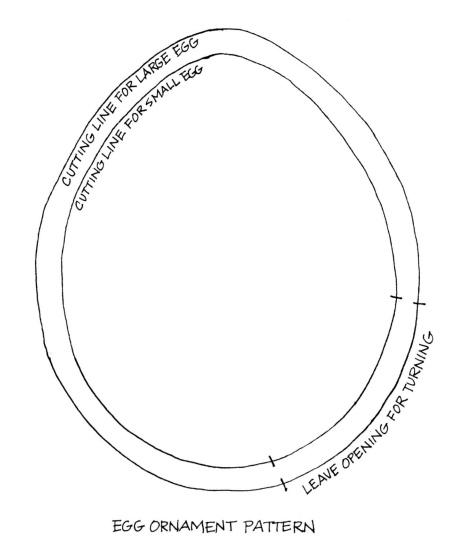

EGG ORNAMENT PATTERN

RIBBON
BOW

DRAW IN
HEART LINE
WITH PEN

APPLIQUÉ PATTERNS

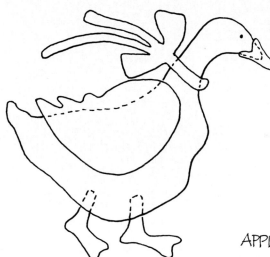

APPLIQUÉ PATTERN KEY

———————— TRACING LINE
— — — — — TRACING LINE
(BUT WILL BE HIDDEN
BEHIND OTHER FABRIC)

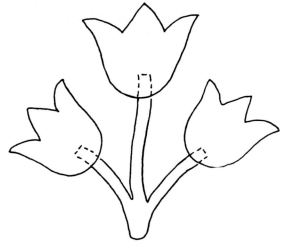

FOR SMALL EGG ONLY

USE EMBROIDERY
FLOSS TO ADD
HAIR TO GIRL

FOR SMALL EGG ONLY

# Easter Eggs Galore

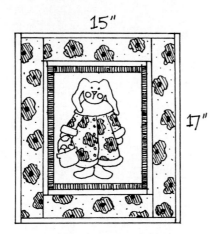

EASTER BUNNY QUILT LAYOUT

15"

17"

## The Easter Bunny

Finished Size: 15 × 17 inches

**Materials and Cutting**

Prewash and press all of your fabrics if you anticipate that you may want to launder your appliqué project. Using a rotary cutter, see-through ruler, and cutting mat, prepare the pieces as directed in the chart below.

|  | YARDAGE | CUTTING | |
|---|---|---|---|
|  |  | **NO. OF PIECES** | **DIMENSIONS** |
| **Background** | ¼ yard | 1 | 8½ × 10½-inch piece |
| **Appliqué Pieces**<br>Coat<br>Other Features | ⅙ yard (6 inches)<br>⅛ yard pieces<br>or several coordinated scraps |  |  |
| **Border One** | ¼ yard | 2<br>2 | 1 × 8½-inch strips<br>1 × 11½-inch strips |
| **Binding** |  | 2<br>2 | 1 × 14½-inch strips<br>1 × 17½-inch strips |
| **Border Two** | ⅛ yard | 2<br>2 | 1 × 9½-inch strips<br>1 × 12½-inch strips |
| **Border Three** | ¼ yard | 2<br>2 | 2½ × 10½-inch strips<br>2½ × 16½-inch strips |
| **Backing** | ½ yard | 1 | 16 × 18-inch piece |
| **Batting** | ½ yard | 1 | 16 × 18-inch piece |

Appliqué film
Tear-away paper (machine appliqué only)
Black, extra-fine point, permanent felt-tip pen (Penstitch only)

## Appliqué

**STEP 1.** Refer to Timesaving Techniques for Appliqué on page 16, and decide which technique you will use (Penstitch, machine, or buttonhole embroidery appliqué). Cut appliqué designs from assorted scraps of fabric using the **Easter Bunny Appliqué Pattern** on page 223.

**STEP 2.** Center and appliqué the bunny design to the background fabric piece. Refer to the **Appliqué Pattern** and the **Appliqué Pattern Key** for guidance in placing the pieces.

**STEP 3.** Embroider the bunny's nose using the satin stitch. With green embroidery floss, add leaves to the tops of the carrots sticking out of bunny's pocket. French knots can be used for the eyes and the buttons. Or, for an extra-special Easter outfit, handsew tiny beads on the coat for buttons.

## Borders

### BORDER ONE

Sew the 1 × 8½-inch strips to the wallhanging top and bottom. Press all seams to the border. Sew the 1 × 11½-inch strips to the sides. Press.

### BORDER TWO

Sew the 1 × 9½-inch strips to the wallhanging top and bottom. Press all seams to Border Two. Sew the 1 × 12½-inch strips to the sides. Press.

### BORDER THREE

Sew the 2½ × 10½-inch strips to the wallhanging top and bottom. Press all seams to Border Three. Sew the 2½ × 16½-inch strips to the sides. Press.

## The Binding

Sew the 1 × 14½-inch binding strips to the wallhanging top and bottom. Press all seams to the binding. Sew the 1 × 17½-inch strips to the sides. Press.

## Finishing

**STEP 1.** Use the finished top as a pattern to trim the backing piece and batting to fit.

**STEP 2.** Position the top and backing with right sides together. Lay both pieces on top of the batting and pin all three layers together. Sew together, leaving a 3- to 4-inch opening for turning.

**STEP 3.** Turn right side out, press, and handstitch opening.

**STEP 4.** Machine or hand quilt around both sides of all the borders.

# Easter Egg Wallhanging

Finished Size: 13½ × 15 inches

## Materials and Cutting

Prewash and press all of your fabrics if you anticipate that you may want to launder your appliqué project. Using a rotary cutter, see-through ruler, and cutting mat, prepare the pieces as directed in the chart below.

## Appliqué

**STEP 1.** Refer to Timesaving Techniques for Appliqué on page 16, and decide which technique you will use (Penstitch, machine, buttonhole embroidery, or hand appliqué). Cut nine egg appliqué designs from coordinated fabric scraps using the **Easter Egg Appliqué Pattern** on page 222.

**STEP 2.** Center one egg onto each of the nine 3½ × 4-inch background pieces and appliqué in position.

## Assembling the Blocks

**STEP 1.** Lay out the blocks in a pleasing arrangement with three rows of three blocks each. Sew the blocks in each row together.

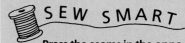
**Press the seams in the opposite direction every other row, so you'll have opposing seams. See Diagram 1.**

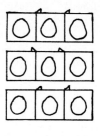

DIAGRAM 1

**STEP 2.** Sew the three rows together. Press seams down.

| | YARDAGE | CUTTING | |
|---|---|---|---|
| | | **NO. OF PIECES** | **DIMENSIONS** |
| **Eggs** | ⅛ yard each or coordinated scraps approximately 3½ × 4 inches for nine eggs | | |
| **Background Pieces** | ⅛ yard each or coordinated scraps of nine fabrics | 9 | 3½ × 4-inch pieces |
| **Corner Squares** | ⅛ yard | 4 | 2 × 2-inch squares |
| **Border One** | ⅙ yard (6 inches) | 2 | 1 × 9½-inch strips |
| | | 2 | 1 × 12-inch strips |
| **Binding** | | 2 | 1 × 13½-inch strips |
| | | 2 | 1 × 16-inch strips |
| **Border Two** | ⅛ yard | 2 | 2 × 10½-inch strips |
| | | 2 | 2 × 12-inch strips |
| **Backing** | ½ yard | 1 | 16 × 18-inch piece |
| **Batting** | ½ yard | 1 | 16 × 18-inch piece |

Appliqué film
Tear-away paper (machine appliqué only)
Black, extra-fine point, permanent felt-tip pen (Penstitch only)

## Border One

**STEP 1.** Sew the 1 × 9½-inch border strips to the top and bottom. Press all seams to the border.

**STEP 2.** Sew 1 × 12-inch border strips to the sides. Press.

## Border Two

**STEP 1.** Sew the 2 × 10½-inch border strips to the top and bottom. Press all seams toward the border.

**STEP 2.** Sew the 2 × 2-inch corner squares to each end of both 2 × 12-inch border strips. Press.

**STEP 3.** Pin in position and sew border strips to the sides. Press.

## Binding

**STEP 1.** Sew the 1 × 13½-inch binding strips to the top and bottom. Press all seams to the binding.

**STEP 2.** Sew the 1 × 16-inch binding strips to the sides. Press.

## Finishing

**STEP 1.** Position the top and backing with right sides together. Lay both pieces on top of the batting and pin all three layers together. Trim the batting and backing to the same size as the top. Sew together leaving a 3- to 4-inch opening for turning.

**STEP 2.** Turn right side out and handstitch opening.

**STEP 3.** Hand or machine quilt around the eggs or egg blocks and in the ditch around all the borders.

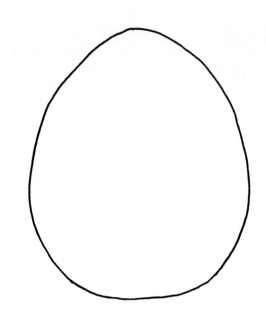

EASTER EGG APPLIQUÉ PATTERN

APPLIQUÉ PATTERN KEY

———————————— TRACING LINE

– – – – – – – – TRACING LINE
(WILL BE HIDDEN
BEHIND OTHER
FABRIC)

· · · · · · · · · · SEWING LINE
(USE MACHINE
SATIN STITCH TO
CREATE THESE
LINES ON
THE DESIGN)

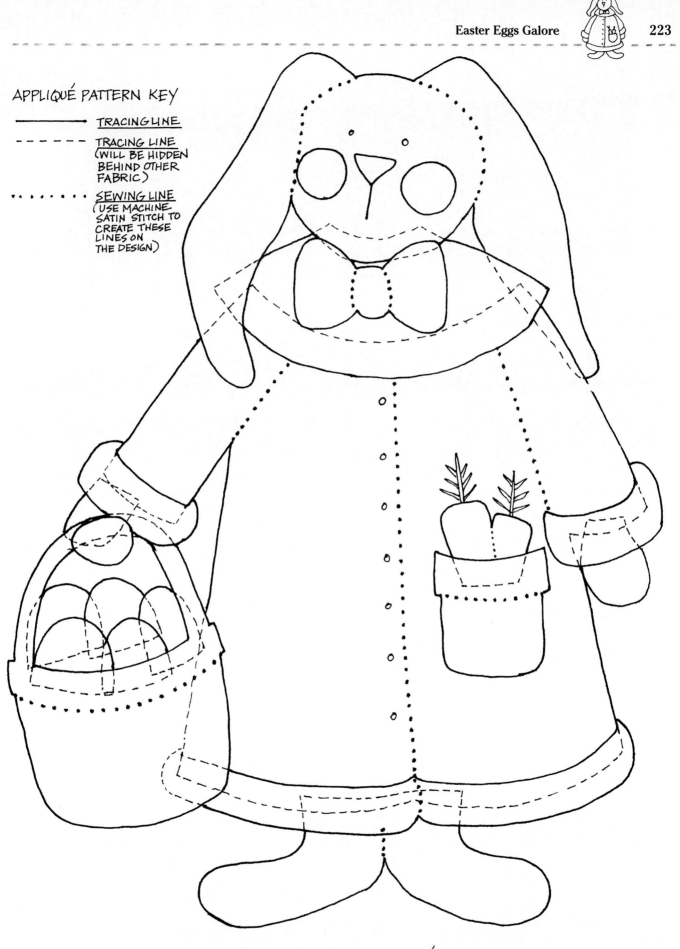

EASTER BUNNY APPLIQUÉ PATTERN

# Holiday Stockings

Here are some holiday stockings sure to catch Santa's eye! You have your pick of three designs, featuring a plump-cheeked angel, teddy bear and his Christmas tree, or jolly kitty wearing a wreath. These stockings are nice and roomy so Santa can really pack them full of goodies! For a fun twist on tradition, you can choose to mount your stockings on a wallhanging. The stocking tops are open, ready to fill with stocking stuffers. As an extra treat, this project also includes directions for a Sassy Cat Wallhanging, shown in the photo on page 229. You can make these cats out of holiday fabrics, or as I've done, stitch them out of fabric scraps for a wallhanging to enjoy year-round. (All of the quilts shown in the photos were done in machine appliqué.)

## Stockings

Finished Size: 9½ × 15 inches

### Materials

**STOCKING AND LINING**   ½ yard
for each stocking

**APPLIQUÉ DESIGNS**
Note: Coordinated scraps can also be used for these appliqué designs.

TEDDY BEAR
| | |
|---|---|
| Tree | ¼ yard |
| Bear | ⅛ yard |
| Feet and star | ⅛ yard |
| Turtleneck and hat | ⅛ yard |
| Sweater | ⅛ yard |

ANGEL
| | |
|---|---|
| Dress | ¼ yard |
| Hands, head, feet | ⅛ yard |
| Apron, wings, petticoat | ⅛ yard |
| Cheeks | ⅛ yard |
| Hearts | ⅛ yard |

CAT
| | |
|---|---|
| Cat head and body | ¼ yard |
| Wreath | ⅛ yard |
| Bow | ⅛ yard |
| Cheeks | ⅛ yard |

**Appliqué film**

**Tear-away paper** *(for machine appliqué only)*

**Black, extra-fine point, permanent felt-tip pen** *(for Penstitch only)*

**Tracing paper or ⅓ yard nonfusible interfacing**

## Cutting

Trace the **Stocking Pattern** on pages 232 and 233 onto tracing paper or nonfusible interfacing to make your pattern. *Position the fabric right sides together* and cut out two sets of stockings; one set is for the outer stocking, and the other set is for the lining. Cut out two sets for each stocking you are making.

## Appliqué

**STEP 1.** Refer to Timesaving Techniques for Appliqué on page 16, and decide which technique you will use (Penstitch, machine appliqué, or buttonhole embroidery). Cut appliqué designs from assorted fabrics using the **Cat, Teddy and Tree,** or **Angel Appliqué Patterns** on pages 231, 234, and 235.

**STEP 2.** Center and appliqué the designs to the stocking fronts. Use the **Appliqué Pattern Key** and the **Appliqué Patterns** as a reference for the order in which to place the pieces.

**STEP 3.** Add the finishing details with color-coordinated embroidery floss. Use French knots for eyes and the angel's hair. Embroider the cat and bear noses with the satin stitch. Add mouths to the angel and the bear with the outline or stem stitch.

## Assembling the Stockings

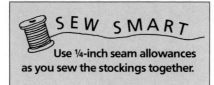

**SEW SMART**

Use ¼-inch seam allowances as you sew the stockings together.

**STEP 1.** With right sides together, sew the stocking front to the front lining along the top edge as shown in **Diagram 1.** Press seam allowance open. Repeat, sewing the stocking back to the back lining along the top edge. Press.

**STEP 2.** With right sides together, pin and sew the stocking front/lining piece to the stocking back/lining piece. Leave a 3- to 4-inch opening in the lining for turning right side out. See **Diagram 2.**

**STEP 3.** Clip all curves, then turn and press. Handstitch the opening.

**STEP 4.** Push the lining down into the stocking and give it a final pressing.

**STEP 5.** Fill with holiday goodies!

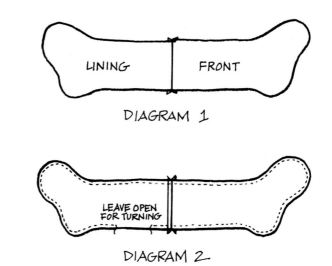

LINING     FRONT

DIAGRAM 1

LEAVE OPEN FOR TURNING

DIAGRAM 2

# Stocking Wallhanging

Finished Size: 38½ × 24 inches

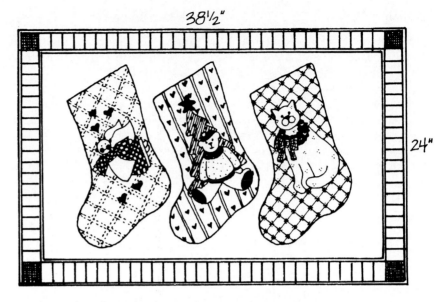

STOCKING WALLHANGING LAYOUT

## Materials and Cutting

Prewash and press all of your fabrics if you anticipate that you may want to launder your appliqué project. Using a rotary cutter, see-through ruler, and cutting mat, prepare the pieces as directed in the chart below.

| | YARDAGE | CUTTING | |
|---|---|---|---|
| | | **NO. OF PIECES** | **DIMENSIONS** |
| **Background** | 1¼ yards | 1 | 19½ × 34-inch piece |
| **Backing** | | | remaining fabric |
| **Half-Inch Border** | ½ yard | **Before You Cut:** From these border strips, cut two 1 × 34-inch strips and two 1 × 20½-inch strips. | |
| | | 3 | 1 × 44-inch strips |
| **Binding** | | 4 | 2¾ × 44-inch strips |
| **Scrap Border** | Coordinated scraps of Christmas fabrics | 10 | 1½ × 25-inch strips |
| **Corner Squares** | Fabric scraps that contrast well with the scrap border | 4 | 2 × 2-inch squares |
| **Stocking and Lining** | ⅓ yard *each* of *three* fabrics (½ yard for directional prints) | | |
| **Appliqué Designs** | Refer to Appliqué Design fabric requirements listed on page 225 for Stockings | | |
| **Batting** | ¾ yard | 1 | 25 × 39-inch piece |
| **Appliqué film**<br>**Tear-away paper (for machine appliqué only)**<br>**Black, extra-fine point, permanent felt-tip pen (for Penstitch only)**<br>**Tracing paper or ⅓ yard nonfusible interfacing** | | | |

## Cutting

Trace the two-part **Stocking Pattern** on pages 232 and 233 onto tracing paper or nonfusible interfacing to make your pattern. *Position the fabric right sides together* and cut one set of stockings from each of the three stocking fabrics. (In each set of stocking pieces, one stocking shape is the front and the other is the lining.)

## Appliqué

Center and appliqué designs to the stocking fronts. Refer to Steps 1, 2, and 3 under Appliqué in the preceding Stockings project on page 226.

## Attaching the Stockings

**STEP 1.** With right sides together, sew each of the stocking fronts to the matching stocking linings. Leave stocking tops open for turning. Clip curves, turn, and press.

**STEP 2.** Turn stocking top under ¼ inch, press, and topstitch closed.

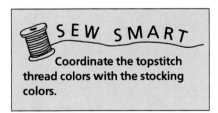

**S E W   S M A R T**

Coordinate the topstitch thread colors with the stocking colors.

**STEP 3.** Center the three stockings on the background fabric and pin in position. Topstitch in place. Leave the top open so you can stuff with lots of treats.

## Half-Inch Border

**STEP 1.** Sew the 1 × 34-inch strips to the quilt top and bottom. Press toward the border.

**STEP 2.** Sew the 1 × 20½-inch strips to the sides. Press.

## Scrap Border

**STEP 1.** Arrange the ten 1½ × 25-inch coordinated strips in a pleasing order and sew them together. As you sew, press all the seams in one direction. See **Diagram 3**.

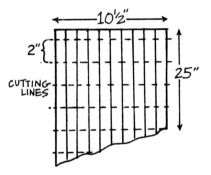

DIAGRAM 3

**STEP 2.** From this strip set, cut eleven 2 × 10½-inch strips, referring to the cutting lines in **Diagram 3**. Sew two of these strips together end to end to make a 2 × 20½-inch border strip for one side. Repeat to make a second side border strip. Sew three of the 10½-inch strips together to make a 2 × 30½-inch border strip for the top. Repeat to make a second strip for the bottom.

**STEP 3.** Fit and sew the scrap borders to the wallhanging sides. See Hints on Fitting a Scrap Border on page 28 for pointers on how to fit the border to the quilt. Press seams toward the half-inch border.

**STEP 4.** Fit the scrap borders to the top and bottom, up to but not including the side borders. Add ¼ inch to the ends of each strip so they will fit correctly after the corner squares are added. Use a seam ripper to remove any excess border. Sew a 2-inch corner square to each end of the border strips. Press to border.

**STEP 5.** Pin and sew the scrap borders to the top and bottom of the quilt. Press seams to the half-inch border.

## Layering the Quilt

Arrange and baste the backing, batting, and top together following the directions for Layering the Quilt on page 32. Trim the batting and backing to ¼ inch from the raw edge of the quilt top.

## Binding the Quilt

Using the 2¾ × 44-inch strips cut from the binding fabric, follow the directions given under Binding the Quilt on page 33.

## The Finishing Stitches

Machine or hand quilt along the outside edges of the stockings to reinforce them and keep them from pulling out when you add all the holiday treats. You may also want to fill the background with a 1- to 2-inch grid of quilting. (If you machine quilt, do so before adding the binding.)

# Sassy Cat Wallhanging

Finished Size: 24 × 14 inches

## Materials and Cutting

Prewash and press all of your fabrics if you anticipate that you may want to launder your appliqué project. Using a rotary cutter, see-through ruler, and cutting mat, prepare the pieces as directed in the chart below.

| | YARDAGE | CUTTING | |
|---|---|---|---|
| | | **NO. OF PIECES** | **DIMENSIONS** |
| **Background** | ⅝ yard | 1 | 19½ × 9½-inch piece |
| **Backing** | | | remaining fabric |
| **Half-Inch Border** | ¼ yard | **Before You Cut:** From these strips, cut two 1 × 19½-inch strips and two 1 × 10½-inch strips. | |
| | | 3 | 1 × 44-inch strips |
| **Binding** | | **Before You Cut:** From these strips, cut two 1 × 23½-inch strips and two 1 × 14½-inch strips. | |
| | | 3 | 1 × 44-inch strips |
| **Scrap Border** | Fourteen coordinated fabrics from your scrap bag | 14 | 1¼ × 20-inch strips |
| **Corner Squares** | Fabric scraps that contrast well with the scrap border | 4 | 2 × 2-inch squares |
| **Appliqué Designs** | Refer to Cat Appliqué Design fabric requirements listed on page 225 under Stockings. | | |
| **Batting** | ½ yard | 1 | 16 × 26-inch piece |
| **Appliqué film**<br>**Tear-away paper (for machine appliqué only)**<br>**Black, extra-fine point, permanent felt-tip pen (for Penstitch only)** | | | |

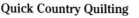
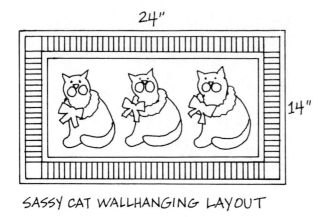

24"

14"

SASSY CAT WALLHANGING LAYOUT

## Appliqué

**STEP 1.** Refer to Timesaving Techniques for Appliqué on page 16, and decide which technique you will use (Penstitch, machine, or buttonhole embroidery appliqué). Cut three cat appliqué designs from assorted scraps of fabric using the **Cat Appliqué Pattern** on the opposite page.

**STEP 2.** Center and appliqué the cats to the background piece. Use the photograph as a reference for how to place the cats on the background. Use the **Appliqué Pattern Key** and the **Cat Appliqué Pattern** as a reference for the order in which to place the individual pieces.

**STEP 3.** Embroider noses on the cats using the satin stitch in color-coordinated embroidery floss. Use French knots for the eyes.

## Half-Inch Border

**STEP 1.** Sew the $1 \times 19\frac{1}{2}$-inch border strips to the top and bottom of the quilt. Press toward the border.

**STEP 2.** Sew the $1 \times 10\frac{1}{2}$-inch strips to the quilt sides. Press.

## Scrap Border

**STEP 1.** Arrange the fourteen $1\frac{1}{4} \times$ 20-inch coordinated strips in a pleasing order, and sew together to make an $11 \times 20$-inch strip set. As you sew, press all seams in one direction.

**STEP 2.** From this strip set, cut eight $2 \times 11$-inch strips. Sew two of those strips together end to end to make a $2 \times 21\frac{1}{2}$-inch strip for the side border. Repeat to make a border strip for the other side. Sew two of the 11-inch strips together end to end to make a $2 \times 21\frac{1}{2}$-inch strip for the top edge of the quilt. Repeat to make a border strip for the bottom.

**STEP 3.** Fit and sew the scrap border to the quilt sides. (See Hints on Fitting a Scrap Border on page 28 for pointers on how to fit the border to the quilt.) Use a seam ripper to remove any excess border. Press seams to the half-inch border.

**STEP 4.** Fit the scrap borders to the top and bottom of the quilt, up to but not including the side scrap borders. Add ¼ inch to the ends of each strip so they will fit correctly after the corner squares are added. Use a seam ripper to remove any excess border. Sew a 2-inch corner square to each end of the border strips. Press to the border.

**STEP 5.** Pin and sew the scrap borders to the quilt top and bottom. Press seams to the half-inch border.

## Binding the Quilt

**STEP 1.** Sew the $1 \times 23\frac{1}{2}$-inch strips to the top and bottom edges of the quilt. Press all seams to the binding.

**STEP 2.** Sew the $1 \times 14\frac{1}{2}$-inch strips to the sides. Press.

## Finishing

**STEP 1.** Use the finished top as a pattern to cut out the backing. Position the top and backing with right sides together. Lay both pieces on top of the batting and pin all three layers together. Trim the batting to the same size as the top and backing. Sew together, leaving a 3- to 4-inch opening for turning.

**STEP 2.** Turn right side out and handstitch the opening. Press.

**STEP 3.** Machine or hand quilt in the ditch on both sides of the scrap border and around the kitties. You could also do some stitching in the background if you like.

APPLIQUÉ PATTERN KEY

———————— TRACING LINE

— — — — — — TRACING LINE
(WILL BE HIDDEN
BEHIND OTHER
FABRIC)

• • • • • • • • • SEWING LINE
(USE MACHINE
SATIN STITCH TO
CREATE THESE
LINES ON THE DESIGN.)

CAT APPLIQUÉ PATTERN

232

CUTTING LINE

STOCKING TOP

MATCH WITH STOCKING BOTTOM TO COMPLETE PATTERN

STOCKING PATTERN

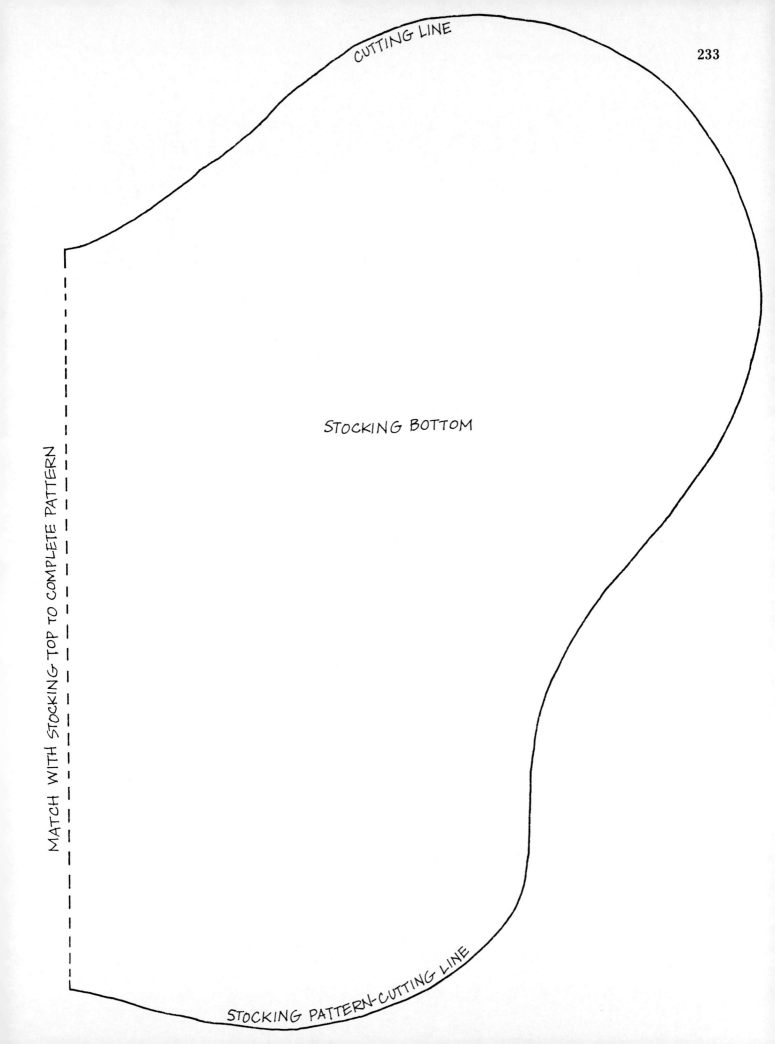

233

CUTTING LINE

STOCKING BOTTOM

MATCH WITH STOCKING TOP TO COMPLETE PATTERN

STOCKING PATTERN-CUTTING LINE

APPLIQUÉ PATTERN KEY

———————— TRACING LINE

– – – – – – TRACING LINE (WILL BE HIDDEN BEHIND OTHER FABRIC)

• • • • • • • SEWING LINE (USE MACHINE SATIN STITCH TO CREATE THESE LINES ON THE DESIGN.)

TEDDY AND TREE APPLIQUÉ PATTERN

ANGEL APPLIQUÉ PATTERN

# Merry Medley for Christmas

Nothing conveys the spirit of the season better than a welcoming wreath on your front door decked out with ornaments you've stitched yourself. Choose from a selection of twelve seasonal and country appliqué designs to make a whole host of ornaments to dress up your wreath or Christmas tree. You can also pick six of your favorite designs to use on a Noel Door Banner (shown in the large photograph). All in all, a very Merry Christmas medley!

## Christmas Ornaments

**Materials**

**ORNAMENT BACKGROUND**

Two 3½-inch squares per ornament (⅛ yard makes six ornaments)

**APPLIQUÉ DESIGNS**

Coordinated scraps or ⅛ yard each of several coordinated fabrics

**FLAG ORNAMENT**

Scraps of red, white, and blue fabrics

**TRIM, BRAID, PIPING, OR LACE**

½ yard per ornament

**RIBBON HANGER**

½ yard per ornament

**Black, extra-fine point, permanent felt-tip pen**

**Appliqué film**

**Stuffing** *(Use a smooth stuffing like FiberFil, not shredded foam.)*

## Appliqué

Penstitch Appliqué works especially well with these appliqué
designs. See page 18 for details on
this technique.

**STEP 1.** Cut two 3½ × 3½-inch
squares or two hearts for each
ornament you wish to make. Cut
with fabrics placed right sides
together. Use the **Heart Ornament
Pattern** on page 241.

**STEP 2.** Trace the appliqué designs
of your choice from the ten **Appliqué Patterns** on pages 242 and
243 onto appliqué film. For the
heart ornament, draw small square,
rectangular, or triangular patches
freehand on the appliqué film.
Fuse to scraps of fabric, then cut
the shapes out of the fabric. Fuse
the designs onto the ornament
background pieces. Use the **Appliqué Patterns** and **Appliqué Pattern Key** as guides for placing the
pieces. When everything is in
place, use the black pen to draw in
facial features on the snowman,
goose, and teddy bear.

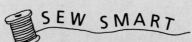

> ### SEW SMART
> For the watermelon orna-
> ment, cut a full wedge-shape
> piece from each of three colors
> (the sample on the wreath in the
> large photograph uses red, white,
> and green). With the black pen,
> draw seeds on the appliquéd
> watermelon shape. Position the
> watermelon diagonally on a 3½-
> inch square.

## Assembling the Ornaments

**STEP 1.** Cut two 8- to 9-inch pieces
of ribbon for a hanger for each
ornament. Pin and sew to the
right side of the front ornament
piece as shown in **Diagram 1**.

DIAGRAM 1

If you wish to use lace or trim on
your ornaments, choose between
the methods described in Steps 2

and 3. If you are not adding any
trimming to your ornaments, see
Steps 4 and 5.

**STEP 2.** Pin lace or trim to the
ornament front and stitch ¼-inch
from the raw edge. See **Diagram
2.** Place ornament back on ornament front with right sides facing,
and sew together. Leave an opening at the bottom for turning. Fill
with stuffing and handstitch the
opening closed.

DIAGRAM 2

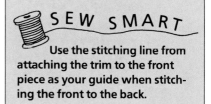

> ### SEW SMART
> Use the stitching line from
> attaching the trim to the front
> piece as your guide when stitch-
> ing the front to the back.

**STEP 3.** Here's a no-sew option for
attaching trim. Sew the front to
the back leaving an opening for
turning. Stuff, and handstitch the
opening closed. Using a hot glue
gun, glue braided trim around the
edge of the ornament.

**STEP 4.** For ornaments you wish to
leave plain, with no trim, simply
sew the front to back with right
sides together, leaving an opening
for turning.

**STEP 5.** Here's another finishing
option. For a pinking-sheared
edge, sew the ornament front to
back with the *wrong* sides together.
Leave an opening at the top as

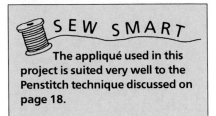

shown in **Diagram 3.** Use pinking shears to trim the edge all the way around the ornament. Fill with stuffing. Pin two 8- to 9-inch ribbon pieces in position at the top for hangers. Now finish stitching across the top.

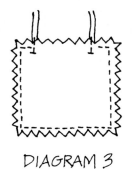

DIAGRAM 3

### The Flag Ornament

**STEP 1.** Cut eight ¾ × 4-inch strips of fabric (four of red and four of white). Stitch together the eight strips, alternating fabrics. Trim seam allowances to ⅛ inch to reduce bulk.

**STEP 2.** Cut one 1¾ × 1¼-inch piece of navy blue fabric. Fuse and Penstitch appliqué this piece to the striped fabric so the bottom edge is lined up with the fourth seam line. See **Diagram 4.**

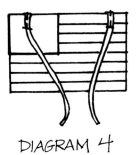

DIAGRAM 4

**STEP 3.** Sew two 8- to 9-inch ribbon hangers to the right side of the ornament front. Use the front as a pattern to cut the backing piece out of a scrap of fabric. With right sides together, sew the front to the back leaving an opening for turning. Turn right side out.

**STEP 4.** Cut a heart out of red fabric using the **Heart Appliqué for Flag Pattern** on page 241. Center, fuse, and Penstitch appliqué the heart to the center of the navy fabric.

**STEP 5.** Fill with stuffing and hand-stitch the opening.

# Noel Door Banner

Finished Size: 10¾ × 14½ inches

## Materials

| | |
|---|---|
| **BACKGROUND** | ⅛ yard |
| **BACKING** | ⅓ yard |
| | cut into 12 × 17-inch piece |
| **LATTICE, HANGING STRIPS, TRIANGLE** | ¼ yard |
| **NOEL APPLIQUÉ** | ⅛ yard or scraps |
| **APPLIQUÉ DESIGNS** | ⅛ yard or scraps of several coordinated fabrics |
| **BATTING** | ⅓ yard cut into 12 × 17-inch piece |

**Appliqué film**

**Black, extra-fine point, permanent felt-tip pen**

**Bell for bottom of banner**

## Appliqué

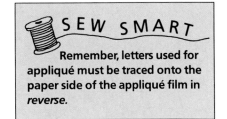

SEW SMART

The appliqué used in this project is suited very well to the Penstitch technique discussed on page 18.

**STEP 1.** Using a rotary cutter and see-through ruler, cut six 3½ × 3½-inch squares and one 3½ × 10½-inch piece of background fabric.

**STEP 2.** Choose six of your favorite appliqué designs from the **Appliqué Patterns** on pages 242 and 243. Trace onto appliqué film. Fuse the film onto the assorted scraps of fabric, then cut the appliqué shapes out of fabric. Fuse and Penstitch appliqué one design to the center of each of the six 3½-inch squares.

**STEP 3.** Center, fuse, and Penstitch appliqué the word *NOEL* to the 3½ × 10½-inch piece of background fabric. Use the appliqué letters on page 241.

SEW SMART

Remember, letters used for appliqué must be traced onto the paper side of the appliqué film in *reverse.*

**STEP 4.** Using the **Triangle Template** on page 243 as a pattern, cut one triangle and sew it to the bottom edge of the NOEL appliqué piece.

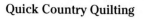

## The Lattice

**STEP 1.** Cut two 1 × 44-inch strips of lattice. From one strip, cut four 1 × 3½-inch strips and two 1 × 10½-inch strips. From the second strip, cut one 1 × 10½-inch strip and cut the remainder of that strip in half.

**STEP 2.** Sew the 1 × 3½-inch strips to each side of the two center appliqué squares. See **Diagram 5.** Press all seams toward the lattice.

DIAGRAM 5

**STEP 3.** Sew another square to each side of the two center squares as shown in **Diagram 6.**

DIAGRAM 6

**STEP 4.** Sew a 1 × 10½-inch strip above the top row of appliqué squares, between the appliqué rows and between the NOEL and second row of appliqué squares. Refer to **Diagram 7.** Press all seams to the lattice.

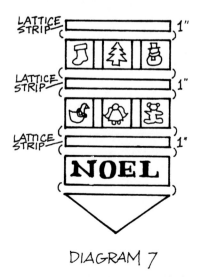

DIAGRAM 7

**STEP 5.** Sew each of the remaining two lattice strips to the sides of the door banner. Trim the bottom of each strip at the same angle as the edges of the triangle. See **Diagram 8.**

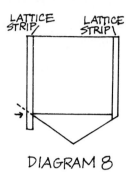

DIAGRAM 8

## The Hangers

**STEP 1.** Cut two 2 × 16-inch strips of the lattice fabric. Fold in half the long way with right sides together and sew along the length. Leave the ends open and turn so right sides are out. Press.

**STEP 2.** Pin to the right side of the front panel with raw edges even as shown in **Diagram 9.** Stitch ¼ inch from the raw edges.

DIAGRAM 9

## Finishing

**STEP 1.** Use the completed front panel as a pattern to trim the backing and batting pieces to fit.

**STEP 2.** Position the top and backing with right sides together. Lay both pieces on top of the batting and pin all three layers together. Sew together, leaving a 3- to 4-inch opening in the side for turning.

**STEP 3.** Clip corners, turn right side out, press, and handstitch opening.

**STEP 4.** Machine or hand quilt in the ditch around the background pieces.

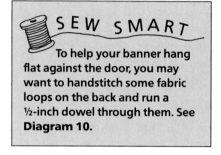

**SEW SMART**

To help your banner hang flat against the door, you may want to handstitch some fabric loops on the back and run a ½-inch dowel through them. See **Diagram 10.**

DIAGRAM 10

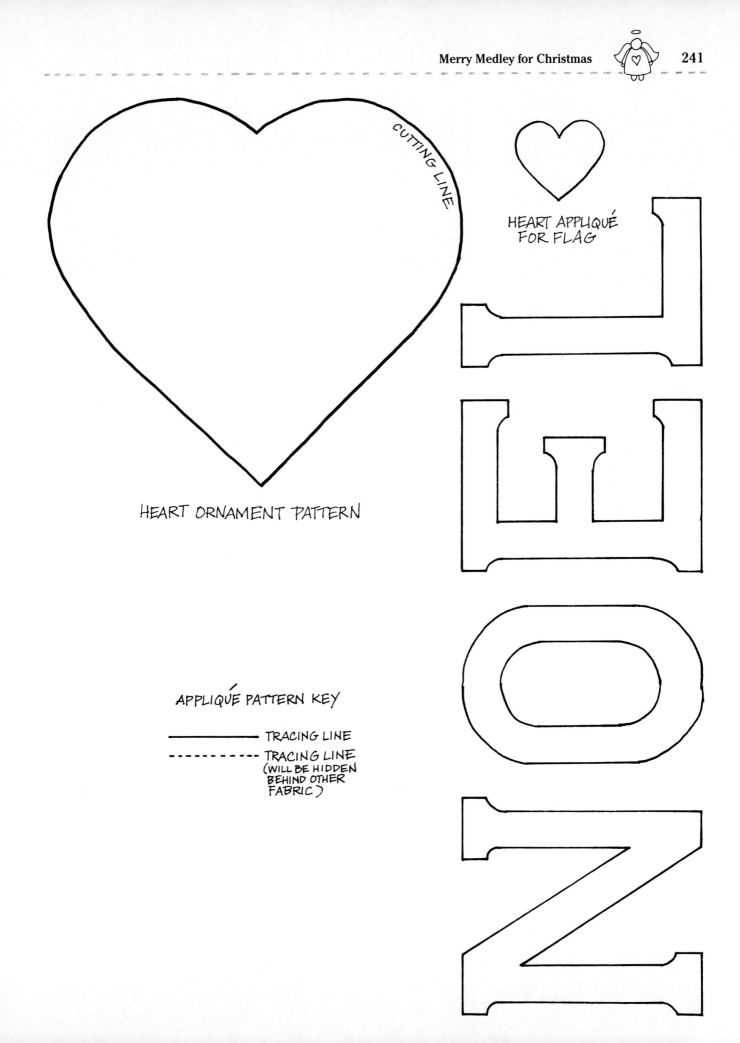

CUTTING LINE

HEART ORNAMENT PATTERN

HEART APPLIQUÉ
FOR FLAG

APPLIQUÉ PATTERN KEY

———————— TRACING LINE

- - - - - - - - TRACING LINE
(WILL BE HIDDEN
BEHIND OTHER
FABRIC)

N O E L

APPLIQUÉ PATTERNS

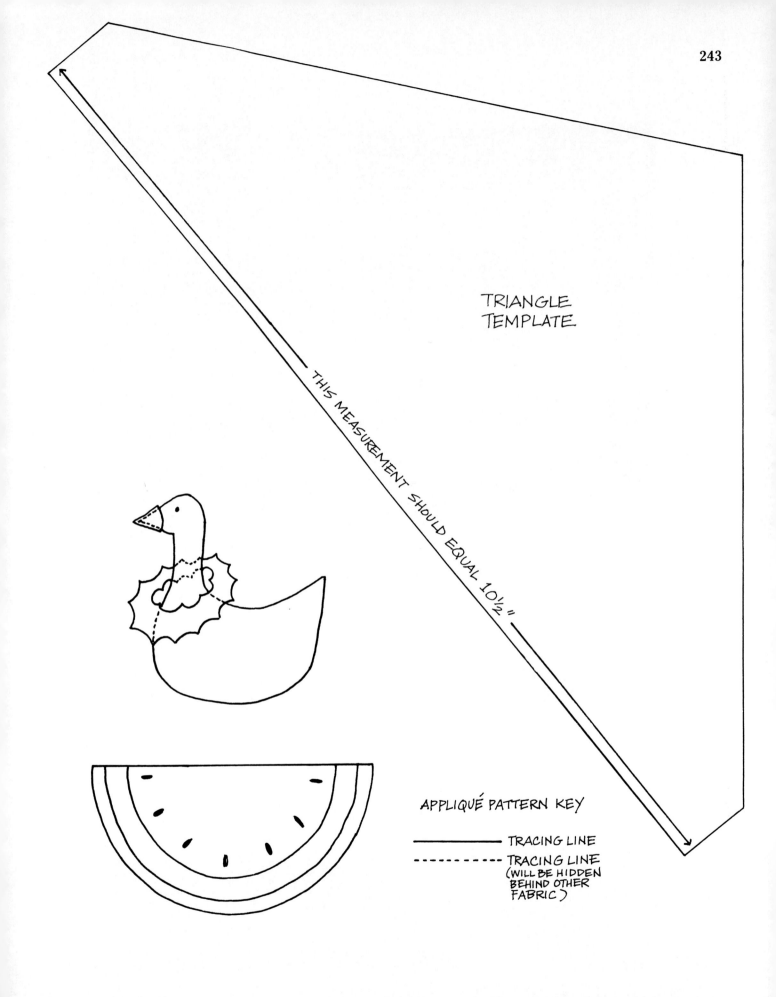

243

TRIANGLE
TEMPLATE

THIS MEASUREMENT SHOULD EQUAL 10½"

APPLIQUÉ PATTERN KEY

———— TRACING LINE

- - - - TRACING LINE
(WILL BE HIDDEN
BEHIND OTHER
FABRIC)

# Santa's Season

18"

23"

SINGLE SANTA QUILT LAYOUT

## Single Santa

Finished Size: 18 × 23 inches

### Materials and Cutting

Prewash and press all of your
fabrics if you anticipate that you
may want to launder your appliqué
project. Using a rotary cutter,
see-through ruler, and cutting mat,
prepare the pieces as directed in
the chart below.

| | YARDAGE | CUTTING | |
|---|---|---|---|
| | | NO. OF PIECES | DIMENSIONS |
| Background | ⅓ yard | 1 | 11½ × 16½-inch piece |
| Half-Inch Border | ¼ yard | 2 | 1 × 11½-inch strips |
| | | 2 | 1 × 17½-inch strips |
| Binding | | 2 | 1 × 17½-inch strips |
| | | 2 | 1 × 23½-inch strips |
| Appliqué Pieces | Several coordinated scraps or ⅛-yard pieces | | |
| Santa Coat | ¼ yard | | |
| Santa Bag | ¼ yard | | |
| Scrap Border | Several coordinated scraps | | Cut into 3-inch lengths of varying widths to create two 3 × 12½-inch and two 3 × 22½-inch strips. |
| Backing | ⅝ yard | 1 | 19 × 24-inch piece |
| Batting | ⅝ yard | 1 | 19 × 24-inch piece |

Appliqué film
Tear-away paper (machine appliqué only)
Coordinated machine embroidery thread (machine appliqué only)
Black, extra-fine point, permanent felt-tip pen

## Appliqué

**STEP 1.** Trace pieces for Santa appliqué onto appliqué film using **Single Santa Appliqué Patterns** on pages 248 and 249. Because Santa was too plump to run on a single page, you will need to make a tracing of each page and join the two pieces of his coat together before proceeding. Fuse the film onto the assorted pieces of fabric, then cut the appliqué shapes out of fabric.

**STEP 2.** Lay out all the pieces on the 11½ × 16½-inch background piece. Refer to the **Appliqué Pattern, Appliqué Pattern Key,** and **Single Santa Quilt Layout** for placement guidance. When you're sure they're positioned correctly, fuse. Then machine appliqué the design to the background piece.

**STEP 3.** With the black pen, add a twinkling eye to Santa's profile.

## Half-Inch Border

**STEP 1.** Sew the 1 × 11½-inch strips to the top and bottom of the wallhanging. Press all seams to the border.

**STEP 2.** Sew the 1 × 17½-inch strips to the sides. Press.

## The Scrap Border

**STEP 1.** Cut several coordinated scraps into 3-inch long pieces of varying widths (I used pieces from 1 to 3½ inches wide). Sew these pieces together to make two 3 × 12½-inch strips and two 3 × 22½-inch strips.

**STEP 2.** Sew the two 3 × 12½-inch strips to the wallhanging top and bottom. Press all seams to the half-inch border. Sew the two 3 × 22½-inch strips to the sides. Press.

## The Binding

**STEP 1.** Sew the two 1 × 17½-inch binding strips to the top and bottom. Press all seams toward the binding.

**STEP 2.** Sew the two 1 × 23½-inch strips to the sides. Press.

## Finishing

**STEP 1.** Use the finished top as a pattern to trim the backing and batting to size.

**STEP 2.** Position the top and backing with right sides together. Lay both pieces on top of the batting and pin all three layers together. Sew together, leaving a 3- to 4-inch opening for turning.

**STEP 3.** Turn right side out, press, and handstitch the opening.

**STEP 4.** Machine or hand quilt in the ditch on both sides of the half-inch border and binding.

# Santa Quartet

Finished Size: 14½ × 16½ inches

## Materials and Cutting

Prewash and press all of your fabrics if you anticipate that you may want to launder your appliqué project. Using a rotary cutter, see-through ruler, and cutting mat, prepare the pieces as directed in the chart on the opposite page.

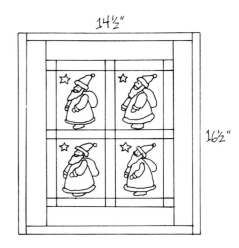

SANTA QUARTET QUILT LAYOUT

## Appliqué

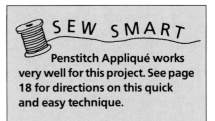

**STEP 1.** Trace pieces for the four Santa and star appliqués onto appliqué film using the **Santa Quartet Appliqué Pattern** on page 248. Fuse the film onto assorted fabric scraps and cut the appliqué shapes out of the fabric.

**STEP 2.** Center, fuse, and Penstitch appliqué one small Santa to each of the four 5 × 6-inch background

| | YARDAGE | CUTTING | |
| --- | --- | --- | --- |
| | | NO. OF PIECES | DIMENSIONS |
| Background | ¼ yard | 4 | 5 × 6-inch pieces |
| Lattice | ⅛ yard | 6 | 1 × 5-inch strips |
| | | 6 | 1 × 6-inch strips |
| Appliqué Pieces | Several coordinated scraps or ⅛-yard pieces | | |
| Corner Squares | Coordinated scraps | 9 | 1 × 1-inch squares |
| Border | ⅛ yard | 2 | 2 × 11-inch strips |
| | | 2 | 2 × 16-inch strips |
| Binding | ⅛ yard | 2 | 1 × 14-inch strips |
| | | 2 | 1 × 17-inch strips |
| Backing | ½ yard | 1 | 15½ × 17½-inch piece |
| Batting | ½ yard | 1 | 15½ × 17½-inch piece |
| Appliqué film<br>Black, extra-fine point, permanent felt-tip pen | | | |

pieces. Refer to the **Appliqué Pattern** and **Appliqué Pattern Key** for help in positioning the pieces. As shown in the **Santa Quartet Quilt Layout**, add a star to the upper corner of each block.

**STEP 3.** With the black felt-tip pen, add an eye to each Santa.

## The Lattice

**STEP 1.** Sew a 1 × 6-inch lattice strip in between the two Santa blocks in the top row. Sew a strip to the outside edge of each block. See **Diagram 1**. Repeat for the bottom row. Press all seams to the lattice.

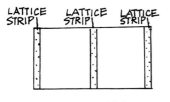

DIAGRAM 1

**STEP 2.** Sew three corner squares and two 1 × 5-inch lattice strips together to make a 1 × 11-inch strip that looks like the one shown in **Diagram 2**. Repeat to make a total of three 1 × 11-inch strips.

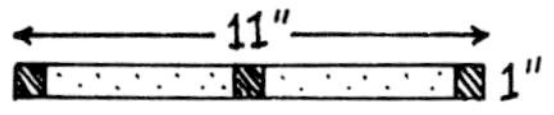

— 11" —
1"

DIAGRAM 2

**STEP 3.** Pin and sew a lattice strip from Step 2 to the top and bottom of the top row and below the bottom row of Santas. If you have accurately cut and sewn these horizontal strips, the corner squares should align exactly with the vertical lattice strips. Pin and sew the two rows together. Press seams to the lattice.

## The Border

**STEP 1.** Sew the 2 × 11-inch border strips to the top and bottom of the wallhanging. Press all seams to the border.

**STEP 2.** Sew the 2 × 16-inch strips to the sides. Press.

## The Binding

**STEP 1.** Sew the two 1 × 14-inch strips to the top and bottom. Press all seams to the binding.

**STEP 2.** Sew the two 1 × 17-inch strips to the sides. Press.

## Finishing

**STEP 1.** Use the finished top as a pattern to trim the backing piece and batting to fit.

**STEP 2.** Position the top and backing with right sides together. Lay both pieces on top of the batting and pin all three layers together. Sew together, leaving a 3- to 4-inch opening for turning.

**STEP 3.** Turn right side out, press, and handstitch the opening.

**STEP 4.** Machine or hand quilt in the ditch around both sides of the lattice and the binding.

**STEP 5.** Get out the milk and cookies because Santa Claus is coming to town!

APPLIQUÉ PATTERN KEY

——————————— TRACING LINE

- - - - - - - - - - - TRACING LINE
(WILL BE HIDDEN
BEHIND FABRIC)

SANTA QUARTET APPLIQUÉ PATTERN

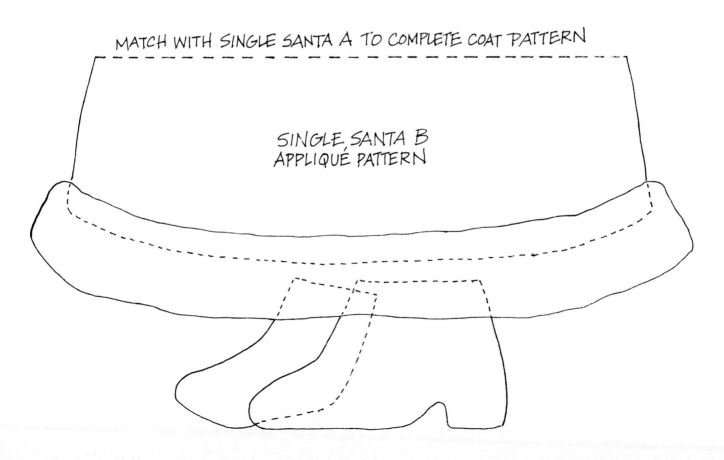

MATCH WITH SINGLE SANTA A TO COMPLETE COAT PATTERN

SINGLE SANTA B
APPLIQUÉ PATTERN

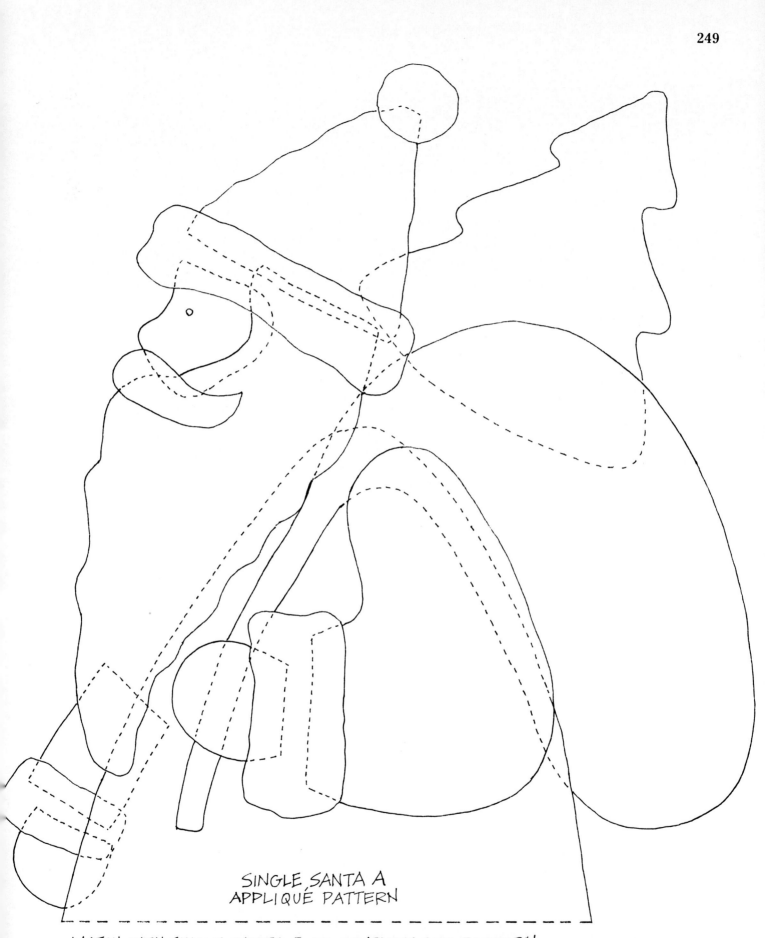

SINGLE SANTA A
APPLIQUÉ PATTERN

MATCH WITH SINGLE SANTA B TO COMPLETE COAT PATTERN

# Appendix:
# Quilting by Mail

**Cabin Fever Calicoes**
P.O. Box 550106
Atlanta, GA 30355
1-800-762-2246
*Tools and supplies for quilters, including batting, 100 percent cotton fabrics, fabric marking tools, pins and needles, quilting hoops and frames, sewing and quilting thread, template plastic, and thimbles*

**Clotilde, Inc.**
1909 S.W. First Avenue
Fort Lauderdale, FL 33315
(305) 761-8655
*Sewing notions and quilting supplies, including Heat 'N Bond appliqué film, embroidery floss, fabric marking tools, magnetic pin holders, scissors, seam rippers, quilter's ¼-inch masking tape, and quilt soap*

**Keepsake Quilting**
Dover Street, P.O. Box 1459
Meredith, NH 03253
(603) 279-3351
*Appliqué film, white and dark batting, 100 percent cotton fabrics, extra-fine point, permanent felt-tip pens, pins and needles, needle grabbers, quilting hoops and frames, rotary cutters, cutting mats, see-through rulers, and thimbles*

**Mumm's the Word**
W. 211 Cleveland Avenue
Spokane, WA 99205
(509) 325-5317
*Screen-printed panel used in Nursery Rhyme Time on page 197. The panel includes both rhymes, "Hey Diddle Diddle" and "Star Light, Star Bright." To order, send $3.00 (includes shipping).*

**Nancy's Notions**
333 Beichl Avenue, P.O. Box 683
Beaver Dam, WI 53916
1-800-765-0690
*Primarily sewing notions, including appliqué film, embroidery floss, magnetic pin holders, scissors, seam rippers, sewing machine attachments (including the walking foot), tear-away paper, template plastic, and tracing paper*

**Osage County Quilt Factory**
400 Walnut, Box 490
Overbrook, KS 66524
(913) 665-7500
*Appliqué film, white and colored batting, 100 percent cotton fabrics, fabric marking tools, quilting thread, rotary cutters, cutting mats, see-through rulers, and template plastic*

**Quilts & Other Comforts**
Box 394-7
Wheatridge, CO 80034
(303) 420-4272
*Notions and supplies for quilters, including coordinated fabric packets, see-through rulers, reusable self-adhesive quilting templates, quilting hoops and frames, quilting thread, collectors' thimbles, and quilters' tote bags*

# Credits

## Photography Location

The photographs in the book were shot at the Walnut Valley Guest House, an eighteenth-century stone cottage nestled in the heart of Amish farmland. Fully restored, the Walnut Valley Guest House offers up-to-date comforts amid early American decor. It is conveniently located for exploring Amish quilt country, and visitors are welcome year-round. Reservations may be made by the day or by the week.

**Walnut Valley Guest House**
**Keith and Bev Haselhorst**
**380 Hammertown Road**
**Narvon, PA 17555**
**(215) 445-7121**

## Props Used in the Photographs

The following people and stores very generously donated the use of the decorative items that appear along with the quilts in the photographs.

**Barbara Jorda Antiques**
**Malvern, PA 19355**
  *Quilt rack, house*

**The Cranberry Moose**
**232 South Washington Street**
**Naperville, IL 60540**
  *Clay snowmen, wooden snowmen, Merry Christmas box, teddy bear, drum*

**Dilworthtown Country Store**
**275 Bintons Bridge Road**
**West Chester, PA 19380**
  *Man and the moon, bag of blocks, ears of corn and basket, flag case, sheep, oats, seed box, horse, Humpty Dumpty*

**S & S Antiques**
**Malvern, PA 19355**
  *White wicker high chair*

**The Shops at the John B. Good House**
**Sandy Lane Antiques**
**Route 625 and Maple Grove Road**
**Bowmansville, PA 17507**
  *North Carolina tobacco barn; Merry Christmas plaque; teddy bears; wool bear; Randy Smith cow, cat, and bear; wagon and blocks; Christmas cards; Santa Claus doll; green rocking chair*

**Strauz Antiques**
**2083 Main Street**
**Churchtown, PA 17555**
  *Child's chest, birdcage*

**Vintage Textiles & Tools**
**P.O. Box 265**
**Merion, PA 19066**
  *Toy Singer sewing machine, toy German painted sewing machine, toy German red sewing machine, large sewing box, Clarks ONT thread sewing box, sewing bird, sewing clamp, revolving thread caddy, sewing basket*

**Wallace Antiques & Craft Shop**
**R.D. 6, Box 250**
**Coatesville, PA 19320**
  *Heart wool wreath, jar with thread spools, ironing boards, red barn, drying rack, wreath, Merry Christmas sign, watermelon, feather tree with spools, fabric bows*

**Design Discovery**
**782 Hillview Road**
**Malvern, PA 19355**
  *The balance of the props were provided by Design Discovery.*

## Fabric Shown on the Cover of the Book

The Victoria Print shown on the cover, from P & B Textiles, is no longer available. Look for other P & B Textiles fabrics at your local quilt shop.